# THERE'S A GERMAN
# JUST BEHIND ME

# THERE'S A GERMAN
# JUST BEHIND ME

CLARE HOLLINGWORTH

THE RIGHT BOOK CLUB
121 CHARING CROSS ROAD
LONDON, W.C.2

*This edition 1943*

MADE AND PRINTED IN GREAT BRITAIN BY
MORRISON AND GIBB LTD., LONDON AND EDINBURGH

# PREFACE

FROM the fall of France in 1940 until the beginning of the war with Russia a year later, the Balkan States were the principal object of Germany's designs. The aim of this book is to give a true picture by an eyewitness of events in that area of Europe as they developed. Obviously these events are too recent for any final judgment to be passed. But I hope that an exact report of what I saw may serve as a basis for those who will have the opportunity of writing a more fully documented history in the future.

But for the efficient help of Rosa Wessely, who typed my script through the heat of a Cairo summer, this book would still be in the form of my own detailed diary, plus a mass of press cuttings and copies of despatches.

Several officials who were *en poste* in the Balkans, especially those who served in the Legation at Bucharest, have given a great deal of help and advice, for which I am deeply grateful.

The reader may wonder why Greece and Romania are treated at such great length in comparison with Hungary and Bulgaria. The reason is that Romania for over a year provided one sensation after another, and Greece took the unusual line of fighting the Axis, whereas in Bulgaria and Hungary the Germans walked slowly through without causing a stir or giving rise to ' nerves '.

May I plead the indulgence of readers for obvious omissions ? Those who have tried to write on the war since the Germans invaded Poland, and more especially since the fall of France, will know that the rules of censorship in the Middle East are without parallel in world history. As one correspondent said : " The Russians could learn a lot from these bureaucrats."

Christopher Buckley, the special correspondent of the *Daily Telegraph* in Greece during the War and thereafter in the Middle East, is to a great extent responsible for the section on Greece, and has given incalculable help with every other chapter.

CAIRO, *October* 1941.

# CONTENTS

|  |  | PAGE |
|---|---|---|
| PREFACE | . . . . . . . | 5 |
| TABLE OF DATES | . . . . . . | 7 |
| **CHAPTER** |  |  |
| I. PARIS TO THE BALKANS | . . . . | 9 |
| II. YUGOSLAVIA—BALKAN GATEWAY | . . . | 14 |
| III. CRUMBLING ROMANIA | . . . . . | 32 |
| IV. HUNGARY—ARISTOCRACY'S LAST STRONGHOLD | . | 53 |
| V. ROMANIA—CAROL ABDICATES | . . . | 68 |
| VI. ROMANIA—IRON GUARD | . . . . | 90 |
| VII. ROMANIA—PETROLEUM, PENETRATION, ARRESTS | . | 106 |
| VIII. GREECE—THE SHADOW AND THE BLOW | . . | 122 |
| IX. ATHENS—ALBANIAN FRONT—ATHENS | . . | 147 |
| X. ROMANIA—CIVIL WAR | . . . . | 177 |
| XI. BULGARIA—GERMAN STALKING-HORSE | . . | 199 |
| XII. GREECE—CRUMBLING DICTATORSHIP | . . | 215 |
| XIII. YUGOSLAVIA—THIRTEENTH-HOUR REPENTANCE | . | 246 |
| XIV. GREECE—THE END OF AN EPIC | . . . | 268 |
| XV. RETREAT TO AFRICA | . . . . | 283 |
| INDEX | . . . . . . . | 296 |

# TABLE OF DATES

## 1940

June 10. Italy declares war on Britain and France.
,, 22. France accepts German armistice terms.
,, 28. Romania accepts Soviet ultimatum demanding cession of Bessarabia and Northern Bukovina.
July 1. Romania renounces Anglo-French guarantee.
,, 4. Tatarescu Cabinet resigns. New Romanian Ministry, including Horia Sima, formed by Gigurtu.
Aug. 15. Greek warship *Helle* torpedoed off Tenos.
,, 16. Hungarian and Romanian delegates meet at Turnu Severin to discuss Hungarian claims to Transylvania.
,, 21. Romania agrees to cession of Southern Dobrudja to Bulgaria.
,, 22. Britain promises naval and air aid to Greece if attacked.
,, 24. Hungary breaks off Turnu Severin negotiations.
,, 30. Romania, under German pressure, agrees to the cession of large parts of Transylvania to Hungary (Vienna Diktat).
Sept. 6. King Carol abdicates.
,, 14. Gigurtu Cabinet resigns. Antonescu forms Cabinet.
Oct. 4. Meeting of Hitler and Mussolini on Brenner Pass.
,, 12. German troops enter Romania to reorganize army and ' protect ' oilfields.
,, 28. Italian ultimatum to Greece, followed by immediate hostilities. Britain promises aid to Greece.
Nov. 4. Landing of British troops in Crete announced.
,, 10. Earthquake in Romania.
,, 20. Hungary joins Axis Pact.
,, 21. Greeks occupy Koritza, abandoned by the Italians. Antonescu summoned to Berlin.
,, 23. Romania and Slovakia join Axis Pact.
,, 27. Iron Guard rising in Romania to revenge Codreanu. Numerous assassinations.
,, 30. Greeks occupy Pogradetz.
Dec. 4. Italians abandon Argyrokastro and Premeti. Turco-British Trade Agreement announced.
,, 6. Greeks occupy Santi Quaranta.
,, 23. Greeks occupy Chimara.

## 1941

Jan. 10. Greeks occupy Klisoura.
,, 21. Iron Guard extremists in Romania attempt *coup d'état*. Serious rioting for several days.
,, 27. General Wavell meets Greek commanders in Athens.

Jan.  29.  General Antonescu forms new military cabinet in Bucharest. Death of Metaxas ; Korizis succeeds as Greek Premier.

Feb.  10.  Britain severs diplomatic relations with Romania.

„     11.  Turks warn Bulgaria against acquiescence in German penetration of Bulgaria.

„     14.  M. Cvetković, Premier of Yugoslavia, summoned to Hitler.

„     17.  Turco-Bulgarian non-aggression pact.

„     22.  German troops enter Bulgaria.

„     25.  Eden and Dill arrive in Turkey for consultations.

„     27.  Full agreement announced in Anglo-Turkish talks.

Mar.   1.  Bulgaria signs Axis Pact in Vienna. German occupation of Bulgaria begins.

„      3.  Eden in Athens.

„      5.  Britain severs diplomatic relations with Bulgaria.

„      7.  German pressure on Yugoslavia to join Axis Pact.

„     21.  Cabinet crisis in Yugoslavia. Three Ministers resign.

„     25.  Yugoslavian Ministers sign agreement with Germany in Vienna.

„     27.  Revolution in Yugoslavia. Prince Paul resigns ; Regency abolished. King Peter assumes personal power.

Apr.   3.  Count Teleki, Hungarian Premier, commits suicide.

„      6.  Germany invades Yugoslavia and Greece. Presence of British Army in Greece made known.

„      9.  Germans enter Salonika and capture Uskub and Nish.

„     10.  Germany recognizes independent Croatia under Pavelić. Bulgaria severs relations with Yugoslavia.

„     11.  Hungary invades Yugoslavia and occupies Banat.

„     17.  Germany announces Axis plans for reorganizing Yugoslavia.

„     18.  Greek Premier, Korizis, dies ; Tsouderos succeeds him.

„     20.  British evacuate Mount Olympus.

„     21.  Greek army in Epirus surrenders to Italians.

„     23.  Greek King and Government leave for Crete.

„     27.  Germans enter Athens.

„     30.  Italy annexes Slovenia. Bulgarians occupy Greek Thrace. Germany sets up quisling régime in Greece under General Tsolakoglou.

May    2.  British evacuation of Greece completed.

„     20.  German parachute attack on Crete.

„     21.  Italy annexes Dalmatia.

„     23.  British aircraft withdrawn from Crete.

June   1.  British evacuation of Crete completed.

„     21.  Croatia joins Axis Pact.

„     22.  Germany attacks Russia.

## CHAPTER I

## PARIS TO THE BALKANS

THOSE who knew were aware that the struggle in France was really at an end. But still some shopkeepers smiled brightly and boasted of the French army and its well-known powers of defence. The Maginot Line was so far untouched, but the Germans were penetrating rapidly nearer and nearer to Paris from the lightly fortified Belgian frontier. In Ciro's and the Ritz Bar gaiety had reached that peak of feverishness which I noticed so often in Warsaw, and again in Bucharest before the final crash. Shops were full of new summer models. Polish, Czech and English officers walked around the green boulevards escorting well-known *poules de luxe*. The Englishwomen had been evacuated from Paris long before this ; those who remained were journalists, refugee workers, or women in uniform. Plans were being made for the evacuation of children to the country ; French families were cheerfully sending their children seventy or eighty kilometres out of Paris. No one realized that within a month the cafés of the Champs Elysées would be occupied by German officers. No one took in the gravity of the position.

The Swiss frontier was closed and re-opened again. I was extremely anxious to get through to the East of Europe before it was too late ; so leaving all my treasures, old maps bought in the flea market in Paris, books, ski-ing and riding equipment, I took the Simplon train.

I have always believed in following my destiny and trusting to my instinct. It has got me into tight corners at times, but I have never regretted giving it its head. Never had my instinct said more firmly " Go East ! " I knew that it was desperately important for me to be east of the ' divide ' when Italy should come into the war ; and this was now clearly only a matter of days.

This was due, in part, to the fact that I have always been interested in the Balkan countries and Balkan history. My earliest childhood memories include cutting out and treasuring the maps from *The Times* during the course of the last war, and more particularly those which referred to the Balkans. This interest I have never since lost, and circumstances have enabled me to travel widely in all the Balkan countries and to study Balkan problems on the spot.

There was also the question of refugee work. During the period between Munich and the attack on Poland I had worked in Katowice and Warsaw organizing relief work for the numerous Czech refugees who succeeded in slipping over the frontier in those months. I had managed to get a large proportion of them out of the country with visas for England, Sweden, Russia or America. Now the problem was to take up the work again and continue doing what one could for the Poles. I had spent part of the winter of 1939–40 in Budapest largely engaged on this work, and though there were now other workers there and in Romania, I felt the need to return to see if more required to be done and to write reports for several slow-moving organizations in London.

At the same time, logic told me that the Eastern Front, wherever it might be, was likely to be of a more fluid nature, and therefore more interesting, than the West. At the very beginning of the war I had believed, like nearly everyone else, that we were destined to see indeterminate trench warfare of the 1915 attrition variety in the margin between the Maginot and Siegfried Lines. By the time I had made up my mind to leave Paris it had become clear to me that a deadlock of many months must follow the German conquest of France. I never believed in the probability of the invasion of England, and I knew that a long period must elapse before England would be in a position to counter-attack effectively on the Continent. Convinced that the Channel would become the new Maginot-Siegfried line, I made off for what has so often been the cockpit of eastern Europe.

The Balkans were obviously in Germany's direct line of south-eastern expansion. The *Drang nach Osten* is as much a reality to-day as in 1914, and the Balkan States were no more prepared to meet it in 1940 than in that year. Britain's interest in the Eastern Mediterranean involved her in counter-measures. Russia, also interested in extending her influence over the Balkans, was liable at any time to appear as the champion of Pan-Slavism. Italy, having thrust her foot in by the conquest of Albania, was on the look-out for further aggression-without-tears.

The chances of Balkan unity in the face of all these gathering shadows were never very bright, and by the summer of 1940 they were non-existent. Just as the larger experiment of pooled security in Europe had broken down over the unwillingness of member States to face the risks of collective action—involving dangers immeasurably smaller than those to which so many of these States have since succumbed—so in their corner of Europe the efforts of the more enlightened Balkan statesmen, such as Titulescu and Venizelos, to achieve Balkan unity against aggression remained stillborn after the signature of the Balkan Entente in 1934, a Treaty between Romania, Yugoslavia, Turkey and Greece to be effectively valid only in the event of unaided Bulgarian aggression against one or more of them. Against external aggression there was no likelihood of unity among the Balkan nations, and they lay more or less directly in the eventual line of conflict of the warring Powers. Across Germany's line of advance Britain, with France concurring, had erected the showy but quite insubstantial barrier formed by the guarantees to Turkey, Romania and Greece. The pivot of this system was the Anglo-Turkish Treaty of Alliance signed in October 1939. With France dropping out, the guarantees became heavy liabilities, but the Balkans were a field on which British and German interests must assuredly clash, even if British policy and British strategy could look forward only to a retreat by stages to the Mediterranean. This, in fact, is what happened. How far, with the dice heavily loaded against us, we conducted, diplomatically and militarily, a successful Fabian rearguard action from the summer of 1940 to the summer of 1941, and how far we were in fact unceremoniously hustled from one point to another, never once possessing the initiative, with the result that Germany was able to advance from the upper Danube practically to the shores of the Aegean without firing a shot, it will be the purpose of this book to show. Still more important will it be to study how far British policy was stultified by its failure to support the democratic elements in these countries (particularly in Greece), its support of King Carol in Romania, of Metaxas in Greece, or its pathetic faith in Royalty—the honesty of Boris of Bulgaria, the strength and reliability of Prince Paul of Yugoslavia.

The course of my Balkan travels took me first to Romania, and it was there that I spent the greatest proportion of my time. I thought when I left Paris, and events fully justified me, that no Balkan country lay more directly in the line of the converging interests of the Great Powers than this ill-welded, inchoate nation of twenty millions, so richly gifted by nature, so poorly equipped in terms of human material to defend its heritage. Germany needed its very great oil resources, and would certainly bring diplomatic and military pressure to bear to obtain them. Britain had a corresponding interest to prevent this. Romania was also, as I shall show, the country where, after Poland, German and Russian interests and German and Russian lines of expansion most obviously crossed one another. "Watch Cernauti!" a well-informed fellow-traveller, whose identity I never discovered, said to me once when crossing the Channel in August 1936. "The first great clash of the Second World War will occur there." Writing these lines to-day on the second anniversary of the German-Soviet Pact, his words seem more prophetic than I thought them two years ago.

Romania, lying like a walnut between the pincers of two great Powers, was also regarded with predatory eyes by two smaller Powers, Hungary and Bulgaria, each of whom had territorial claims to press when the hour should be opportune. It had acute minority problems, a régime corrupt to the core and intensely unpopular and every sign of imminent internal debility. One did not need to be a prophet to read the signs of the times and to know that Romania was, in the words of one of Kipling's characters, "an eligible central position for the next row."

So I booked my ticket for Bucharest.

In the dim light of the *Gare de Lyon*, friends seeing me off gave me all their French money, so that if I was not allowed to enter Switzerland I might have enough to return to Paris. I had little luggage, and my visas were in order. During the journey German bombers flew over; the train stopped, the passengers were alarmed, but no bombs were dropped. When we arrived at the Swiss frontier everyone who had not a diplomatic visa was thrown out of the train. Although my Swiss visa was not diplomatic, it was issued by a Legation and not by a Consulate, and I bullied the official at the frontier to let me in. The Swiss in Lausanne, where I stopped to visit my bank, were far more depressed than the French had been. Trade was bad, the large hotels empty, there had been no season for winter sports; but these were excuses, and in their hearts the Swiss were afraid the Germans might occupy the country at any moment. I was glad to leave. But greater gloom overcame me in Italy.

There has never been much romance in the industrial cities of Northern Italy. The train attendants treated me as though I were dirt, and though all talked of coming into the war against us within a few days, the Italians admitted, quite openly, that it was not what they wanted to happen. Milan and Trieste were full of Germans, many of them complaining about the food, which even then was bad. The hotel-keepers had a curious point of view; they seemed reluctant to give me a room because I was English, but they too told me that Mussolini was dragging them unwillingly into a war.

The frontier between Italy and Yugoslavia was closed, but it was possible to get out of the country over the short and narrow bridge which divides Šušak from Fiume. This town, which was divided into two after the last peace treaty, has a mixed population on both sides of the frontier, and local people were forced to cross in streams all day long. I stood in my bedroom in Šušak and threw a pebble across the narrow stream into Italy. As no planes were running I had to take the train for the dull journey to Zagreb I know so well.

## CHAPTER II

## YUGOSLAVIA—BALKAN GATEWAY

THE railway from Šušak to Zagreb is the gateway to the Balkans. Through the first stage of the journey one climbs steadily over the Carso and the northern spurs of the Dinaric Alps. At one point I saw remains of Italian trenches dating from the last war carved out in the hard rock. The reflection that within a few days these trenches would, metaphorically speaking, be facing the other way sent me into a depressing reverie about the futility of war. Though I was en route for Bucharest, I looked forward to stepping off at Zagreb, a town I know well, and getting the feel of the local situation. Moreover, reactions to the Battle of France, now entering its final stage, would be particularly interesting in this region wedged in an angle between Germany and Italy.

Yugoslav trains, owing to their inferior coal, have a peculiar and unpleasant smell of their own. At every station people were buying newspapers, and little groups of peasants stood collected round men wearing collars and ties who were able to read and who could explain what was happening in France. Every paper had a map with a daily-increasing black bulging line, indicating the German advance.

Within the two months since my last visit Yugoslavia had changed. Always an indication of popular feeling and trust, the Black Market for money had fallen and whereas I had previously bought dinars at 360 to the pound sterling I could now get only the official rate of 200.

Yugoslavia is a good ' specimen ' Balkan State. Like Romania it is a ' Succession State ', and both its area and population were more than doubled as a result of the 1919 Peace Treaties. It is as troubled as Romania by minority problems. In theory it is a Triune Kingdom of Serbs (about six and a half millions), Croats (about four millions), and Slovenes (something over one million). Between these races, theoretically enjoying equal rights and an

14

equal position in the kingdom, there has been a constant antagonism, more particularly between Serbs and Croats. But in addition to the problem of running these three races in harness, there are quite a number of genuine minorities. There are more than half a million Germans, mostly descendants of the eighteenth-century colonists settled in southern Hungary by Maria Theresa as a frontier guard against the Turk. Half a million Magyars are found in the Backa and Bachka provinces, an area which geographically is a part of the great Hungarian plain and ethnographically is almost entirely Magyar, but was allotted to Yugoslavia in order that the town of Subotica (Mariatheresiopol in the old days) in the extreme north, which is inhabited by Bunjevacs (Catholic Serbs), might fall within the boundaries of the Southern Slav kingdom. Half a million Albanians form a Moslem fringe in the west and south-west. A quarter of a million Romanians in the Banat of Temesvar are balanced by a much smaller Serb population in the Romanian part of the Banat.

In addition to these minorities there is the formidable problem of the Macedonians, of whom at least 600,000 live in the southern part of the kingdom (Skoplje, Veles, Monastir, Strumnitza, etc.). The Bulgars have always claimed these for their own, and consider that Bulgaria has established a moral claim to the whole of Southern Serbia up to Lake Okhrida.

Macedonia is one of the vexed questions of Europe, and so long as there is a ' Macedonian question ' there will always be the raw material for a first-class international row ready to the hand of any Power prepared to take advantage of it. Almost all who have given attention to the study of the country and people are agreed that the inhabitants of Macedonia bear more resemblance in language and racial characteristics to the Bulgars than to the Serbs or Albanians. On the other hand, it is maintained in some quarters that the Bulgars were merely lucky in being the first to make the Macedonians ' race-conscious ' and to inject them with the dubious stimulant of nationalism in the latter part of the last century. " Come along," they said in effect to these bewildered but more or less amenable herdsmen and brigands, " you are Bulgarians ! You are not Serbs or Albanians. Just remember that ! " This of course is to simplify the situation down to the level of " 1066 And All That ", but there is some truth in the contention. In any case the question of Macedonia is a permanent bar to the establishment of friendly relations between Yugoslavia and her eastern neighbour. The real trouble lies in the fact that both countries have allowed themselves to develop ' historical consciousness ' in connection with Macedonia, owing to the fact that at various times during the Middle Ages this region formed a part both of the Serbian empire of Dushan and the Bulgarian kingdom of Simeon, and each country appeals to history, a tiresome Balkan habit employed also by Romanians and Magyars in buttressing their respective claims to Transylvania.

The Bulgarian claim is also based on two abortive treaties or ' arrangements ' of more modern times. By the Treaty of San Stefano in 1878 a Greater Bulgaria had been erected, including the whole of Macedonia, but this Treaty was quashed by the subsequent settlement at Berlin, both Disraeli and Bismarck fearing that ' Greater Bulgaria ' would be nothing but a Russian puppet. Again, in the negotiations which led up to the formation of the Balkan League against Turkey in 1912, though the allotment of what was referred to as the ' contested zone ' was left to the arbitration of the Tsar, Bulgaria, which has always maintained that the inhabitants of this region are pure Bulgars, certainly understood that Macedonia would in point of fact be assigned to her, while Serbia would obtain an outlet on the Adriatic coast. The intervention of the Powers, or rather of Austria, prevented this latter solution to the problem, as Vienna, backed of course by Berlin, absolutely vetoed the extension of Serbia to Durazzo, and none of the other Powers were very actively concerned to oppose her. Serbia therefore filed a claim to the bulk of Macedonia and, after the Second Balkan War, which arose out of the dispute over the spoils between the victors, she got it, except for what went to her Greek ally. It is only fair to state that by the treacherous midnight attack which the Bulgarian armies made on the Serbs and Greeks the Sofia Government rather prejudiced its case in the eyes of the world. After the 1914–18 War, Serbia, now part of Yugoslavia, received certain strategic rectifications of her frontier in the Pirot and Strumnitza regions. These, though inhabited purely by Bulgars, are small in area and constitute an aggravation rather than an additional problem.

Internationally, Yugoslavia is, like Romania, a pivot State, having been a member of those two ill-fated alliances, the Little Entente and the Balkan Entente. As one of the chief beneficiaries of the break-up of the Austro-Hungarian Empire she had a vested interest in the maintenance of the *status quo* after Versailles. Her obvious enemies, besides Bulgaria, were Hungary, from which she had obtained a solid wedge of purely Magyar territory, and Italy, which coveted the Dalmatian coast (half of which had been promised her by the secret Treaty of London—April 26, 1915—and formed one of the inducements to persuade her to enter the first World War). Against this, Yugoslavia has unsatisfied claims in Istria and the Isonzo region. It was therefore in the interests of common self-protection, rather than, as is sometimes maintained, through the Machiavellian diplomacy of France, that Yugoslavia moved into alliance with Romania and Czechoslovakia.

In the Balkans, after the settlement and exchange of populations between Greece and Turkey, the major international problem had been the mutual safeguarding of their interests by Turkey, Greece, Yugoslavia and Romania. All these States desired to maintain a Balkan *status quo*, and as all of them had territories coveted by Bulgaria (the Enos-Midia line, Thrace, Macedonia and Southern Dobrudja respectively), the Balkan Alliance, finally signed in 1934, about which more will be said in a later chapter, tended to take the form of an alliance against Bulgaria by four nations all of which had something to lose to her.

Serbia's three wars with Bulgaria since 1878 had driven a deep wedge between Serbs and Bulgars, effectively killing all real hopes of a Pan-Slavonic federation, the most satisfactory solution for this part of Europe. The idea of a single Slav State

2

extending from the Adriatic to the Black Sea nevertheless had a certain attraction for young intellectuals in both countries, for whom it exercised the same sort of curious fascination that Federal Union has more recently had in Britain and America. Just as there were those who strained at the gnat of the League of Nations and subsequently swallowed the camel of Federal Union, so among the young hopefuls of Balkan political circles there were those who imagined that because the kingdom of the three nations worked uneasily and creakily, the addition of a fourth nation would in some unexplained manner render everything gloriously simple.

But the idea of a federalized union to include Bulgaria also made a particular appeal to the Croats, who hoped by political co-operation with the Bulgars to curb the dominance of Belgrade. Since the formation of the Triune Kingdom there has always been this dual tendency in Yugoslavia—the endeavour to run the three peoples in harmony and the attitude of many Serbs who frankly regarded the additions made by the Peace Treaties as a mere extension of Serbia to be ruled by and for the benefit of the Serb people. This latter view was in accordance with the general spirit of the Vidovdan Constitution of 1921 ; it was the fixed policy of Nicholas Pašič, Serbia's wartime Premier, who had reached the position of Grand Old Man of Balkan politics, and it was the policy of King Alexander.

The Croats have never sat down under this interpretation of the Constitution. Until the end of the last war they were ruled from Budapest ; they have continually resented being ruled from Belgrade, and they desire a wide measure of autonomy. They speak the same language as the Serbs, but having always looked westwards for their culture they are Roman Catholics, while the Serbs are members of the Orthodox Church. The Croats employ the Latin alphabet, while the Serbs write with the Cyrillic. The Croats are proud of the centuries-old tradition of their great University at Zagreb ; they look down on the Serbs as an almost savage people, and complain bitterly that all their taxes are spent on building in Belgrade, and in supporting a civil service and a diplomatic corps which contain no Croats.

Their impoverished aristocracy and small but rich middle class, who in the past paid frequent visits to Vienna and Budapest and took their colour from them, resent the dominance of the more unlettered Serbs, whose rule has usually been arrogant and always tactless. The Croat peasants, who are fortunate in having one of the richest areas in Europe to till, were led in their opposition to the Serbs first by Radić and subsequently by Maček.

Up to his death in the fight in Parliament in 1928, Stepan Radić had been the leader of the Croats. In the pleasingly direct manner in which southern Slavs conduct their differences a Serb Deputy, rising in his seat in the Skupstina, drew a revolver and shot the Croat leader and two colleagues. Radić's memory is now sacred to the Croats, largely because his death was that of a martyr. In Zagreb in August, on the anniversary of his death, large black flags fly from every house, the shop windows display his portrait covered with black crêpe, and there are processions of mourners. Some friends of mine who were out of town on one of these anniversaries, and whose house consequently lacked the symbols of respect for the dead leader, had their windows broken by an angry crowd.

Radić had serious faults, though they were forgotten after his death. His political associates found him unreliable and not always truthful. No doubt he felt that the cause for which he was fighting justified any means he might employ; he went so far as to join forces, when he thought it expedient, even with the Serbian Government which was the obstacle to his desires. His hold upon his people was too strong for him to fear the criticism of Zagreb in regard to himself and his tactics, for the peasants loved him as one of themselves; they remembered that he was the first man to realize that the chief sufferers in a Croatia ruled from Belgrade were not the grumbling bourgeoisie of Zagreb but the peasants, who were the greatest part of the population. Radić was, moreover, a wonderful speaker and, whatever contradictions and foolish statements he might make, he could always put across his main thesis with vigour and clarity and make an audience of peasants understand political problems.

The shooting of Radič, coming as the climax of a long period of political confusion and racial antagonism, convinced King Alexander that some degree of personal dictatorship was inevitable. The Croats had withdrawn from the Skupstina after the slaughter of their leader and there was a real prospect of their breaking right away from the Triune Kingdom. Consequently, at the beginning of 1929, King Alexander, in the nterests of holding the State together, as he judged, proclaimed royal dictatorship. It is interesting to recall that *Punch*, which has not shown itself specially aware in recent years of new political trends, devoted a full-page cartoon to this incident. Over the caption " THE NEW FASHION " it displayed the Café des Dictateurs, outside which Mussolini and General Primo de Rivera are sipping their *apéritifs* when King Alexander of Yugoslavia saunters in. " H'm ! " grunts Mussolini. " My little place is becoming less exclusive ! "

As Alexander occupied a dominating position in Yugoslavia for fifteen of the twenty years between the two wars, it is well to devote some attention to his character and career. Undoubtedly he had been much influenced by his boyhood at the Court of the Russian Tsar. He was the second son of King Peter, not destined for the throne, and his father could not allow him much money. To his companions in St. Petersburg he was poor, the son of a not very important king of a not very civilized country, and their Tsar was charitably giving him a free education. His position was somewhat humiliating. The result was to develop in him something of an inferiority complex, and a determination to make Serbia a larger and more important State. Well grounded in rigorous Court etiquette and military discipline, he sought to make the Serbian army efficient, and took as his model the army of the Tsar.

It is said that Alexander did not get on well with his father. Between him and the succession stood the Crown Prince George, a man of hasty and violent temper, like his ancestor, Black George, the pig merchant. Alexander's enemies say that it was by his contriving that Prince George was declared a lunatic, deprived of his right of succession to the throne and confined in an asylum. The evidence suggests that George, though by no means a fit person to rule the country, was not in reality a dangerous lunatic.

Alexander has been represented both as a saint and as a devil. In truth he was neither, but a man striving to rule an excessively difficult country in the way that seemed best to him. The fact that many people consider his method unsound is no reflection upon his sincere devotion to the interests of his country ; though many believe that the failure of the party system under the Vidovdan Constitution was due to his machinations. He was, in fact, a typical middle-class Serbian officer, with definite ideas for the welfare of his own people, the Serbs, but with no understanding of the interests of the Croats. With a police force backed by an army, he ruled as a Dictator ; the parliamentary opposition was part of the machinery of government ; the real opposition, the Croats, he ruthlessly suppressed.

As Regent during the 1914–18 War, Alexander had borne hardship and poverty. It was natural that he should desire to make money for himself and his heirs, both for the power that money would give him on the throne and as a provision for his old age, should he ever be dethroned. He was not so skilled in money-making as Carol of Romania. In this respect, as in his affection for his wife and children and his capacity for hard work, he was in no way different from ordinary men. Such popularity as he enjoyed was due to personal contacts with the peasants ; he would stop his big Packard in a village and enter into conversation with his people upon matters that they understood. His charm, however, was assumed.

The terror of the King was assassination. Death by violence had overtaken almost all his predecessors upon the throne of Serbia, including his ancestor, Black George. His father had obtained the throne through the murder of Alexander Obrenović in 1903 ; the enlargement of Yugoslavia was due to a war begun by the murder of the Austrian Archduke Franz Ferdinand by an over-zealous Serbian. Alexander's right-hand man during his dictatorship was Zivkovič, who had admitted the former Alexander's assassins to the palace.

King Alexander, knowing that the one likely means to the hand of his enemies for destroying his work was murder, nearly always wore a bullet-proof waistcoat. His failure to do so for the short drive from the quay to the railway station at Marseilles may have cost him his life. Only on rare occasions did he venture into the streets of Belgrade ; then, with a set face, accompanied by his aide-de-camp, he would walk for half an hour along the main street while hosts of secret police watched over his safety. Rumours of his fear of death achieved terrific dimensions in Belgrade. The Macedonian Terrorists had been substantially suppressed by the Bulgarian Government in the summer of 1934 ; but the more violent elements among the Croats had by that time begun a Croat terrorist movement, organized in secret societies, which even now publish newspapers in America, such as the *Croatia Press*, which appears in English and, repudiating the more or less constitutional methods of Maček, openly states that Alexander was slain in pursuance of the will of the Croat people. Cernozemsky, the assassin of the King, had in fact been lent to the Croats by the leading Macedonian Terrorist, Ivan Mihailov.

Mihailov is one of those figures who seem to take to Balkan terrorism as a First in Greats takes to the Civil Service. From 1914 he had been one of the organizers of the Macedonian Terrorists who, working from Sofia, aimed at stirring up disorder in the region which had so recently passed to Serbia. The movement was originally led by Protogerov and Feodor Alexandrov. Both of these were subsequently assassinated by the agency of Mihailov, who succeeded to the leadership of the organization in 1920. From his hide-out at Djumaya, just inside the Bulgarian frontier, this pleasing brigand exercised authority over the local villagers, taxing them for the upkeep of his band. The Serbs believe him responsible for the murder of Stambulisky, the enlightened Agrarian Prime Minister who had worked for a policy of close co-operation with Yugoslavia. After he had been condemned to death on ten separate occasions, his movement was liquidated in August 1934 by the Gheorgíev Government and Mihailov fled, first to Turkey, where he lived for some time on the island of Prinkipo, famous as one of Trotsky's numerous asylums, and later to Poland. After the Germans had conquered Poland he came under their protection. The Nazis saw in him a valuable tool for the task of di-integrating Yugoslavia, and the Bulgarian Government was .nstructed to grant him a full pardon. In May 1941 he was put in charge of the administration of the newly conquered region of Skoplje. This picturesque figure, who is said periodically to liquidate his closer collaborators, was very recently reported to have committed suicide—a most improbable termination to so swashbuckling a career of rascality. In judging the work of Alexander it is always important to remember that the raw material out of which he had to build his kingdom contained many such elements as the unspeakable Mihailov.

The enemies of Yugoslavia had hoped that the death of Alexander would result in the immediate break-up of the Triune Kingdom. The Croats were expected to seize the opportunity of the temporary leaderlessness of the Serbs to revolt and smash the State to pieces. This hope was at first expressed in the Italian newspapers ; but the Government at Rome, fearful, apparently, of being implicated in the assassination, hastily issued instructions to the Press to adopt a different tone.

The Croats, whatever their grievances against the Serbs, had no desire to fall into the lap of Italy, which was already attempting to denationalize the large Slovene minority in the Julian Marches ; the protection of the Yugoslav army, though it was run by Serbs, was preferable to Italian or Hungarian domination. Maček had succeeded Radič as leader of the Croat nationalists. He, too, was worshipped by the Croatian peasantry, but he lacked his predecessor's gifts of leadership. From his prison, however, he sent messages of condolence to the Royal Family, and described the death of the King as a loss to the whole nation. Korošec, the Slovene Catholic leader, who like the Bosnians played sometimes with the Serbs and sometimes against them, had been banished by Alexander to the island of Hvar, where he lived in great luxury. Although never formally released, he was first seen among the mourners at Zagreb station when King Alexander's corpse passed through. There was thus an opportunity for reconciliation in the generous mood of the Croats, but Prince Paul and the Prime Minister Jevtič preferred to do nothing and to continue repression. The Croats and the Slovenes, disappointed, resumed their opposition.

For some years now, Maček has been a name to conjure with in Croatia, and so, though I have never had any excessive admiration for this tubby little man, I was glad to accept an invitation to his house.

Maček himself pretends to be a peasant, but is not. He wears peasant costume and lives in a peasant house, sitting round a table not only with his young wife and children but with all the local inhabitants from the neighbouring cottages. When I had lunch with him we all dipped our bowls into one big central dish composed of meat and vegetables covered with gravy, which we ate with slabs of bread. We drank water. Maček's house is small, and better kept than those of his neighbours, but the only distinguishing feature was a large and powerful radio in the corner.

Maček had been a successful lawyer in Zagreb. He speaks German, and just as it is impossible for an Englishman to understand the power of such an ugly little man as Hitler over the German people, so it is impossible to comprehend why a fattish man of about sixty, wearing thick spectacles, with a rather unpleasant voice, should wield such power with the Croat peasants. They certainly adore him. Everything he says is law to them. Any stranger travelling in the countryside around Zagreb soon becomes convinced of this. Cries of " Sliva Maček ! Sliva Maček ! " greet him in every village. As an indication of the strength of feeling for and against Maček, I will quote the experience of two friends of mine who were motoring down through Croatia in the summer of 1936. In each village which they passed through they were greeted with " Sliva Maček ! " and being amenable people, they soon got into the habit of replying in similar words and even anticipating the salutation themselves. They chanced, however, to pass through the village of Srb, which, as its highly consonantal name implies, is a

Serbian settlement situated in Croatian country. Racial feeling runs strongly in such miniature enclaves. My friends, unaware of the name of the village, cheerfully greeted the first inhabitants with " Sliva Maček ! " only to be met with black hostile looks. Worse still, their car broke down rather badly before they were clear of the village, and when the customary knot of curious bystanders noted that they were thoughtlessly wearing Maček badges, a concession to the proselytizing spirit of some chance encounter earlier in the day, the atmosphere became really ugly. Night was coming on, and it was only with the greatest difficulty and by the display of thick wads of dinar notes that they obtained a night's lodging in the village and some very inexpert assistance with the car. Nor were either of these favours granted until they had torn off their Maček badges as a concession to local feeling.

Maček was frequently in trouble with the Serbs, who imprisoned him soon after he succeeded Radič. Some people believe him to be shrewd, cunning, far-sighted, perhaps a little double-dealing. Maybe he is double-dealing, but my impression of him over a period of years is that he is a stupid old man whose power over the peasants is used by his supporters for their own ends.

One of his right-hand men was Bicanič, and the other was Cosutič. Bicanič is about forty, an economist who speaks English well. He is a man of sound pro-Allies sympathies and democratic views, but he has a somewhat unbalanced devotion amounting almost to worship for Maček, with whom he had been in prison for two years. Cosutič, although he pretended to be very democratic, I believe to be a man of definitely pro-German sympathies. Both these men pulled Maček hither and thither until the old man became a peasant director talking of democracy who rode round rather ludicrously on his famous white horse.

Maček was not changed by becoming a member of the Government. He did, I believe, wear a morning suit and top hat in Belgrade, but never in Zagreb. He was proud, with reason, of having effected, after so many years of strife, an agreement between the Serbs and the Croats which had given the latter some local autonomy and made several of them cabinet ministers.

There were, however, two figures of international reputation who remained outside Yugoslav politics at this time. One was the attractive but *difficile* sculptor, Mestrovič, who after Prince Paul became Regent was so tired and disillusioned by politics that he refused even to discuss them save when he was in one of his notorious bad tempers. The other, Dr. Stampar, though less well-known than the creative Mestrovič, was the man who organized the health services in Yugoslavia after the last war. Through his activity the worst malarial belt in south Serbia was rendered innocuous. Every town had its clinic, and the larger towns had enormous hospitals. That in Skoplje, which is made of steel and concrete and gave the impression of enormous efficiency, was one of many I saw. The Rockefeller Institute helped him to build a large hospital in Zagreb. His work became well known at Geneva. The King either became jealous of his power and popularity or annoyed by his Liberal democratic views. Stampar was put out of office, and progress in health administration then stopped. He thought it advisable to leave the country, and took an important post with the League of Nations Health Service in China. He returned quietly to Zagreb about 1935 and found, to his horror, that his eldest children, through the influence of their schoolfellows, had become completely Fascist-minded. This he explained, quite reasonably, to have been caused by insidious and continuous propaganda coming from the nearby frontiers of Germany and Italy and working largely on an anti-Semitic line. It is no exaggeration to say that the rich bourgeoisie of Zagreb is eighty per cent. Jewish. The remaining twenty per cent. Pavelič, the present puppet Dictator in Zagreb, relies on for his support. Two or three per cent. before the German occupation were supporters of Maček and should now, I fancy, if alive, be fanatically flag-waving for Pavelič.

． ． ． ． ． ．

In this black month of June 1940 the peasants were complaining, as peasants all over Europe were complaining, of the appalling rise in the cost of living, which was, though they little knew it, caused by the vast quantities of food which were being sent out of Yugoslavia to Germany every day. Contrary to the belief prevalent in more sophisticated and better politically educated countries, the peasants really had no idea of what was going on. Drinking wine on one of the mountainside cafés of the Slem, the beautiful peak district to the north of Zagreb, the peasants complained of the rise in the price of matches, newspapers, soap and machine-made clothes, while they were still able to sell eggs only at six a penny. The Croat with whom I had been dining explained to them that all their eggs, butter and cheese were going to Germany, but that Germany paid a low price for them, and paid that price often in raw materials and manufactured goods unwanted by the peasant but nevertheless increasing the price of matches and paper. It was impossible to make the peasants believe that the country was being bled for Germany. Like most small traders, when the objects they wish to sell are in the hands of the higglers they have no further interest in their destination. The Yugoslavs were receiving, in exchange for their agricultural produce, second-class military equipment, cameras, motor-cars and aspirin ; and although they had no need of these goods, except the armaments, they were too afraid of Germany either to refuse to allow their food to go there or to make a stand about the goods they received in exchange. The harvest had been a bad one, and the condition of the peasants in the poorer districts had become acute.

All the Yugoslav towns had been improved during the previous six months by the building of large travel bureaux, that at Zagreb twice as large as any other shop, filled with advertisements for trips on the Hamburg-Amerika Line, and invitations to ski, swim or kiss in Germany, capped by photographs of Nordic youths being embraced by handsome females carrying flowers. These shops were carefully guarded by the Yugoslav police, who were unable to stop the almost daily breaking of the windows by passers-by with carefully concealed bricks. Terrorism has always been a pastime in Yugoslavia,

and while I was in Zagreb all the telephone booths in the town
were blown up by bombs which had been placed there by the
extreme Croat Party, who were dissatisfied with the measure of
autonomy that Maček had secured. There is no doubt that
these people were financed and supplied with arms by Italy,
whose Consul-General opened a large Cultural Institute which
was as little frequented as the German travel shops.

Bicanič, who, owing more to his ability than his friendship
with Maček, had obtained an influential job in the Government,
had just returned from Russia, where he had been to sign a pact
establishing, after twenty years, consular representation between
Moscow and Belgrade and providing for two per cent. of the
total foreign trade of Yugoslavia to go to Russia. His description
of the journey was amusing. He said that during the negotiations Molotov (known to journalists as Auntie Molly) had
been unable to speak any language except Russian, and the
interpreter provided was a young Polish youth from Pinsk,
whose French was not too strong ; in fact Bicanič found it easier
to speak Serbian to Molotov and Molotov to reply in Russian
rather than use this fourth-class interpreter.

It was significant, as was proved some weeks later, that all
the maps which this Yugoslav delegation saw included Bessarabia
within the Russian, and not the Romanian frontiers. At that
time, Bicanič had the impression that the Russians, if attacked,
would defend the Ukraine, but that beyond small snippets of
territory in the Balkans they had no imperialistic designs in
Europe. The Yugoslavs themselves were apprehensive at the
possibility of being isolated with Italian Albania on their southern
frontier ; the Adriatic was almost an Italian lake, and they
feared with reason that the continual bad news from France,
coupled with the knowledge that Italy would come into the war
at any minute, would disturb their neutrality, as they were not
sure which way Romania, Hungary and Bulgaria would turn ;
in fact they felt they would all turn very strongly towards the
Axis.

At that time the Yugoslavs felt that the Italians would invade
Greece, taking Salonika and cutting Yugoslavia off entirely,

but the Yugoslavs firmly refused to make any military agreement with any other Balkan State, and Prince Paul, that sad specimen of Oxford-educated humanity, was playing hard on both sides. As the brother-in-law of the Duchess of Kent he was in close touch with the English royal family, and he spoke English to his wife. He convinced the British Minister, Mr. Ronald Campbell, that he, as the chief Regent for the young King Peter, held the reins of government firmly and used them in a way which could only do good to the Allied cause. There seems little doubt that he was saying the same to the Germans. Those of us who had known Prince Paul over a period of years remembered how frequently he had let down his friends. As a nobody in Yugoslavia before the assassination of King Alexander in Marseilles he had befriended artists and Left politicians. As soon as he became Regent, the only artist he met was Mestrovič, a man of international reputation whose works Paul bought but never paid for.

Prince Paul had the look of a man without charm or reliability, a man whose unstable habits, not so much of physical as of mental disloyalty, caused his wife great unhappiness. Prince Paul enjoyed being the First Regent, and had little intention of giving up his power when the young King came of age. He was not only unreliable, but a bad ruler in the technical sense; his secretaries were inefficient; he allowed them to keep papers from him. For example, he once told me that, although he had himself carefully ordered *The Times*, his secretaries generally prevented him from seeing it, and he was too busy to make a fuss. His programme was often mishandled. He told me again that some important English guests had been turned away as he was totally unaware of their arrival. He was so much influenced by the White Russian elements of his wife's family that he hated the long-awaited recognition of Russia and objected to the propaganda campaign of books and pamphlets written in Serbian with which the Russians had flooded the country. I told him they were far better than the illegal leaflets which the Communist Party had previously distributed.

Although the Yugoslavs realized the danger of their position and to some extent the inadequacy of their army, they were unable to come to any decision as to the line of defence they should take up. Military experts said it was impossible to defend the mountains of northern Yugoslavia, and that the best line of defence would be the line of the Sava River. This cut Croatia in two, and the Croats said " Unless we defend Croatia we do not fight ! " So even after an emergency meeting of the Defence Council on May 16, no decision as to plans for defence could be made.

One evening whilst I was in the hideous modern town of Belgrade I took a droski over the bridge built by King Alexander which crossed the Sava, past the old frontier station which used to mark the limits of Serbia and Austria-Hungary, to the German villages around the principal military airport. Here the feeling was tense ; the Germans in the cafés were making some show of suppressing their celebrations over the gradual collapse of France, and the Yugoslavs were avoiding them. Unquestionably these Germans, who had been colonists of some years' standing in Yugoslavia, but like all Germans had remained pure German, were wonderful material for Hitler's fifth column. They and others like them established themselves at all the more important strategic points in the country.

There is only one pleasant part of Belgrade, and that is standing on the fortress which was occupied by the Turks for four centuries, which overlooks the junction of the rivers Sava and Danube. Otherwise this modern town, hideously built with little town-planning and but gradually replacing the tin huts put up after the last war, has little to recommend it. I can feel little sadness that the Germans have now destroyed it by bombing.

I should have liked to visit Skoplje and Okhrida, towns in the south of the country, very different from Belgrade in their mountainous surroundings. Little of the Turkish influence has passed away. Here, unlike Turkey, which has tried to modernize herself in a few years, the women are still veiled and still live in harems. Brigands come down from the mountains at night and attack houses in order to steal the livestock, which in those places is always given preferential treatment to the children. Dirty, insanitary and dusty, these towns and villages seem a different country, their people of a sturdier stock than the Serbs of Belgrade. On the Dalmatian coast, now so well-known by holiday-makers, is a further type, which contains much Italian blood and where art treasures of the sixth century prove that whilst the peasants in the interior of the country were practically cannibals, those on the seaward side of the almost impenetrable Dinaric Alps were enjoying a cultured and pleasant life and trading by sea with Venice and other Mediterranean ports.

I had to leave Belgrade on a German plane; there was no other. I was a little self-conscious, and the Germans were a little self-conscious; the Swastika was hidden by the sign of the Aeroput Air Line, which this plane was for the moment supposed to represent. But I at least had the comfort of knowing that the German plane would arrive in Bucharest, whereas the Aeroput ones frequently crashed. We flew over the Iron Gates where the Danube runs into a narrow gorge, and into the plain of Romania.

## CHAPTER III

## CRUMBLING ROMANIA

BUCHAREST in June 1940 had not changed in any fundamental way since the beginning of the war. The inhabitants were perhaps a little depressed owing to the anticipated fall of France, but the same people were there enjoying the same gay life. Every night the restaurants and night-clubs were packed with members of the diplomatic corps, journalists, oil magnates and Romanian politicians in power. The bar of the Athenée Palace Hotel, both before lunch and before dinner, was the international meeting-place. Here Walter Duranty, king of all the journalists, gave his daily comment on events which everyone crowded round to hear. Princess Elizabeth Bibesco, daughter of Lord Oxford and Asquith but the wife of a Romanian, came in every day to hear the news. Junior diplomats collected there the information for their despatches, which were sent by most secret cypher, but which arrived actually two or three days after the same information had been printed in the local papers.

The carefree atmosphere of Bucharest, no matter what crisis might occur in the outside world, gave foreigners a freedom they had never experienced before. Everyone might live in open sin without criticism; an official was criticized for the woman he lived with only if she happened to be a Romanian thought to be working for the enemy. But beneath all this gaiety it was quite obvious that things were going wrong.

The British Minister, Sir Reginald Hoare, had lost a great deal of his power. Before the war began he had been an intimate friend of Armand Calinescu, prime minister until his assassination just after the downfall of Poland. The British Minister had been able to ring Calinescu up at any time of the day or night to obtain advice or information. A few days after I had left Poland, on my way out to lunch, I was held up by a crowd; they were explaining how a farmer's cart had blocked the route of the Prime Minister's car on his way home from lunch, and whilst the luxury car was slowing down his body and that of his private detective had been riddled with bullets by the Iron Guard.

Calinescu was immediately made a public hero; his body was laid out in state surrounded by candles, dressed in purple velvet. The members of the Iron Guard who shot him were taken out in a lorry to the spot where the incident happened, and were there shot one by one, with half an hour's interval between each shooting. Their dead bodies were allowed to lie in the dust for forty-eight hours; newsvendors, orange sellers, gipsy fortune-tellers, and particularly sellers of hot food did a great trade meanwhile. A law was passed providing that any policeman recognizing a member of the Iron Guard might shoot him on sight. Calinescu was buried amid great pomp and ceremony; but not only was Calinescu dead, but the Anglophile influence over King Carol was at an end, and the intimate contact which the British Legation had had with the Cabinet, through their Minister, Sir Reginald Hoare, was for ever over.

The Minister never quite realized this, and invited the same small group of Anglophile or Francophile people to dinner with him as before. He made no attempt to become friendly with the new men who surrounded the King. Admittedly they were ruffians, and hardly perhaps suitable friends for a British Minister, but they were the men in power; and they were neglected entirely and completely by our representatives. One exception alone stands out. Whilst he remained in power Gafencu, the Foreign Secretary, was in contact with both British and Americans.

Gafencu is physically one of the most attractive men I have ever had the good fortune to see. He married when young a Frenchwoman, who it is said was brought to Bucharest as the mistress of an elderly rich industrialist who tired of her. She then became a cabaret dancer, and, rumour has it, used to be carried naked on a pseudo-golden plate into one of the night-clubs of Bucharest. Here Gafencu met her and married her,

3

and presumably has never regretted it, as she makes a lively and charming wife.

Gafencu has a noticeable but slight scar on the left side of his face. When he becomes angry or uncertain the scar goes a deep red, and after that nothing at all can be done with him. He is a man of convictions, but not of convictions sufficient to carry him through the German political attack on Romania. He was criticized for having left the party of Maniu without having changed his Left democratic pro-Allies beliefs, but he had agreed to serve under Carol. He never quite dared to go the whole hog, and he failed the British particularly badly over the question of the destruction of the Romanian oilfields.

Long before war had been declared the Romanians and the British had decided jointly that when danger of the Germans taking the oilfields became acute, they would destroy them. Plans for this destruction were drawn up by both Romanian and English oil experts and by the General Staffs of both countries. Nearly everyone in power in Romania was mixed up in them in some way or another, but the difficulty with the oil wells was to say precisely at what moment they fell into German hands.

Many legendary stories have been put about, some on the German wireless. They concern a man known as Sindbad the Sailor, which title was given to all the Legation files connected with the now famous or infamous Giurgiu incident, who set out with a brilliant but ill-conceived plan for blowing up the Iron Gates, in order to prevent oil being taken by barges from Romania to Germany. Germany needed this oil to carry on the war, as the oil she was herself making was of second-rate quality compared with that which she imported from Romania.

Sindbad's plan was roughly that three or four ships should go up armed with a good load of concrete. If the worst came to the worst they could be sunk at the Iron Gates, making other traffic difficult, if not impossible, for the next few months; while if luck were on their side they would take a small part of the bank on either side of the Iron Gates, thus further securing that no oil should arrive in Germany.

To this end he got together a number of Englishmen, one or two of whom were men of outstanding ability with knowledge of local conditions and fluent in the Romanian language; as additional help, men were sent from the British Navy. Naturally these men thought this not only a great joke but a great adventure. They had been sent out from England with only their naval uniforms, so, as no officer of a foreign Power may wear his uniform in a neutral country, they had to be fitted up with odd grey bags and sailor sweaters at the various ports along the Black Sea. Thus the party, heavily equipped with big ropes and ammunition, sailed up the Danube.

The Romanians were a little surprised to find well-fed handsome English sailors manning boats on the Danube which are generally managed by rough bargees who speak a few words of Greek, Serbian and Romanian, whose nationality and morals are always undeterminable, but whose manners and mode of life are among the roughest ever seen. This, however, might have passed had it not been for one or two of the British so-called hush-hush men, who under the influence of women and alcohol boasted in public of the possible results of this Danubian picnic.

The Minister, luckily for him, was in London to discuss with Lord Halifax, the Foreign Secretary, and all the ministers from the Balkans, future British policy in that area. The Hon. R. M. A. Hankey, the brilliant son of Lord Hankey, then a member of the War Cabinet, who was First Secretary, was acting as Chargé d'Affaires, and all had been arranged with the Romanian authorities so that these ships were to be allowed up the Danube, in any case an international waterway.

Careful enough preparations were not made, and the party stopped at the small and godforsaken Danubian port of Giurgiu to refuel. This took longer than was expected, and the sailors made themselves conspicuous by drinking beer and flirting with the local damsels in the town, so much so that the port authorities decided they must inspect the goods which these mystery ships were carrying up the Danube. There can be no doubt that the German Secret Service had obtained information, probably given quite unwittingly by one of the British hush-hush men, that the mission was a serious one and the cargo deadly contraband. In any case, the ship which was not to be examined *was* examined by a petty official and its cargo discovered, and the expedition came to an abrupt end. Certain members of the Romanian Cabinet, who were pro-German, were more than delighted, and Gafencu had not the courage to stick up for the British, who were, to say the least of it, in a very nasty position. All the hush-hush men involved were quite rightly and hurriedly sent back to England. The Press was badly handled, and owing to lack of information many stories damaging to the Allied cause were despatched from Bucharest. The Romanians who were involved backed out, and effective British sabotage was at an end. One or two of the cleverer people managed to stay out their time.

A most remarkable personality in Bucharest was Major Ratay, the American Military Attaché, a man of enormous wealth, who had built a luxury house in the town where he entertained lavishly, giving a great deal of pro-German information. He was reported to have fought bravely in the last war, and since then had become an expert on China, even writing a standard text-book on the Chinese language. He also worked for some time in the American Military Attaché's department in Berlin. Big, hairy, looking rather like a bear in his beautifully cut dress clothes, he nightly outlined Germany's aims. Stoutly maintaining that he was not pro-German, but, unlike the English, realized the strength and power of Germany, he did his work. He was right about Poland; everything he prophesied happened. Immediately after the Polish campaign I dined with him and the American Military Attaché from Warsaw. He then prophesied the Norwegian campaign and the fall of France as a result of the Blitzkrieg through Holland and Belgium. As his prophecies were proved correct, his prestige increased.

After the Giurgiu incident he said that France would fall, that Italy would join the war, Italy would attack Greece, Germany would occupy Hungary and Romania without a fight, and would finally attack the Ukraine. He spoke with authority, for he had known Hitler in 1926 when Hitler was sixth man in the National Socialist Party. He was constantly going to Germany to meet high officials. He said that our British agents were no good, as they had obviously given bad information on Poland and France before the war. He always compared them to paid women, who gave what was expected of them, and said that in Germany they were fed with information by the Gestapo. They were shown tanks that had broken down, uniforms that had rotted in the rain. Ratay always maintained that the Germans were feeding the British with false information in Romania.

His own information was stupendous. On one occasion he telegraphed a speech of Hitler's to Washington one week before it was made ; he spoke of the special food given to the Nazi infantry. He realized that he was unpopular, and was thought by many to be solely a German agent, but he did not care. His influence with the Romanians was so great, much greater than that of the American Minister, that the British tried to unseat him, but without success.

Great consternation was caused on June 1, 1940, when a royal decree announced the resignation of Gafencu ; it announced at the same time that Gigurtu, previously Minister of Communications, was to become Foreign Secretary. This change was obviously a result of the continual French defeats and the immediate prospect of Italy joining the war. Military precautions were taken in Romania, troops were called up, and it became impossible to cross on the main road through the heavily guarded oilfields without a special permit. It was impossible to go to Brasov on business or for a walk in the Carpathians without spending hours and hours in the Prefecture of Police in order to obtain permission.

The number of soldiers everywhere was enormous, but they did not seem to alarm the village people, whom I watched taking their Sunday evening stroll, looking contented and happy in the sun. The soldiers were by no means contented and happy. Many had been mobilized for a long time. The conditions under which they lived, even when it is acknowledged that all Balkan armies are likely to live in a manner which would shock a British or American soldier, were appalling. Those privates who could afford it hired beds in peasants' cottages; the rest slept in stations, in barns, in cowsheds or in the open. No facilities were provided for washing; they were nearly all covered with lice. Few outside Bucharest had complete uniforms. One would have army boots, another a cap, a third trousers, and a fourth a rifle. They marched about, discontented and unhappy, longing to get back to their homes to work on the land. They caused a great deal of discontent in the country because, apart from their unhappy mode of life, their pay was less than 20 lei a month, and this was rarely paid. The lei must be calculated at 850 to the dollar or 1500 to the pound sterling. Discontent was also rising through fear of a Hungarian attack on Transylvania.

It is not true that Transylvania is purely Hungarian or purely Romanian. There is a Hungarian majority in some parts. The award of Transylvania to Romania took place after the last war. But the people of Transylvania are in truth merely Transylvanians, like the people of Silesia, who did not think of themselves as Germans or Poles but as Silesians. Even the leader of the Hungarian minority in Transylvania, Count Bethlen, told me that though he was a Hungarian, and his title was given him by the Hungarian King, he was foremost and essentially a Transylvanian.

I thought it worth while to visit the city of Cluj, the natural capital of Transylvania, to see what was happening. I drove along Romania's one good road, which runs through the pass of the Carpathians at Sinaia; this was the road afterwards used by the German troops for their advance into the Balkans. Everything in Cluj, menus, newspapers, official notices, was written in three languages, Romanian, Hungarian and German. The German minority was carrying on its usual game of causing more trouble than already existed between the Hungarians and the Romanians, and many of them, who were Saxon colonists from the time of Maria Theresa, were known to be members

of the German fifth column. I was told that a large number
of Romanian officials, who had been sent there from Bucharest,
had been bought up by this fifth column. There were stories,
which I did not at the time believe, that the King had been bought
by the Germans too.

The population complained that the fortifications which
were being built against Hungary were built only where they
showed to passers-by from the road or railway, while in other
places the money was going into the pockets of the directors
and the fortifications were never touched. Everything one
bought had stamp taxes : taxes for the Romanian Air Force,
taxes for the Army, and the people, especially the people in
Cluj, complained of this enormous waste of money.

I could not help comparing the atmosphere in Cluj to that
of Silesia before the war. On Corpus Christi Sunday there was
a large procession through the town to the Catholic cathedral in
the centre square—most Romanians, of course, are Orthodox.
The procession was headed by the local dignitaries in ill-fitting
morning suits, but they walked only after the road had been
strewn with grass and flower petals. There were parties of
priests, of children in white dresses, and nuns in grey with white
caps ; then paraded the Straja Tarii, King Carol's Youth
Movements of girls and boys, and finally came the bishop under a
canopy surrounded by priests and carried by boys in white
trousers with blue sashes. Thousands of people watched this
semi-religious, semi-nationalistic procession, at which Romanian
national songs and religious hymns were sung, echoed all over
the town by blazing loudspeakers.

Count Bethlen, with his beautiful white-haired wife, had for
many years been the leader of the Hungarian minority. The
Romanians, terrified of him, refused to allow him to lead the
Hungarian movement, and placed in his stead the tame Count
Banffy, with whom they could do as they pleased. Most of the
Hungarian counts, including Count Banffy, still lived in large
houses round the centre square, where no tramlines had been
laid, as the nobles in the days of their power had complained
of the noise and had the lines removed. The dislike between

the two races was obvious to anyone walking through the streets of Cluj, and continual incidents occurred.

I went to see the Royal Resident, the King's representative for the whole region. He knew trouble was coming, but could do little to counteract it or stop the insidious German propaganda from egging on one section of the population against another.

The German minority was divided into two. The younger section, who were pure Nazis, were armed, and the Romanian officials dared not confiscate the arms they knew were hidden. Rifles and ammunition were brought across the Hungarian frontier from Germany in empty petrol lorries and stored in barns and empty buildings round the city. The other section consisted of older Germans who had not entirely succumbed to Nazi ideology.

Transylvania, though the most important item in the programme of any Romanian politician, was a mere unimportant pawn in the German game, though the Romanians never saw it. A peasant I met one Sunday afternoon summed up Romania's position so shrewdly that his remarks are worth repeating. He said : " We were friends with the English and the French, but we have on our doorstep the Germans and the Russians, who both want our oil and our rich agricultural plain. England and France were too far away to help, and so we had to choose for ourselves. We chose Germany because we hate and fear Bolshevism and want to continue to have our own plots of land to till." This summing up of the peasant was true also for the bourgeoisie, essentially Francophile in their culture, all speaking French and writing French, even amongst themselves. When France fell they instinctively chose Germany, because by so doing they felt they would be able to retain their motor-cars and their middle-class way of life. The German propaganda was clever in continually dangling the Bolshevist bogey before the nose of the Romanians. Stories of misery in Russia were always current in Romania, and few Romanians believed in the permanence of the agreement between Germany and Russia which took place in August 1939.

The politicians—and they very frequently changed—who replaced Calinescu and Gafencu in the Romanian Cabinet were all men with strong anti-Bolshevist and pro-German sympathies. We English never really knew them, and, wrongly, we remained aloof. The worst dinner, or the most miserable, I ever had in my life was a formal meal to which the Minister of Propaganda invited all the journalists. It was given in one of the restaurants outside the town. By all the laws of nature it should have been warm and pleasant, but a howling wind was blowing and drizzle coming down. We were put under cover but with no walls. As the only Anglo-Saxon woman journalist, I was on the left of the Minister, and on his right was the notorious Fräulein von Kohle, who passed as a journalist but had never been known to send a despatch to her newspaper. Although middle-aged, she was beautiful, with fair hair plaited round her head in a truly Nordic manner. She had already been attacked in many English newspapers as one of the most prominent German spies. Whether her spying was successful, it is difficult to say, but as the bed companion of cabinet ministers she must have beaten all records. At the time when I sat on the Minister's left she had just become his mistress, and he was the fourth Minister of Propaganda in Bucharest with whom she had lived. The whole room packed with journalists watched this difficult and unpleasant situation. As an Englishwoman I could not speak to her, but the Minister had to speak to me occasionally, so the disjointed conversation continued while the wind blew ever louder. By 11.30, a very early hour in Bucharest, we were released because the Minister himself felt cold. Months afterwards the German Press, in attacking me, hinted that I had tried on this occasion to put Fräulein von Kohle out of her job.

The stress as the attitude in Romania and the Press rapidly changed to a pro-German one was relieved by a visit from the most intelligent man I have ever been privileged to meet, Sir Stafford Cripps, then on his way out as Ambassador to Russia. People who a month previously would have called him a Bolshevist and a Red, were clamouring for invitations in order that they might have a cup of tea with him, so much had his new ambassadorial status changed the attitude of the world. He made a profound impression in Bucharest; officials said rather patronizingly, " He cannot be such a Red after all ". Sir Stafford received me with his usual quiet courtesy and helpfulness; he had learned that by trusting journalists with valuable information you could prevent them trying to find unreliable and dangerous stuff to write. He answered all my questions carefully and well. At that time he was optimistic about his mission to Russia, although later he said that he had been sent two years too late. At that time (June 1940) he knew that Germany and Russia were still working very close together.

One of the immediate effects of Sir Stafford Cripps' appointment to Moscow was the nomination there of new and better diplomats. Ex - Foreign Minister Gafencu was appointed Romanian Minister there, as part of the scheme of improved relations with the U.S.S.R. In any case it was a little embarrassing for the Romanian Government to have anyone as important as Gafencu sitting around doing nothing. They feared, quite wrongly, that he might get together with Maniu and form a serious opposition party to the Government. One might even give the Cabinet credit for the feeling that his talents should be utilized. Rather reluctantly Gafencu accepted the post; Moscow did not attract him greatly, and he would have preferred almost any other country.

Sir Stafford's visit coincided with the nomination of the new Russian Minister to Bucharest, Monsieur Lavrentiev, and a general movement of rapprochement took place. This was the Romanian method of trying to tide over the Russian danger by being more friendly. The new Minister never had much power. He was allowed by his Government to visit the Foreign Office on State occasions and to call for a very few minutes on his colleagues, but he never mixed with the diplomatic corps. His chauffeur was the man who mattered in the Legation, the G.P.U. (Russian Secret Service) man who had been sent by Moscow to watch and report on the activities of the Russians in Romania. I often wondered how they spent their time behind the high walls

of the large and sinister-looking Legation which has so recently
been completed in Bucharest.

It is certain they had some contacts with the illegal Communists in Romania, but these were either intellectuals who
sincerely believed in Communism, or a few scattered peasants
and miners willing to take risks. Most of the people who in
England or America would be Communists had been driven
to the more hooligan and adventurous activities of the illegal
Iron Guard movement. This movement, financed by Germany
and fanned by the memory of the martyred Codreanu, its leader,
grew with enormous rapidity after the fall of France.

At this time the Germans were making much of their new
' plan ' for Europe. Every day more German ' tourists ' arrived
in Bucharest, some of them, such as Baron von Felsen, important men who had held responsible positions in America for
many years, and who immediately got on to terms with the
American colony. They reported on the plans for the ' new
order ', but the Romanian army remained mobilized and
equally divided between the German and the Russian frontiers.
Everywhere the Germans were being industrious and
clever.

On the Sunday before Gafencu left for Moscow I went with
Walter Duranty to the small Gafencu villa by the side of Lake
Snagove, and spent the entire day  bathing and talking. The
lake is one of a chain which King Carol planned to cover
the malaria-ridden swamps which surrounded Bucharest. He
intended that they should run from Snagove, 50 kilometres to
the north of Bucharest, down to the Danube. Though completed only so far as Bucharest itself, this chain of lakes forms
an agreeable boating-place, and provides sites for clubs and
restaurants for the town. I mention this in such detail as one
of the few constructive things accomplished by Carol during
his reign. On this last Sunday in Romania Madame Gafencu
sat chain-smoking on the terrace, her dyed yellow hair untidy,
wearing trousers as she pestered Duranty with questions about
suitable garments to take to Russia. He told her to take everything, powders, soaps and food for the next six months. Gafencu

was himself outspoken about his position in going to represent a Government of his country which he could not and did not support. He saw quite clearly what was going to happen in Romania, but blamed the English to some extent for not having supplied the country with the necessary equipment to make her army effective. I thought of his remarks many times in later months when the Blenheims which we had sent to Romania at great cost to ourselves were being flown by German pilots, the Romanians never being allowed to use their own machines after October 12, when the German ' mission ' arrived.

After the departure of Gafencu the English and French set played a less important social role. Prince Antoine Bibesco was informed that his services in the Romanian diplomatic corps would not further be required. His sister, Princess Marthe Bibesco, the wife of the head of the Bibesco house, once the ruling princes of Romania, turned more of her social attention to Germans and Italians. In the last war, though in possession of a house in Paris, she had managed to keep on very good terms with the Germans. After the war she managed once again to become on good terms with the King and Queen Marie. Now she gradually dropped the English for the numerous Germans who were arriving every day. Princess Marthe was reputed to have been the intimate friend of Carol's father ; she is now a handsome woman of middle age who runs her house on model lines and whose garden, on which only Bulgarians work, is the finest in the country. Not only was she on such excellent terms with all the officials, but she was known to be a friend of the most powerful woman in Romania, Madame Magda Lupescu. In fact, one of the most sensational exhibits in Madame Lupescu's house, which was opened to public view after the abdication, was a letter from Marthe to Madame Lupescu in which she said, " you are, in fact, the Queen of Romania ".

Marthe had many strange and unexpected friends, one of whom was a dull middle-class Englishman named Pow, who, because he was manager of some unimportant bank, imagined himself to be the leader of the British colony. He spoke with an appalling accent, and his wife's conversation was shocking for its crudity, but Marthe stoutly maintained that she obtained a great deal of useful information from these people, who were constantly in her house. When, however, I tried to obtain information from her concerning my German friends who were also friends of hers, despite my experience as a journalist, I never gained anything.

Madame Lupescu, whom I always think of as I saw her last, well covered but with blazing red hair, did not exercise the anti-German influence over King Carol which one would have expected from a Jewess. Magda Lupescu, who is now about forty-five, was born in Sulina, the daughter of the local chemist. She was a bright child, and quickly learned English from the then large British colony in Sulina. Her vivid personality soon enabled her to get a job in Bucharest, where she met King Carol, and so greatly influenced his life and the history of her country. She had a house in a smart suburb of Bucharest, but had all her meals with the King and played poker with him every night, a game at which she was particularly skilful.

Her house was full of treasures ; she had beautiful clothes and bought a great deal of jewellery in Romania. On a patch of land farther outside the town near to the Baneasa aerodrome she was building herself a large and beautiful country house when the crash came. Pillars for the courtyard were imported from an old château in Italy, doors which opened and closed by electricity, sunken baths and beautiful terraces, all in good taste, were already built, and obviously she had decided to become a hostess, as the kitchen was equipped to cook for at least 200 people. There was a secret path from the house to the airport, where King Carol's plane, rather uselessly, was always in good condition to take off at a moment's notice should a crash arise in the affairs of his country.

The loss of Bessarabia at the end of June 1940 was not only the beginning of the end of greater Romania and its independence, but it set alight the powers opposing the kingship of Carol. A year previously Walter Duranty, after visiting the country to collect material for one of his American magazine articles, wrote that there was little chance of Bessarabia being retained by Romania. The U.S.S.R. had never given more than a grudging consent that it should be Romanian territory (it had been attached to Russia for the previous hundred years). Though the wildest, Bessarabia was the least attractive part of Romania.

Chisinau (Kishinev in Russian days), the capital of the province, is one of the most depressing towns which it has ever been my ill-fortune to visit. Scarcely any of its houses appear to be more than one storey high, and though this is attractive enough in a town like Pinsk, where the houses are all huddled about higgledy-piggledy, in Chisinau, where all the roads cut one another at right angles and are in any case completely characterless, it is unbelievably depressing. Over everything there seems to hang a thin veil of grey dust. Chisinau is just the sort of place where one would go quietly away and hang oneself from sheer *tædium vitæ*. It was the site of the most scandalous of all the Jewish pogroms in the days of Imperial Russia. The only thing that suggested contact with the western world when I was there was a copy of the *Manchester Guardian Weekly* which I discovered on a kiosk. The water-closets at the Hotel Londra, the best in the place, are repellent even by Balkan standards.

There is no hotel in the whole province where one can obtain a bed with less than twenty bugs—this I regard as the maximum number for a possible night. The roads are quite impossible for motor traffic. In the towns there are cobbled streets, but these soon give place to black or dark grey mud tracks in which carts are often stuck axle deep, and in summer the mud turns to the most tiresome kind of dust. The corrupt administrations in Bucharest never made much effort to repair the roads or to build railway lines. The lines had been built for communication with Russia, and this made transport to Bucharest or to the Danube delta difficult. It was not possible to increase the agricultural output when there was no outlet for sales. This accounts argely for the poverty of most of the peasant inhabitants of Bessarabia, who were cultivating some of the richest land in Europe. During the last few years before the war the Lares, the Romanian air line, started a service to Chisinau. This made things easier for politicians and civil servants, but naturally did not affect the life of the peasant. The Romanians, who possessed a fair number of first-class American-built air liners, always used peculiar old machines on the service to Chisinau, and forced landings in out-of-the-way places were so frequent and the danger so obvious that many people preferred to travel by the slower but surer railway. For myself, having travelled by Polish, Yugoslav, Greek and Romanian air lines before the war and having had many uncomfortable experiences, I always make a point of getting a British or a German plane if at all possible.

The population of Bessarabia was rather mixed. In the towns were large numbers of Jews, who lived a kind of ghetto life, wearing the kaftan as do the poorer Jews in Poland. Many of the Jews who had risen above this standard of life were not very pleasant people, and they helped to cause the rise of antisemitic feeling throughout the whole country. Soon after the 1914–18 War the land reform had become efficient enough to allow for a small plot of land for every peasant. But the impossible transport and a series of bad harvests had made life so hard for many of them that they fell into the hands of the Jewish moneylender, mortgaging their land or, worse still, selling it. Thus the peasant made his own lot far harder. The Jews, too, do not show up well in Bessarabia, where they act as agents for selling the produce of the peasant in the large towns. They often made five or six hundred per cent. profit on their transactions. The Germans (who, as related elsewhere, were used as an excuse for bringing German soldiers into Romania in order to transfer these people back to Germany) were the most advanced of all the inhabitants of Bessarabia, and, numbering nearly a hundred thousand, were nearly all agriculturists. They had settled during the hundred years of Russian government, but in a truly German manner, though encouraged by Russians and not discouraged by the Romanians, they had retained their own language, habits and religion.

There are about one hundred and fifty thousand Russians in Bessarabia. Most of them are peasants who were settled there during the period of Russian government, but there are a few older Russian settlers in the delta region, and in the towns a few White Russians who came as refugees, as well as the administrative class which never desired to return to their country after the death of the Tsar. The Romanians give the population in 1930 as 2,864,000, out of which 1,611,000 were Romanian. There were, too, considerable numbers of Ukrainians and a few Ruthenians, as well as Bulgars and Turks.

This mixed population had no say as to who should in future govern them. On June 26, 1940, M. Davidescu received a demand from Molotov that within the space of twenty-four hours Romania should agree to the Russian occupation of Bessarabia. The language of the demand was not even diplomatic. This was the moment of supreme opportunity for Carol. He called a meeting of the Cabinet, but not until he had telephoned to Berlin to ask what help Germany could give Romania should she resist the claim. Hitler said no help would be forthcoming, and advised Carol (whom he had never liked) to give in to the Soviet demands. At this moment, I believe, Carol could have passed the buck back to Hitler and said, " If you don't help me rid my country of the menace of the Russians, then I shall destroy the oil wells the moment my frontiers are touched. You are now militarily supreme, and I need not tell you how much you depend on Romanian oil." Hitler could not afford that the oil should fall into the hands of Russia nor that the Romanians should destroy it. Carol really had the game in his hand, but lacked the guts to play it. He feared that war on Romanian territory would be the end of his personal fortune.

In this Carol represented the great majority of his countrymen, who would have taken the same decision. They would not have dared to destroy the great oil wealth of Romania when not believing that England could possibly win the war, and they feared the truth of the German gossip that any damage to the oilfields would call forth the worst bombing on Bucharest the Third Reich could produce. The one item of real difficulty lay in the presence in Romania of so large a fifth column. The Romanians had never dared to grasp this nettle. They even denied its existence, though repeatedly warned by the British Minister. The ex-Minister for the Interior told a few journalists in July that when he left the Ministry a few weeks previously there were no less than 91,000 Germans in Romania, and the German Military Attaché continually boasted to neutral colleagues that the German minority was in a position to take control of the country at four hours' notice. Carol knew, too, that if he took the risk of fighting the Russians (at that time no one knew anything about the strength of the Russian army except that it had put up a poor show against Finland), Hungary and Bulgaria would attack him in the back unless the Germans stopped them.

Englishmen like to think that had they been in Carol's place they would have taken the risk, told Hitler that they were going to fight to destroy the oilfields, and then waited to see what he said. I think that in that event, though Hitler wouldn't have liked it, his war with Russia would have begun then and there. King Carol was unfortunately only half English, and that was not enough to make him take this brave line.

Before the Cabinet arrived at the palace Carol had decided that Bessarabia and Northern Bukovina should be returned to Russia. The cars swept into the palace yard. A few people knew what the Crown Council was discussing. But an air of fear mixed with a little excitement was blowing around the town. Large numbers of people stood on their balconies expecting something to happen. The Athenée Palace Bar was, of course, full of diplomats and journalists. My tipster in the Foreign Office (Bucharest) could give me no line on what was in the air, but we all knew that a demand had been made for Bessarabia. The censors quite naturally denied this, as they later denied most other stories that were true, and tried to make us send to London untrue stuff obviously intended to mislead. News leaked out from the palace that the Government was going to give in to the Russian demands before the broadcast announcement in the afternoon of June 27. In fact, no one who knew

Romania believed that there was any chance of resistance being shown. The landowners flocked to Bucharest to find out what was going to happen to their estates in Bessarabia and the Bukovina. Many traders were upset that Cernauti, one of the largest and most developed towns in Romania, would fall into Russian hands. Before the last war Cernauti had been part of the Austro-Hungarian Empire, and looked like it. The only buildings were largish hotels with German names and three or four night-clubs. Noisy trams brought the peasants into the markets from the suburbs. Many Bucharest shops had branches in Cernauti, and all the best sausages and meat in Romania came from the Austrian shops in Cernauti. The town had a university and an English professor. As soon as the Romanian radio broadcast what amounted to acceptance of the Russian demand, wild rumours began to circulate. The Government, in a frantic effort to save its face, asked the Russians to name a time when they might talk things over. But the Russians knew that the big idea was to work quickly. They stated in a communiqué issued on the 27th that Bessarabia must be evacuated within four days.

On the day of the demands Russian planes began to appear over Bessarabia, and on the following days to fly over parts of Moldavia and the Danube delta. It was arranged that a Romanian-Russian Commission would sit at Odessa, and there was a wide belief that Russia had no intention of making no further demands. Hot-headed journalists sent stories that the Hungarians and Bulgarians had filed their demands already. As a matter of fact they did within a short time.

Carol knew he was in disgrace with his people after his many high-sounding speeches in which he had said that not one foot of Romanian soil should ever be lost. General mobilization was ordered. This added enormously to the fears of the masses, and a new Government was formed in the hope of calming everyone. As this Government consisted of men who had never been respected by the Romanians—many of its members being well-known swindlers—it was not successful in this object. Maps of Romania swathed in black crêpe appeared in many shop windows. Three days of national mourning were imposed, when all places of amusement were to be closed and the restaurants to have no orchestras. The German Minister left Bucharest for Berlin, but was away only a short time. His visit may have been caused by the numerous incidents which were reported from Bessarabia. Here and there the Romanian soldiers refused to retire and were fired on by the Russians. There was, I believe, at one moment a genuine danger that the Russians would cross some of the Danube delta waters and establish themselves in a position which would control the traffic of that all-important river. Urdarianu, who in private was one of Carol's swindling quartet and in public Minister of the Royal Court and chief of staff to the Party of the Nation, made a broadcast appeal to everyone to be calm and " hold their heads high in the homeland of misfortune ".

On July 1 the new Government denounced the British Guarantee of 1939 and stated that in future Romanian policy would orientate itself towards the Axis. This was no news to the people who lived in Romania, as the King's policy had for some months been exclusively pro-Axis. It was really an appeal to Hitler to protect them against the future demands of Hungary and Bulgaria. But Hitler was not interested, and when the German Minister returned he told Carol in no uncertain terms that Germany was unable to offer a military alliance to Romania.

Confusion, which never really began to sort itself out until the Germans occupied the country, reigned in all departments of state. Masses of refugees arrived at Bucharest. Hundreds of people with homes in Bessarabia and the Bukovina obtained or tried to obtain passes to return. Many were too stupid to apply for their papers within the prescribed time, and others did not do so when they should have done, owing to the reports which though denied at the time were later admitted to be true, that the Russian soldiers had advanced along the Pruth—the Bessarabian frontier. These troops did, however, return after a few days to within the province of Bessarabia. Horia Sima went to Carol and demanded without much hope that an Iron Guard Government should be formed. When Carol said No to this, the three Guardists in the Cabinet resigned. But the men who remained in office were, on the whole, more Fascist than the Guardists ; or perhaps it is truer to say that they were inclined to give everything to Germany and drop all the Romanian nationalist side of the Guardist doctrine.

## CHAPTER IV

# HUNGARY—ARISTOCRACY'S LAST STRONGHOLD

BRITISH Legations seem often to be situated on the tops of hills, from which the Minister rarely sees anything of the life which goes on below him. Ministers are in a difficult and delicate position; they cannot themselves sit about in cafés and find out what the local gossip may be. Sir Nevile Henderson, when Minister to Yugoslavia, solved the problem of finding out what public opinion was by meeting every day a well-known journalist, Harrison of Reuters. Harrison gave him a great deal of information, in exchange for which the Minister gave him an exclusive, though often off-the-second, line on Prince Paul and what inner Cabinet circles were thinking. It is a pity, for the sake of the information at the disposal of our Foreign Secretary, that more British Ministers have not followed Sir Nevile's excellent example!

The Minister in Budapest, O'Malley, rarely went to the bottom of the hill. During the early part of the war he was extremely friendly with the Third Secretary, an ex-Guardee named Holler, who had a beautiful and ambitious wife. Mrs. O'Malley (Miss Ann Bridge, the author of *Peking Picnic*), was in England, so Mrs. Holler became the Legation hostess. She had access to the Minister at any time of day. The only people who were entertained were the charming English-speaking Hungarian aristocracy. They ride, they have lovely estates to which English people are invited, they amuse themselves by ski-ing and skating in winter, they rarely do a regular job, and they are not trusted by their own people. Their estates are broken up, but they still have enough land on which to live. This aristocracy knows it is a dying race, but is enjoying its last days. It is less representative of Hungary than is Lord Londonderry of the British working classes. These Anglophile aristocrats not unnaturally convinced the Minister that Hungary was far from falling into the Axis orbit. The Minister realized that they were not speaking the truth, but failed either to arrange to receive information from the masses or to get it for himself.

In the years to come endless books will be written for and against British policy in the Balkans in the months after the war had begun and before fighting took place on Balkan soil. Personalities will be pulled limb from limb, and some will maintain that, given the geographical position of Hungary, not even the Archangel Gabriel could have prevented her from coming under German domination. Even if this be true, we might have had a better Minister in Budapest, a more energetic man who would have left behind him a memory favourable to the British cause during the years of war. We spend thousands of pounds on the British Council and other forms of propaganda, but neglect the propaganda value of having the right man in posts so important as that of British Minister to the Kingdom of Hungary.

Z. Baranyay, an intelligent Hungarian who had for many years worked at Geneva and in the Press Department of the Budapest Foreign Office, was sent as Consul-General to Chicago. He told me before he left : " This is not promotion, but all the Anglophiles are being pushed off. My son is at an English school, my views are too well known, and the British Legation is doing nothing to counteract German influence." Mr. C. A. Macartney, one of the few Englishmen who speak Magyar and really know the country and people, told me in January 1940 that he indeed met among all classes a great deal of Anglophile feeling, but had to admit that all the trade was quite naturally going to Germany, and that the heart of the bourgeois was where his money was. It was the bourgeoisie that ruled the country.

The Hungarians were far less melodramatic than the Romanians. Week by week they went further into the German camp, but from the point of view of a journalist there was never any news, nor any outstanding event to report. The Budapest Press Bureau always said : " Oh yes, we are really neutral, though slightly in the Axis camp ; we have tried to attach our- selves to the Rome end of the Axis." Occasionally they showed their goodwill to the British, or rather perhaps their sense of solidarity with the Polish aristocracy, to which they have always been bound by close ties, by allowing large numbers of Polish officers who had been interned in Hungary after getting out of Poland at the end of the Polish War to escape from their places of internment and find their way to France. The Hungarian politicians were often hard pressed to explain their adherence to the Axis, as since the Bela Kun Communistic régime Hungarian foreign policy had been based on two main props, opposition to Russia and Bolshevism on the one hand and to the Peace Treaties on the other. Hungarian Governments strongly desired to regain the large extent of territory which had been lost to Yugoslavia and Romania by the Treaty of Trianon at the end of the Four Years' War. Until Germany signed her pact with Russia in August 1939 these aims were not mutually contradictory, for Germany was violently anti-Russian, and supported Hungary in decrying the peace treaties and trying to reclaim her lost lands. When Germany became friendly with Russia, Hungary was forced into sending a diplomatic representative to Moscow, since her acquisition of Sub-Carpathian Russia or Ruthenia, filched with Germany's help from Czechoslovakia at the time of Munich, gave her a common frontier with Russia.

Occasionally the Hungarians made efforts to withstand German pressure. They refused to have a permanent German Military Mission established in Budapest during the early part of the summer of 1940, and as a sop, Germany offered Hungary a large part of her lost province of Transylvania. This she took at the expense of Romania. The Hungarians were most excited at receiving back at last part of the province to whose return all their propaganda since 1921 had been directed, and Germany's stock went up not only in the hearts of the aristocrats, who felt there was a chance of recovering some parts of the estates they had lost, but also among the bourgeoisie and the peasants, who not unnaturally felt that the Germans were really doing something for them.

Transylvania is a self-contained economic unit whose natural capital, Cluj (or Klausenburg), is in a hilly fertile country with a considerable German minority. Whether the Hungarians or the Romanians have the best right to rule the whole or a part of the country, it is impossible to judge fairly. The Romanian claim dates from the time of the Roman settlements; the Hungarians ruled it until the last war. Of the German colonists the older are Saxons, the more recent Swabians. The Saxons (Protestant) and the Swabians (Roman Catholic) have been constantly used as a means for stirring up trouble between Hungary and Romania. The Romanian minority, when Transylvania was part of Hungary, were largely peasants, the German peasants and townspeople, the Hungarian landowners and peasants. The Romanians were badly treated; when they acquired Transylvania they treated the Hungarians very badly in turn. Their estates were split up, Hungarian children were made to learn Romanian in school, and the number of Hungarian schools provided by the Romanian State was supposed to be far too few; but the country was fertile and prosperous, and the poorer peasants' houses were clean and pleasant, and had a far higher standard of comfort than in any other part of the Balkans. They could not be compared with the poorer Turkish villages (Mohammedans always seem to sink to a lower level than Christians, though I do not know why this should be) or the terrible villages of Egypt. Romanians from Bucharest were sent out to administer Transylvania from Cluj; the Hungarians were not allowed to have jobs in the Civil Service, and there was little for them to do but complain. They cannot, however, have been too badly treated, as I was always very lavishly wined and dined by Hungarian Counts when visiting Cluj, where they told me of the horrors of Romanian rule.

The Hungarian landlords, already impoverished by the Four Years' War and in many cases still more by the brief Communist interlude under Bela Kun in 1919, naturally suffered further heavy losses when their Transylvanian estates passed to Romania and, as Romanian territory, were subjected to the agrarian reforms which to a great extent divided up the estates among the peasants. There were cases where the owners of six thousand acres found their holdings reduced to one hundred and fifty. I have no intention here of going into the vexed question of these reforms and provoking a hornet's nest about my ears, though frankly my sympathies lie on the side of the peasants, but I am bound to admit that there were many injustices committed in the transfer of land. In theory the landlord was allowed to choose which part of his estates he could retain, in practice he could not do so. There does not appear to have been an equitable distribution as between Romanian and Hungarian peasants ; nor was all the land that was taken from the landlords (with negligible compensation or none at all) given to the peasants. Large areas were kept as ' State Reservations ', which meant royal parks and forests.

Whatever may be said against the Magyar landowners, their attachment to the soil was sincere enough. They had some of the merits as well as all the defects of a landed oligarchy. Count Banffy once told me that though his estates had been reduced from 1000 to 100 hectares and many Romanians had been introduced on to his lands, yet he preferred to remain, though it involved becoming a Romanian citizen and though frequent efforts were made by Romanian Governments to shift him in view of his position as potential leader of a Hungarian National movement. The attachment of this caste to a completely anachronistic organization of society is sometimes infuriating, sometimes pathetic. Sometimes, also, I have found it a trifle embarrassing, as on the occasion when Count Bethlen, the leader of the Hungarian minority, invited me to dinner. I was told not to dress, and I arrived, having driven that day from Bucharest, in a tweed coat and skirt. I came down to dinner to find my hostess who, though middle-aged, was a beautiful woman, tall and dignified, dressed in green satin with rows of pearls that set off her lovely white hair. They apologized for the poverty of the largish villa in which they lived, but the service seemed to me to be excellent, and the dinner, consisting mainly of chicken paprika, more delicate in flavour than one could have bought in Budapest, was accompanied by Hungarian wine of 1911 vintage from their own estates.

After the war began the German minority, which had been increasingly Nazi for some time, became completely and whole-heartedly pro-Hitler. They had mysterious stores of arms, and were themselves not sure whether these were to be used against the Hungarians or the Romanians. They collected arms, marched about the countryside, kept themselves fit, and waited for orders from Berlin ; but this Fifth Column, huge in size, was never needed. Hungary demanded that Romania give up Transylvania. This was one of the many causes of King Carol's abdication, indeed the one which finally brought about his departure, but the actual occupation of Transylvania by the Hungarians took place with a minimum of incident.

There were very few English people there, and once more Whitehall cannot have been well informed. Our Consul in Cluj, Mr. Peter Pares, son of Sir Bernard Pares, was quite at sea among the intrigues of Germans, Hungarians and Romanians. Bucharest after the Hungarian occupation was soon flooded with ' real ' photographs showing Romanian priests who had been shot and Romanian women who were supposed to have been raped, but I soon saw that these photographs had been previously used by the Romanian press in illustrating the horrors of another tyranny. Romanians were strongly recommended not to leave before the Hungarian occupation, as Bucharest was already overfull with refugees from the Dobrudja, which King Carol had lost to Bulgaria, and Bessarabia, which he had previously lost to Russia.

It was always difficult to evoke any enthusiasm about Tran-sylvania, as one was so pumped by propagandists on both sides. I well remember when the question of ceding Transylvania to Hungary was first discussed. Germany was, of course, putting pressure on Romania to accede to her wishes. It was arranged that a Hungarian delegation should go to Romania to discuss the new frontiers and the methods by which the local administration should be handed over. The Romanians were eager that we journalists should make a good story for them, and for once the Press were well treated. A special coach was attached to the night train from Bucharest to Turnu Severin, a small Danubian port situated as near as possible to Hungary, where the conference was to take place. We got out of the train and stood about in the blazing sun from 8 o'clock in the morning until 11.30, waiting for the arrival of the ship bearing the Hungarian delegates. There was nowhere to sit and nowhere to get a drink, nor indeed any place to shelter from the sun. At last the ship arrived, and in order to be as insulting to their hosts as possible, the Hungarians kept the Romanian officers waiting to receive them on the dock for an hour while they " changed their uniforms ".

Just before one o'clock, in gold brocade and with many medals, the delegates disembarked and walked slowly to the waiting cars. The little Hungarian Press Attaché, rather to my dismay as I was staying in Romania, rushed up to me saying : " My dear Miss Hollingworth, why have you not been to Hungary recently ? You must sit down and let me tell you what is happening, as I am sure you must be very badly informed by the Romanians here." The Romanian Press representative overheard this remark, and my stock, never very high with the Romanians, was to sink lower. We went up a steep and dusty hill to the building where the conference was to take place only to find when we arrived there that the Hungarians and Romanians were so much at loggerheads that it was impossible for them to begin their conference owing to their inability to settle simple questions of procedure.

My story was obviously to be that nothing had happened. I looked for the censor, and he passed the story—not that it mattered whether he did or not, as no journalist with any sense took any notice of the Romanian censor ! I looked for a telephone ; there was one, and about thirty journalists were fighting to get possession of it. Being small, I pushed my way quietly through the crowd until I got to the door of the kiosk by creeping under two people who were fighting to get into it. I got my hands on the telephone, and twined my arms round the mouthpiece so that nothing short of dislocating that could possibly pull me out of the box. The harassed girl at the exchange then told me Rome was on the line. I know I should have handed the instru-

ment over immediately to the correspondent of Stefani, but I
also knew if I did I should never see that telephone again ; so
refusing Rome and refusing to move, I got my call through to
Geneva, and the day's work was over.

It was obvious that the conference would continue for a
week. It was equally obvious that life in Turnu Severin was
going to be most uncomfortable, and that few stories with any
news value would come out of it. Bucharest was a city where
anything might happen, so we all trooped back to Bucharest on
the afternoon train, knowing that the Germans would say,
when they were tired of this child's play between Hungary and
Romania, in what way the province of Transylvania should be
occupied.

The Romanians had great difficulty in finding men willing
to be delegates at such an unpopular conference ; everyone refused,
rightly feeling that at any moment the Romanian population
might turn on them and murder them as people who had betrayed their country, and shoot them up in good Romanian
style. People remembered that Marghiloman, the Germanophile
Premier who had accepted office when Romania was defeated
in 1916, and had done his best at the Treaty of Fossy to temper
the Mitteleuropa wind to the shorn Romanian lamb, had never
been forgiven by his countrymen. It was queer to see how
much emotion and feeling, as genuine as a Romanian ever has,
was put into this absurd wrangling over Transylvania when
each country must have known that its existence depended
entirely on Germany.

How right we were not to stay on in Turnu Severin ! The
conference dawdled on for ten days, and the stupid agency men
who covered it came back thirsty and bug-bitten. The Romanian
police were almost efficient, and refused to allow them any
contact with the Hungarians or even to bathe in the River
Danube, hot though it was.

As the world now knows, Romanian and Hungarian delegates
were called to Vienna in September and the Vienna Diktat
organized by the Germans and Italians was handed out for the
Romanians to accept. The preamble to the award, read by

Ribbentrop to the assembled delegates in the Belvedere Salon, after stressing the disinterestedness of Axis mediation, expressed the optimistic hope that " a firm foundation for lasting and friendly relations between Hungary and Romania had been created ". One would like to know the reactions of the Romanian delegates when they heard this statement.

The interesting feature about the award is that, arbitrary and erratic as the new frontier was, it gave a superficial impression of having actually been conceived with some regard for ethnography. The majority of the proposals for frontier rectification in favour of Hungary had envisaged the shifting of Romania's western frontier some distance farther east, so as to include in the territory to be ceded such towns as Arad, Oradea Mare and possibly Cluj. In the same way, the Romanians, at the height of their demands during the last war, when the Allies with a somewhat naïve belief in the value of their military support were making the most extravagant offers, had obtained a provisional promise of the Theiss frontier, many miles west of the final settlement.

The Vienna award adopted a different principle. Taking account of the compact Székler bloc (of undoubted Magyar race though settled for many centuries in their present homes) which lies in the great bed of the Carpathians at the farthest extremity from the Hungarian border, the Vienna settlement devised a new frontier which, roughly speaking, gave the north and east of Transylvania to Hungary, leaving to Romania the south and west as well as the whole of the Banat. Thus Hungary received Oradea Mare, Cluj and the whole Székler region, but not Arad, Sighisoara or Brasov. Hungary obtained somewhat more than half of Transylvania proper, though Romania was left in possession of more than, in her crumbling and chaotic condition, she could have hoped to retain. A solution had been found for that Székler problem which had baffled so many amateur re-shapers of Central Europe.

Needless to say, the Nazis were not interested in nice points of ethnographical justice. What they wanted was a division which would render both Hungary and Romania more than ever dependent on Germany. The new frontier makes the effective defence of the remainder of Transylvania a strategic impossibility. In other words, the Germans could, if they wished, give the order at any time for the conquest or absorption of the remainder of the province, and the Romanians would be in no condition to resist. Actually, of course, no Romanian resistance was likely in any circumstances, even had Germany allotted the whole of the province to Hungary. The state of confusion and disorientation in Romania at this time is impossible to exaggerate. The will to resist, never the most dominating feature of the Romanian character, had been sapped by the loss of Bessarabia to Russia without any show of fight and by the approaching cession of Southern Dobrudja to Bulgaria. Besides, resistance seemed to imply support of King Carol's person and régime, both now almost universally unpopular; it also implied resistance to the will of Germany, and this no Romanian had ever seriously contemplated. As early as March, before the French collapse, responsible men in Romania had told me: " Of course, though we are pro-Ally, it would be out of the question for us to attempt to resist a German attack."

Much was expected in ill-informed quarters of some effective action, or at least some 'strong declaration' from Maniu. This thin-faced little man, who had been so heavily played up by the Western Powers as the man who would save democracy in Romania, was never in the picture. He flitted irresolutely from Crown Councils in Bucharest to his native Cluj, but his almost pathological fear of responsibility saved him as usual from the embarrassment of action. I have always felt that too much significance has been attributed to this little figure. He was a good democrat, an honest man and a friend of England, but he was the last conceivable person to " ride the whirlwind and direct the storm ". I was very forcibly reminded during these days of crisis of the not dissimilar part played by Herriot in the last days of the French Republic. The same wishfulness enveloped both figures; both were technical Leftists of a brand mild enough to be acceptable to the Right; in both the reluctance to take office in the numerous transient Cabinets of the past few years was regarded in certain quarters as a sign that they were reserving themselves in order to emerge with more authority in crises ; the development of a real crisis in their respective countries showed them both lamentably unequal to the situation.

The partition of Romania, reducing its population, it is estimated, from 20,045,000 to 13,291,000, might stand as a parable of the results for a small power of the abandonment of the Collective System. Since Titulescu, Romania has had no statesman who has fully grasped the vital importance of this organization to the continued independence and integrity of his country, and it was certainly not his fault that in supporting the sanctions policy at the time of Abyssinia he was tying his political fate and that of Romania to a cock that had no intention of fighting — that sinister double-headed cock called sometimes Laval and sometimes Baldwin. Sanctions were dead, the Collective System had been fatally betrayed, and Titulescu was out of office by the late summer of 1936. After that, the only hope for the Balkan countries lay in the never very impressive Balkan Entente, which, superficially providing for mutual guarantees of frontiers by Romania, Yugoslavia, Turkey and Greece, was in fact so hedged round by reservations as to render it virtually invalid in the event of any likely aggression. A secret protocol provided that " if one of the High Contracting Parties is the victim of aggression on the part of a non-Balkan Power, and if a Balkan State joins it in its aggression . . . the Pact will operate with full effect against that Balkan State ". Even this guarded attempt to introduce some reality into the Pact proved too much for its signatories, who forthwith began ' contracting out ' of the responsibility of being involved in war with any non-Balkan Power. Only in the extremely unlikely event of a single-handed aggression by Bulgaria against one of the signatories (all of whom had common frontiers with her) would the Pact have come into effective operation. Yugoslavia, for instance, would never have assisted Romania against Russia, nor would Turkey have stirred out of Thrace to aid Yugoslavia (or Greece for that matter, as was later to be seen against Italy). And naturally no other Balkan country in August 1940 ever contemplated for one moment aiding Romania against a Hungary backed by Germany and Italy.

Romania's reduction to practical impotence and, as an enforced tributary to the Axis, to the loss of independence in her foreign policy, marked the end of a transition in Balkan diplomacy from manœuvres designed to maintain and preserve solid Balkan cohesion for self-defence against outside aggression to an utter chaos of conflicting foreign policies, as each State, with the exception of Greece, whose geographical position in the Mediterranean compelled close connection with England, was driven to clarify its position either within an existing Axis sphere, within a potential Soviet sphere of influence, or in a more or less hopeless compromise between them.

By one of the queer streaks of the Romanian national character, so violently anti-Hungarian, its hatred was not transferred to the Germans after the Vienna award, but continued its age-old direction against the Magyar. The Hungarians occupied their new territory by daily steps, taking eight days in all. At the end of this time the map of Hungary came to resemble that of the ill-fated Czechoslovakia. Neither Hungary nor Romania regards this settlement as final. In order to bribe the politicians of both countries, the Germans have frequently promised the Hungarians that they will eventually own the whole of Transylvania, while at the same time solemnly assuring the Romanians that in exchange for their military support against Russia they would be assured of reoccupying their lost territory.

Germany has most cleverly driven a wedge between Hungary and Italy. She promised Hungary that in return for the use of her territory for the transport of troops and the storage of oil and other war materials, she should resume her sovereignty over the old Kingdom of Croatia (it will be remembered that Croatia was ruled by the Hungarian end of the Austro-Hungarian Empire before the Four Years' War). Italy had cast covetous glances on Croatia, and had spent enormous sums of money on propaganda in that country ; and Germany rather surprisingly allowed Italy its sovereignty. Perhaps she felt that Hungary had already become too powerful.

Admiral Horthy, a man of seventy-three (who still remains Regent of this coastless Kingdom) was, or professed to be, very Anglophile. He has a great following in Hungary, and it seems unlikely that the Germans will interfere with his nominal rule, since in any case he cannot live very much longer. The Hungarians have shown no desire to let his son follow him in the Regency, and it will be very easy for the Germans to put in their own man ; for there is no other obvious successor, save for the Hapsburgs, whom the Hungarians are unlikely to want, as until recently they have been backed very hard by the British.

One of the queer things about this war is the change of feeling among the English upper classes towards the Hohenzollern and Hapsburg families. If certain Conservative Members of Parliament, who incidentally know neither the Hapsburgs nor Central and South-Eastern Europe, had their way, there is no doubt that the monarchs who were turned out of Europe after the last war would be restored after this one. The Nazi Party in Hungary is now strong. Jewish persecution, long fashionable among Hungarians of all classes, has been going at full swing, and the trade and banks of Budapest have automatically passed into German hands through the expulsion of Jews from these professions. The Hungarian aristocracy has never entered professional life save as diplomats, and when the Jews were expelled from newspapers, lawyers' offices and the Civil Service the Hungarians had no alternative but to accept the pressing applications of the Germans, as no Magyars were sufficiently well trained for the job. However old the Romanians may claim to be as a race—and they quite frequently claim direct descent from the Romans—they are a new nation and a new country. The Hungarians, who themselves are not above a bit of bribery and corruption, do, however, give the impression and appearance of a people of long-established culture. Budapest is no tawdry little Paris, as Bucharest is. Budapest, full of night-clubs though it is, manages to look and feel like a capital city. The Hungarians, too, have always had a natural flair for propaganda. Soon after the last war influential Englishmen like

5

Lord Rothermere took up the cause of the revisionists. Hungarian Counts, charmingly mannered and beautifully dressed, have constantly visited England and impressed Englishmen of all classes. The very fact that although Hungarians needed a visa to visit Britain, Britishers did not need a visa to go to Hungary, is an indication of the way the Hungarians put themselves out to attract tourists to their charming capital ; and having got the tourists there they let their propaganda loose on them. Rich young men, or more frequently young journalistic arrivistes who wanted a cheap holiday, got themselves introductions in the country—these were easy enough to obtain— and spent an agreeable time being entertained (and the Hungarians entertain extremely well) in the Horseback Hall of Europe. On their return to England they showed themselves ardent champions of Hungary. Sometimes they even wrote books in favour of Treaty Revision in the Danube Basin, but I have always felt that these books owed their conception to palates warmed and stimulated by Imperial Tokay. The Romanians, naturally enough, soon tumbled to this game ; and they too began to entertain lavishly and to trot potential propagandists of British and French nationality round the country, explaining that all was for the best in the best of all possible Transylvanias. I remember being told by a British confrère, who was being conducted on one of these tours, of the extreme difficulty he experienced in getting into touch with the British Consul in Timisoara, who was suspected, wrongly as it happened, of pro-Hungarian sympathies. At the luncheon given in the visitor's honour he was widely separated from the Consul. During his subsequent tour of the city a little group of the local notables formed a sort of bodyguard round him, preventing any contact from taking place. An arrangement made for a subsequent rendezvous in Bucharest was overheard by one of the local notables, and led to a fortnight of most elaborate manœuvring of the British correspondent round the city, during which his two conducting officials constituted themselves a sort of Rosencrantz and Guildenstern to his Hamlet. It involved at least two intentionally missed railway connections and an almost certainly intentional motor-car breakdown at Cetatea Alba at the extreme opposite end of Romania from Timisoara. Of course, things are not as a rule done as crudely as this; but the episode is indicative of the difficulties that beset the path of the would-be objective observer of Central European and Balkan problems.

## CHAPTER V

## ROMANIA—CAROL ABDICATES

SIX weeks before King Carol was to abdicate he arrested General Antonescu, the man to whom he was to turn at the last moment to save him. Carol knew that his job as King was extremely insecure; he knew that at any moment he might be shot by a member of the Iron Guard, or, if he were lucky, he might merely be asked to abdicate. Many Romanians at the time of the abdication had so much respect for General Antonescu that they could not believe that a great deal of his anti-Carol activities were in fact inspired by personal venom against the King. Antonescu, a little fat man, fat all over rather than paunchy, spoke excellent English, and had been Military Attaché in London. Like Gafencu's, his marriage was, socially speaking, catastrophic, as he married a manicurist whose manners were ill-bred and morals indiscreet. She did, however, dress rather well, as she had once worked in a millinery shop. Madame was much taller than the General, and during their years of ' exile ' she had become strong and healthy, owing to the plentiful exercise which the General insisted on taking in the Carpathian mountains. Antonescu had quarrelled with Carol soon after the latter became King of Romania, and in order to avoid trouble he had gone to live at a villa at Predeal in the Carpathian mountains.

This accounted for the friendship which existed between the American Minister, Mr. Gunther, and the General, as Mr. Gunther used Predeal as his second home. He went there every week-end, and there was generally no one else to talk to but Antonescu. Unfortunately, Antonescu never took the good advice offered by the Americans, but he was willing to talk to them much more freely than he spoke to the British. When Carol had Antonescu arrested on charges of plotting against the State, though the charges were kept very secret at the time, Antonescu was brought from his villa to prison in Bucharest.

Few people outside Romania had ever heard of Antonescu, and those who had regarded the arrest as another clear example of Carol's pro-German tendencies. During the time Antonescu was in prison he built up by illegal methods of communication some kind of organization to keep himself in touch with events in the outside world. But when Carol released him and asked him to form a Government he said : " You must give me two days to find out what has been happening during the time you have kept me in prison."

At this moment the atmosphere of Bucharest was extremely tense. Street demonstrations with firing were then a fairly new experience, and after three nights during which the crowd was fired on at intervals by Romanian soldiers it was apparent that some sacrifice must be made to the mob, and the most obvious sacrifice was Carol.

I hold no brief for Carol ; he was a swindler, a traitor to his country, a disloyal friend and a murderer, but he seemed no worse than the men who followed him. Transylvania was lost through Carol. Antonescu came in on the cry of saving it. The English felt that it would be excellent for the pro-German King to go, and be replaced by a sympathetic, if not exactly pro-British, dictator. Not a soul, apart from the people who were actually making money out of Carol, wanted him to stay. The Iron Guards loathed him for having ordered the shooting of their leader Codreanu. The Transylvanian Peasant Party led by Maniu loathed him because he was a dictator. But, most important of all, the man in the street loathed him and hated the pretentious new palace which was started immediately after the King returned from his state visit to London.

Carol was never to see the fruits of his hard work in palace building. One wing was in the roughest stage with scaffolding, and many of the enormous salons were never even painted. A man from Waring & Gillow was sent out to design and arrange the interior. He stayed at the palace until Carol disappeared. What an example, if one were needed, of Carol's inferiority complex ! He wanted his palace to be larger than Buckingham Palace, and had he remained king it would undoubtedly have ended by being bigger than Windsor Castle. A theatre to hold over 1000 people and a church to hold about 400 were being included among the new buildings. Instructions were given to spare no money. This palace probably did him more harm than the political hatred of Left, Right and Centre combined. Any peasant who returned to his village from Bucharest told his cronies all about the palace and the houses that were being pulled down around it, in order that the King might have a vista; the peasant could not be expected to realize that the vista was really a good sweep for machine-guns.

The rare peasant who visited Bucharest generally boasted to his friends on his return to his native village of the lavish way the King was spending money in the capital. But the cronies who heard the boasting soon turned the traveller to shame when their own poverty was mentioned. It is difficult to re-member that the Romanian peasant when conscripted earned 20 lei a month, when the official quotation was 620 lei, and the unofficial 1500 to 4500 lei, to the pound sterling.

The new palace had long been a stale joke in Bucharest when the peasants began to learn of its existence. The province of Bessarabia had been lost; Dobrudja and Transylvania were soon to go; there was an atmosphere of tension between Russia and Germany, and the more the Romanian State tried to sup-press news inside the country, the more hysterical and uncertain the people became. It was rumoured many times that the Russians were marching towards Bucharest; this story was spread by German fifth columnists. Carol's two crack divisions, which had already been in the capital for some days, were on duty at every strategic point with lorries of water and hose pipes. In the big square in front of the palace they were supported by machine- and sub-machine-guns. The Hotel Athenée Palace, where many of the diplomats and journalists were staying, commanded the only good view of the square. When shooting began against the demonstrators everyone was forbidden to leave the hotel, and lights blazed all night through the first-floor windows as the Cabinet were in session.

We journalists watched from the first floor of the hotel.

The servants were so frightened by the sound of the machine-guns that no one could obtain drinks, so we all collected in Walter Duranty's sitting-room. Large cars drove up to the police cordons and were quickly allowed to pass, driving madly through the square and into the palace gates. Carol's white-uniformed footmen were constantly opening and shutting the swing doors. The soldiers could not disperse the crowd, which hourly increased in size until midnight. One stray rifle bullet was fired into a smart garden restaurant, and all the diners ducked under the tables. When I fought my way through the police, who were trying to stop everyone leaving the hotel, I could learn nothing from the crowd. They did not know what they wanted. Many of them were sad that the country was falling to pieces before their eyes, but they had no policy, no idea what to do. They were watching with emotional interest what was going to happen: watching, too, the personal drama of the King, the tenth anniversary of whose accession they had celebrated only a few months previously.

Despite its negative attitude, the crowd did realize that it was angry about the loss of Transylvania, which was then being occupied day by day by Hungarian troops. Again and again the King had said: "Not one metre of Romanian territory shall pass into the hands of the Hungarians." Now three countries had taken from King Carol just what they wanted. The crowd was angry, but no one shouted that he should go. I drove to other less prosperous parts of the town. It was difficult to move about, as the police were trying to stop traffic circulating. Demonstrations in the slums were far more ugly, and it is certain that they were organized by the Iron Guards, who not unnaturally attracted a large number of discontented young men anxious to join in any kind of disturbance.

The Romanian people, like the Germans, are fond of a show, and Carol had not given them one for some time. They don't much mind whether it is a wedding or a funeral or just a procession with a King or Prince as the centre of attraction. A diplomat who had just returned from representing the British Minister at a funeral once said to me: " The Romanians are corpse-worshippers. The dead man lay in his open coffin in front of the altar. His face was made up with plenty of powder and rouge in the usual style of officers, and he was wearing what had once been his evening clothes. Everyone attending the funeral service had to go up and kiss the body, and how they enjoyed it ! "

Carol had provided nothing in the way of processions for many years. He was afraid to go out lest the Iron Guard should shoot him. But between the time when he asked Antonescu to form a Cabinet and the hour of his abdication he did something to satisfy the desire for excitement and public emotion which every Romanian feels. For the first time since the abolition of political parties the Press had that morning contained several mild attacks on the King.

Antonescu, unable to form a new Government, and fearing serious trouble in the country, had forced the King to sign a decree which greatly limited the powers of the monarch, but gave Antonescu the authority or almost the authority of a dictator. In future Antonescu had " full authority in the conduct of all State affairs ". The King did retain command of the armed forces and the rights of minting money, of granting pardons, appointing diplomatic representatives abroad and concluding international agreements. Changes in the Cabinet, the decree stated, must in future be announced over the double signatures of the King and Antonescu. It was significant that the all-powerful German Minister, Fabricius, took no part in these proceedings, though he was kept well informed by all the parties concerned.

Before Antonescu was asked to form a Government the King had invited the Iron Guards to serve in one, and they had refused, using as their excuse that they could not serve under the man who had lost Transylvania. To those who have never lived in Romania the complete lack of logic in the aims and policy of the Iron Guard is so fantastic that it sounds like a poor joke. But it was not funny. The Iron Guard had always been supported and financed by Germany. It was known as the Romanian Nazi Party. But at the time of the loss of so much Romanian territory as a direct result of the increased German power in Romania and south-eastern Europe generally, the Iron Guardists organized riots all over the country to protest. They even went so far as to shoot some officials well known as supporters of Carol. There was, however, a strong pro-German sentiment in the Party, as well as a strong Romanian nationalist feeling.

Antonescu's first job was to sack his arch-enemy Urdarianu. Years previously Antonescu had left the palace swearing not to return as long as Urdarianu, Minister of Court and intimate friend of Carol, remained. Newspapers described Antonescu's sudden accession to power as a *coup d'état*. Certainly the occupation of Transylvania made the fall of the Gigurtu Government inevitable.

The King's object in falling on Antonescu's neck and succumbing to his terms was probably the hope of saving a certain number of lives, including his own, from the disorderly shooting. Antonescu, as the King well knew, had the support of the army. No one knew what Antonescu's relationship was with the Iron Guard and, before the censorship had time to prevent comment, articles appeared glorifying the Iron Guard, attacking Carol and demanding the ' rehabilitation ' of Corneliu Codreanu, who was compared to Hitler, Mussolini, Kemal and Franco. It was also during these two or three days of Press freedom that Bratianu, the Liberal leader, who took part, though only as an observer, in all the proceedings of that eventful week, was allowed to publish an appeal to the Romanian people. We did not know at the time that when Antonescu assured the Axis Ministers that he would loyally carry out the Vienna Diktat, he also assured them that he would carry out as well those secret clauses which allowed two divisions of uniformed German troops to enter Romania to ' instruct ' the Romanian Army.

It has been said that no dictator in history has ever been able to relinquish part of his power and yet retain his job ; Carol was no exception. I was only surprised that he did not fight longer. King Carol abdicated, and the official story, which is rather different from the true one, which was told me by someone who was present during the whole proceedings, was given by

General Antonescu over the radio to the Romanian people. Antonescu in this address said he had been forced to break his oath to ex-King Carol and to demand his abdication for fear of civil war.

" I took upon myself sincerely to defend the policy and honourably to defend Your Majesty," thus Antonescu reported his conversation with Carol. " But all my attempts to find capable and honest men to participate in the new Government failed. I demand your abdication, for there is such disorder in the country that it may easily turn to civil war. I am not in a position to control the present state of affairs. In demanding your abdication, I express the desire of the whole country. At the same time I wish to draw your attention to the responsibility which may fall upon you in case you refuse to accede to this request, which is both the voice of the people and the desire of the army."

That was the story of Carol's abdication as given the public by Antonescu. What really happened, however, was much more dramatic, and here is the real story.

It was known that the King did not want to abdicate ; apart from the financial advantage of being a king, Carol enjoyed the job and was loath to give it up. Antonescu bullied, cajoled, and finally at the critical moment took the King to a window on the first floor of the palace and let him look out on the assembled mob which was being restrained with difficulty by the machine-gun nests. When the crowd saw Carol they hissed. Antonescu quickly drew the King into the room.

" I cannot be responsible for your life (he dropped the ' Sir ') if you stay on," he told the King. " But if you leave I will guarantee that you and Madame Lupescu arrive safely on the far side of the frontier. In one hour the soldiers will be unable to control that surging mob, ammunition will run out, the palace will be broken into, and your body will receive the same treatment as those of the Tsar of Russia and the King of France."

Carol walked across the room and stood for two or three minutes talking to Madame Lupescu. He returned to Antonescu.

" Yes, I will go," he said. " There are two things I want :

one, that you should help me to persuade my son Michael to come with me, and, two, that you should realize that I know you could have formed a Cabinet and prevented this situation. I know you are a good enough soldier to have had the military under sufficient control to make this last melodramatic threat superfluous."

King Carol then asked that Michael should be brought in. He appealed to Michael to come with him. Magda Lupescu appealed too. But it was in vain; Antonescu had won over this confused young man before his father had decided to abdicate.

Magda Lupescu made a desperate effort to have the young Prince accompany them, for their safety, as she was far more alarmed than Carol. She felt that the Romanian mob would never fire on the boy. She may, too, have experienced a feeling of feminine jealousy at the boy's going back to his mother. It had taken Lupescu years to win Michael's affection, and probably she quite genuinely did not want to lose it again.

Michael, in pompous phrases, told his father and his father's mistress that he would stay and be King a second time. The draft of the abdication was swiftly drawn up, strangely enough in the presence of one or two of the more respectable Romanian politicians, such as George Bratianu, as well as of the gangsters who were in office. Those of us who had been waiting up all night wondering how Carol would withstand the storm, were quite suddenly informed that the deed of abdication would be issued in a special communiqué at 7.30 in the morning. King Carol had had two hours in which to answer Antonescu's demands.

Official communiqués were General Antonescu's favourite device for self-deception. He issued six or seven most days, and if they stated that the country was once more prosperous and that order had been restored, Antonescu believed it himself, even though no one else ever did. This communiqué announcing the abdication was the last to be believed.

Order was quickly restored. Michael took the oath as the new King " to preserve the integrity of the Romanian frontiers " at 9.30 on the morning of September 6. Immediately afterwards the young man signed decrees for a political amnesty and for the limitation of his own royal prerogatives.

The new King drove round the streets in an open car, and the emotional Romanian crowd were rather excited about him. It was also announced that the Queen-Mother, King Carol's ex-wife, was returning to Romania, and preparations to receive her began. The English were delighted that she was coming back with the title of Queen-Mother. They thought that as a friend of Princess Marina and sister of the King of Greece she would have a pro-English influence at Court. They thought, too, that she had been ill-treated by Carol, and that she was what is known as a good woman. Their hopes were dashed, despite the messages of warm congratulation from the British royal family. The Queen imported her Italian Count within a week of her return.

I felt rather sorry for the young King as I saw him standing on the balcony receiving the cheers of the curious mob. He looked lonely and unhappy, as well as young and beset with bovine stupidity. He came out on to the balcony at 8.30, and from that time he appeared every half-hour hatless and alone. In the centre of the crowd was a contingent of orderly Iron Guardists, who marched into the square with flags and a picture of Codreanu. Throughout the morning they sang patriotic songs, led by Codreanu's father. They were distributing a manifesto which accused King Carol once again of killing their leader, Codreanu. It included a good deal of rubbish about the mystic side of the movement, which translated into English meant very little, if anything, but which may have appealed to the more democratically minded of the peasants.

King Michael was popular, for it was impossible for any adult to dislike a boy who was king of a country with neither Government nor Constitution. The crowd kept asking one another " Will the boy with the support of the army be able to hold the country together ? Where is Horia Sima, and what does he think of this ? Will the Iron Guard continue their support ? "

Nevertheless Carol still remained the centre of interest for foreign news correspondents. The abdicating King delayed his departure for two or three days, presumably in order to pack an enormous amount of valuables and clothes to take away. A special train with all his baggage and jewellery was sent on ahead. On September 10 he left amid great secrecy. No sooner had the train lurched out of Bucharest station than vanloads of police arrived outside Lupescu's house. They took no notice of six enormous Blenheims which were chained in their kennels, and, whilst the neighbours in the Parcul Philipescu were being disturbed by the noise of these dogs, 164 packing cases were carried out on to lorries. There seems little doubt that Lupescu had meant to carry these cases away with her, but at the last minute had been forced to leave them behind. The house was ransacked by hooligans after the police had gone, and somewhat later restored and opened to the public.

The return of Queen Helen, too, was held up by various delays.

The spirits of sorrow, rejoicing and tension merged into one another so much at this point that the shopkeepers of the capital did not know whether to smile or look miserable. The nation was supposed to be weeping for the loss of Transylvania. The famous gipsy bands in the restaurants were silent, cinemas and night-clubs were shut. Even hotel bars were not allowed to open, and restaurants were closed at the highly inconvenient hour of 11. In Bucharest, where one normally does not begin dinner until 9.30 or 10, it is irritating to be thrown out into the streets at 11 without one's coffee. The Romanian national flag, swathed with yards of black crêpe, was flown from every window. Official mourning was put on in a big way, yet there was supposed to be rejoicing at the Queen's return to her dismembered State.

The looks of this perfectly ordinary woman were described as though she were some fairy princess, whilst shops brought out from the storeroom pictures of her taken at the time of her marriage to Carol some twenty years previously. Photographs of Michael from the day he was born almost until the day his father abdicated were also shown, draped with the Romanian colours.  A little piece of paper bearing the words " His Majesty King Michael " was stuck over the previous inscription, " Prince of Alba Julia " which distinguished those printed during his father's period of office.  King Carol's photographs, which had alone been the focal point of every shop window, and one of which stood on a large trestle table draped in green velvet in the Athenée Palace Hotel, were quickly relegated to lavatories.  Every Romanian householder has a nail on which he hangs the photograph of the man in office, even after he is in office no longer.  It seems thriftless to throw them away unless their originals are dead, so they are kept invariably hanging on odd nails in the water-closet.

The air of sadness hanging over the city did not diminish as flags appeared in the streets.  Many of the State employees, important and humble, were nervous as to their future position. They had retained their jobs only by becoming at least nominally supporters of King Carol and members of the National Renaissance Front.  They had to some extent prospered during what was now termed " ten years of tyrannical government ".  Many of them were corrupt, and, as Antonescu was being played up as extremely honest, they all feared what was worse than dismissal —arrest.  Already Tatarescu, ex-Prime Minister, and Melaxa, great industrialist and friend of Carol, had been arrested, as well as large numbers of minor politicians of no importance whatever, who were for the most part killed in the Civil War the following January.  Although officials denied it, the American head of the telephone company in Romania assured me it was true that the Iron Guard held the telephone exchange at Brasov and the troops would make no effort to overcome the rioters. The chief of police of Brasov said, " We shall take action when we know what is going to happen in Bucharest ".

The German Minister, Fabricius, carefully refrained from commenting on the Iron Guard riots or disorders.  He did say to an American friend of mine : " Carol abdicated because he had to, not out of his love for his country, as he said.  I hope and believe that General Antonescu will be able to restore order and aid consolidation in South - Eastern Europe."  When

Fabricius was questioned as to whether the guarantees which the Axis had offered Romania to preserve her mutilated frontiers were conditional on the abdication of King Carol, Fabricius replied, "Events in Romania—domestic events—are purely the affair of the Romanian people". The German Press, which we saw regularly in Bucharest, refrained from attacking King Carol.

It is strange now to write that, as the King was abdicating and Iron Guard and hooligan demonstrations were occurring in various parts of the country, the Germans were setting up an elaborate organization along the Danube valley which was nominally to transfer the German minority from Bessarabia back to the Reich. The German Commission which had previously worked in Poland arrived in Bessarabia with the full consent of the Russians. They then built large camps in Galatz and in Yugoslavia at Zemun (just to the north of Belgrade). Several hundred German army lorries with soldiers and nurses in uniform arrived with the Commission, in order that the German minority in Bessarabia might be medically examined whilst in the temporary camps, and the whole evacuation be carried out with great speed. It was stated officially that the number of Germans in uniform was so large in order that the whole transfer of immigrants from Romania's ceded territory of Bessarabia and Bukovina should be accomplished in six weeks.

All this distress, emotion and fear were felt by many Romanians to be worse than being at war, " for at least there was some certainty about war ". Shopkeepers, maids and Legation servants were all saying : " Poor Romania, nothing could be worse than this." But in another month there was a grim and tragic earthquake, and four months later a civil war.

Officials were genuinely relieved when Antonescu formed a stopgap Government in which all the former Ministers except Gigurtu were to remain in office until they had seen through the occupation of Transylvania and the Dobrudja. Observers noticed that the stock of the Iron Guard was going up, that members of the Party who had been killed in the disorders were to be given State funerals. The Iron Guard newspaper

*Buna Vestire* (Good News), which had previously been banned, was to reappear, and it was rumoured, truly I believe, that the Iron Guard had placed sentries at all Romanian airports and at the frontiers to prevent the escape of " persons opposed to a Guardist régime ". Certainly such sentries were at the airport a week later, as I saw them myself, acting as if they had full control over the ordinary State officials.

I called on all the intelligent people I knew in Romania, ranging from Prince Antoine Bibesco and a few other land-owning princes to Jewish tailors in the Ghetto and a Communist newspaper-seller. The Communist and the Jew were the only exceptions to the general view that " we must all rally to the support of Antonescu ; if you were a Romanian you would say the same ". This was the view of the intellectual Left, of members of what once had been small trade unions in Romania, and of Liberals. Constantine Bratianu, brother of George Bratianu, announced that his party would support General Antonescu and refrain from any party meeting or agitation. General Antonescu told a Romanian friend of mine that it was expected that Maniu would issue a somewhat similar manifesto. This, I think, damns Maniu finally.

Maniu is a pleasant enough little man, intelligent, and although by no means good-looking, with the same facility as Hitler and the peasant leader of Croatia, Maček, for inspiring tremendous devotion in his followers. Throughout the period of the abdication, and before that at the time of the Vienna Diktat, all his followers, in Transylvania especially, had been waiting, sitting around begging, and lastly demanding that he should speak at protest meetings and demonstrations. Maniu, looking small and sad, continued to eat his meals with a large group of his followers at the restaurant ' Cina ' in the square opposite the royal palace. When the demonstrations were mentioned to him, his hand holding a cigarette trembled nervously. He promised he would speak on a certain day, but when that day arrived his intimate supporters were forced to agree with him that it was too late and that the hour for constructive demonstrations was over. Unlike Maček he did not walk around in peasant costume. Maniu was always available to the Press, though he rarely had anything worth while to say apart from high-sounding phrases about democracy.

Being unable to leave Bucharest myself, I sent a woman (the wife of one of the British Council teachers in Romania) to Cluj to see what was happening. Being entirely inexperienced, she completely failed to sense any feeling from walking about the streets, but she did manage to see Maniu as he was leaving his house in Transylvania for what he thought was to be the last time. Everyone, including Maniu, cried. When asked if he had anything to say, he only murmured, " My heart is broken ".

When he arrived in Bucharest I asked him several times why he never made any effort either to resist in Transylvania the Vienna Diktat, or to combine with George Bratianu and the Liberals to form a semi-democratic government with Antonescu and the army, which should, for a time at any rate, have prevented the Iron Guard régime and its outrages and have relieved the population of the burden of being the employees of a limited company organized to support the King, his expensive mistress and three or four friends.

After King Carol had left Romania facts leaked gradually to the public ear as to the way in which he had ruled the country. Romania had become a business, and the King regarded himself as the managing director, anxious to make as much money as possible out of the concern. During his first exile he had lived in Paris and in Kent as a poor man with an expensive mistress. Although he did manage to keep his seat on the Romanian throne for ten years, the whole period was one of considerable uncertainty, in which he expected to be thrown out at any moment. His schemes for money-making are worthy of consideration by our great industrialists.

The King began in a small way by saving his money and buying a factory here and a factory there, until he was introduced to the Greek-born Romanian Stavitski, Melaxa. Melaxa began life as a humble mechanic on the Romanian railways. He had the charm common to both Greeks and Jews, and the ability to push. In 1923 he started a small company of his own for

6

making railway trucks, and had probably knowingly backed a winner in the form of his partner, who the following year became Under-Secretary of State for Railways. Melaxa at once secured a ten-year contract for locomotives from the Romanian State, and as his capital had increased from about £5000 to the equivalent in lei of £250,000 sterling, he was able to join the Court circle and become a friend of Madame Lupescu.

Both she and the King were struck by this clever little man, and he fascinated them by his big ideas for making money. Melaxa suggested to the King that the Romanian railways should be motorized. The Cabinet soon agreed to this suggestion, and the King sent Melaxa to Germany to buy a patent in order to carry out this work. The King then shared with Melaxa and Madame Lupescu the fat rake-off made when the patent was sold to the Romanian State at an enormous profit.

The fourth member of the palace quartet which formed one of the greatest swindling organizations of the century, Urdarianu, at this time joined the other three. A minor bank was declared bankrupt by the State. It was bought by the quartet (the names of the King and Madame Lupescu never appeared) at a very low price, and they sold it after a few months at 300 per cent. profit to the National Bank of Romania.

The quartet also bought a textile factory, which manufactured the uniforms worn by the one legal party in Romania, the National Renaissance Front, to which every person holding any kind of a job, from a tobacconist to a permanent Under-Secretary of State, must belong. Impoverished officials at wayside country stations saved up their money week by week in order to buy the uniform which it was essential for them to have if they wanted to belong to the party. If they did not belong to the party they had to revert to their peasant holdings, which is the horror of all humble labourers, who always aspire to white-collardom. But as soon as the humble worker had bought his uniform it was changed. Perhaps King Carol, now living in luxury in South America, owes his life to the fact that these humble little men never knew that the King owned the textile factory which made the uniforms for his own national party, and that whenever trade was slack the King changed the uniform.

The facts are even worse than they sound. No other firm could compete with the King in the textile or any other business, as he alone could buy foreign currency at the official rate. For example, the official rate for the pound sterling was something like 620 lei, but if a Romanian wished to buy sterling he could do so only on the Black Market—the National Bank would not think of selling him any ; and to buy sterling on the Black Market cost during the year 194 anything from 1250 to 4500 lei. But the King was the only man in the country who could and did buy lei at the official rate, and with his pounds he imported raw materials free of duty, for which other people paid not only the duty but the higher price caused by buying the goods outside the country with money bought at Black Bourse rates. The King in fact ran the Black Bourse, which was strictly illegal and very much against the interests of his country.

The arrival of the Germans in Romania was something of an anti-climax, for two reasons. The first was that it was no surprise, but merely the logical end to the period of peaceful penetration followed by the appearance of soldiers in uniform assisting with refugee work. The second reason was that the Press gave out the news long before it happened, not as a forecast but as a fact. The truth was that many of the two divisions of German soldiers who were later to occupy Romania went into Transylvania not in uniform but with the Hungarian troops when that province was occupied at the beginning of September. There they remained until they entered Romania on October 12. There were at the time many well-known journalists in Bucharest apart from Walter Duranty ; Cedric Salter of the *Daily Mail* was making a big name for himself in England, and Sulzberger of the *New York Times* was ' hitting ' the front page daily. We all knew that these troops were there in waiting to enter the country. We all wrote despatches anticipating the occupation many times. What caused the anti-climax was when the United Press wrote the story of the entry of German troops, giving eyewitness accounts of soldiers crossing the frontier at least three days before it occurred. Naturally it was big news, and splashed about front pages all over the world. The Romanian Legation in Berlin who were asked to comment on it could not have read their instructions properly, as they immediately confirmed the story that two German divisions were entering their country. That they denied it a few hours later was of no importance, as no one ever reads denials in newspapers. Romanian Legations throughout the rest of Europe denied the story. The Ministry of Propaganda issued a statement from the Ministry of Foreign Affairs which denied the U.P. story entirely. Incidentally, the Ministry of Propaganda, which was in complete control of the censorship, had passed the story for publication. They did not allow any other agency to send it. The reason for this I have never discovered, unless it be that the local U.P. man, who was not a real journalist, had worked in the palace and knew so much about so many people that he could perhaps use blackmail. But this is pure guesswork. So far ahead of time was the publication that when the German Generals were received at the Royal railway station by General Antonescu and Horia Sima no one bothered to write about it. In other words the story was dead before it happened.

During the first few days of their stay in Bucharest the Generals wined and dined with Romanian cabinet ministers, Generals and the King. Between whiles they consumed large meals in the Hotel Athenée Palace. It was fun to hear them order " English breakfast with bacon and eggs ". But that was not enough. By the middle of the morning they were all eating again, and how they enjoyed themselves !

Gradually the soldiers arrived, most of them being billeted outside the capital. Large army lorries unloaded heavy boxes in the hotel. Officers' wives appeared, but these did not prevent the local beauties from spending many hours in the hairdresser's shop. The windows commanded an incomparable view of the hotel entrance. At first the officers were welcome guests, but after a short time the Romanians found their ' guests ' a little tiresome.

From the time of the German occupation of Romania until the severing of diplomatic relations everyone expected that there would be a complete breaking-up of the Romanian State and that Germany would declare a protectorate. The German Minister, Fabricius, was recalled soon after the arrival of the troops, and replaced by von Killinger, who had previously been well known as the ruthless German Minister in Slovakia. Fabricius, a tall good-looking man with a pleasant manner and little brain, had been probably maintaining his job because his wife was Goering's sister. Until his private life, like so many private lives in Bucharest, became involved with two women, the first of his mistresses, Edigh von Kohler, was politically the more important. She was the obvious beautiful blonde German spy. She drove around in high-powered cars, dressed beautifully, drank champagne freely, until she was suddenly recalled to Berlin. I gather that there was some difficulty about the large sums of money which had passed through her hands and for which she could not account. She accused Fabricius of having this money when she was finally flung into prison, and although Fabricius stoutly maintained his innocence he was recalled. The Civil War between the army and the Iron Guard considerably delayed his departure. The second mistress of the German Minister, Madame Butculescu, was of no political interest, but strained the relationship of Fabricius with his wife.

The real German behind the scenes was the sinister Neubacher, whom I saw only on two or three occasions at Sinaia. He was a cripple, wheeling himself round in his own special invalid chair. His face made the Romanian urchins, who pester one so much for money, run away from him at sight. His deformity had so poisoned his mind that he liked nothing better than to see others suffer. His spare-time hobby was designing torture chambers for concentration camps. During the Civil War in Spain he paid several visits at Franco's side to see what effect on political prisoners could be obtained by revolving discs of varying colours and triangular shapes at which the prisoner was forced to look until he went mad or made a confession. He visited the prisons of Romania when he first arrived, and the bug-ridden dirty buildings were not enough for him. He devised the method of twisting arms and slowly pulling out toenails which was practised on British subjects. Where his power came from in Germany is unknown. He was the advance guard of the Gestapo, looking over the land and reporting on the organization and numbers of men which he was likely to need. The army and the diplomats were almost as afraid of this evil-looking man as if they had been Jewish refugees. He seemed entirely devoid of any human kindness. Unlike so many murderers and torturers he had no soft feeling for dog or cat, no daughter or wife whom he loved. He was never known to smile, and rarely went out into society, but lived in a lonely villa on the side of the Carpathians between Sinaia and Predeal. The German headquarters were at Sinaia, and General Hansen, the commander, paid a daily visit to the crippled man. Antonescu always visited him during the week-end when he went for a few hours' rest to his house at Predeal.

The Germans admitted that he was the most powerful of them all in the Balkans. He arranged in October that the Gestapo should take over the buildings which had been used by Carol's own secret police, and I saw German lorries bring up filing cabinets and thousands of loose files. When the Germans were planning the attack on Russia it was Neubacher, and not the Minister nor Field-Marshal von List, who entertained Antonescu and his nephew, Michael, to dinner, and told him that Romanian soldiers would be needed in the German attack on Russia. He told Antonescu that he would find the troops ; there were plenty already trained by the Germans who would make excellent shock troops for the retaking of Bessarabia by Romania. Antonescu wanted Bessarabia back far less than Transylvania or the Dobrudja, and said so, but Neubacher promised that if Bessarabia were taken he would see that Transylvania were restored to Romania. Neubacher, like so many evil men, went about in fear of his life, and generally had about ten German soldiers to form a bodyguard.

Before Neubacher arrived in Romania he had been running a minor Gestapo within the Romanian Police Force, quite unknown to Carol or any other Romanian statesman. One got quite used to Romanian statesmen being unaware of what the

Germans were doing in their country. The Romanian War Office was rarely informed of the fresh arrival of German soldiers, and the Romanian Chief of Staff himself often had no idea how many German divisions there were inside the country. It was Neubacher's men who spied in the camps of Polish refugees. These Poles, most of whom were soldiers, marched into Romania at the end of the Polish War merely to be interned, were often discontented. They lived in vile and miserable conditions with nothing to do all day long; they often had no books to read, no paper on which to write letters, no games to play. The braver ones planned their escape, which hundreds successfully carried out, while the cowardly were influenced by Neubacher's men to go back to Germany. I know reliable refugee workers who frequently saw Neubacher talking to the pseudo-helpers who visited the camps. All the Polish camps were filled with German propaganda, and it is greatly to the credit of those Poles who escaped and found their way by obscure means to France or England that they resisted the insidious propaganda of German agents. All the airmen escaped, and many other highly-trained technicians. Only a few discontented women returned to Germany. The stories of individual escapes were often thrilling, but on many occasions the guards helped the Poles by giving them money to get away.

The British Legation always appeared to be full of Poles from the end of the Polish War in September 1939 until the day when we broke off diplomatic relations in February. Mr. Brown, whom I would be less willing to offend than the Minister, was from Warsaw; he spoke Polish, had a Polish wife, and although he was perfectly capable of telling a duchess that the First Secretary was engaged and would be engaged for the next few hours or days, no Pole however poor was ever turned away until Brown had seen that he had had full attention from the diplomatic staff. All the negotiations for evacuating the civilian Poles had to be carried on through the British Legation, as the Romanians refused to take any notice of the Poles. Gafencu showed up very badly in this respect. Before the war he had been a personal friend of Colonel Beck. When Beck was interned in Romania as the ex-Foreign Secretary of Poland, Gafencu was either too weak or too mean to take any risk that would aid and abet Beck to escape to a safer or more politically comfortable country. After Gafencu went out of office Beck's position was intolerable. Smigly-Rydz managed to escape, it is said, across the frontier dressed as a woman, but no one appears to have seen or heard of him since that time. Beck saw him once just before the escape was planned, and I gathered that the two men did not feel very friendly to one another. Beck said he was ill, and he probably was, with the damp mists of Brasov. He came to Bucharest to see his dentist. I saw him in his hotel bedroom, which was sordid and miserable, but although he was followed by an armed guard he said he was happier than in Brasov. Obviously Beck was too tall and had too conspicuous a nose to be able to disguise himself to escape. His wife was ill with fear ; she was certain that the Germans were out to kill Beck, especially as he, like so many Poles, had refused a German offer to go back to Poland in comfort and style and presumably to rally Poles to the support of the Third Reich.

Beck made one desperate effort to escape soon after the arrival of the German soldiers. How he organized it I do not know, except that Poles have a knack of being good at underground organization. He was then in an isolated villa on the banks of Lake Snagove, about fifty kilometres to the north of Bucharest. He had seven guards, and, having once tried to escape, his daily exercise of rowing across the lake to the restaurant on the far side had been stopped. When I saw him I ran up to speak to him, though the guard tried to stop me. Beck saw in my hand a packet of cigarettes, and grabbed them—literally snatched them without asking my pardon, as a hungry man might grab food. He escaped in disguise, having grown a moustache, in a car with a German number-plate. He had obtained a British passport, bribed everyone in his way, and was well on the way to the frontier on a fine Sunday afternoon when Neubacher's men stopped him and took him to Bucharest, where he has been in close confinement since. Before the Balkan War began his daughter paid frequent visits to Istanbul to sell jewellery in order that she and Madame Beck might live. Beck's imprisonment was the greatest success the Germans had; otherwise the German Consul at Constanza had to sit and watch hundreds of Poles leaving the country, and to know that it was from this harbour that Polish gold, which had been so dangerously brought away from the Germans in Poland, passed out of his control into British hands.

The Romanians were only too delighted for the Poles to escape, as it meant so much the less trouble for them. Romanians are usually ready to do the good-natured thing, particularly if they are well paid for it. Although I would be the last to underestimate the suffering of a large number of Poles in Romania, there were those who managed to get themselves extremely comfortable jobs. When the question of evacuation of the civilians to Cyprus was in the air, one Polish girl said, " I cannot go to Cyprus with the raff and the riff, I must be looked after ". Of course she *has* been looked after. Although unable to write shorthand and scarcely able to type, she found good jobs in Bucharest, Istanbul and Cairo, while hundreds and thousands of British refugees from the Balkans were sent off to India. The same occurred with the refugees from Greece. There were many who were not politically endangered and who had no reason to leave Greece at all except that they thought it would be more fun to live with English people and to have good food and plenty of it rather than face the unpleasantness of life in an occupied territory.

## CHAPTER VI

## ROMANIA—IRON GUARD

EVERYONE who has heard of the Iron Guard associates with it the name of its founder Codreanu, killed early in 1938. The manner in which Codreanu met his death has been the subject of much discussion in Romania, as well as of a judicial court of inquiry. The Guardists maintain that he was killed in a most horrible manner. After his arrest, they say, he was taken gagged and bound, in a covered lorry, through the streets of Bucharest. Some of his followers believe that he was slowly strangled, others that he was wounded and allowed to die slowly. However, if we accept, what all the Guardists assert as truth, that his remains were destroyed—or very nearly destroyed—with prussic acid and then buried in deep concrete, we can only speculate on the methods by which he met his end. Antonescu ordered a retrial of the dead man, which naturally made him more and more of a hero in the local Press, and was, in fact, a trial of the men who it was believed had been involved in the leader's death.

Codreanu was killed, no one really knows exactly in what manner, by the orders of King Carol. This accounts to some extent for the Germans' hatred of Carol, despite his effort to follow a pro-German policy. Codreanu was a peasant by origin, a good-looking lusty man of the soil, with the pale mystic eyes that Hitler would like to think he possessed. The photographs which were kept in the water-closets of Romanian houses when he was out of power always portrayed him in peasant costume covered by a sheepskin coat. Unfortunately I never spoke to Codreanu, but I give him the benefit of the doubt as to not having uttered the many strange, mystic, mad sentences which are now attributed to him by the leaders of the day. The movement was strongly tinged with Puritanism, a remarkable phenomenon in a country so rootedly un-Puritan as Romania has always been and, I suspect, always will be. The Iron Guard is not a movement of a kind to win the sympathy of a Western democrat, liberal in political and social views, but it seems fairly certain that both Codreanu and Horia Sima were inspired by a quite genuine antipathy to the easy-going morals and corrupt political practices of their nation. " I need neither wine nor women to enable me to fulfil my mission " was an oft-quoted saying attributed to Codreanu. This, however, scarcely applied to any considerable proportion of his followers, who gave one the impression of having strayed from Rasputin's camp, and appeared to have adopted that teacher's canon: " Achieve salvation through sin ". After the abdication, Magda Lupescu's house was turned into what was modestly described as a ' Rest House ' for Iron Guardists. In this building twenty young men and twenty girls of the wilder sort lived in complete promiscuity, changing partners almost nightly and making the building the repository for property looted from Jews and opponents of the Guard. To describe the building as a ' Rest House ' was, in fact, a remarkable example of litotes.

A letter written by Codreanu early in 1938, which fell into the hands of his opponents, throws an interesting light on the nature of his mind and ideas. It deals with two subjects. One is the suffering through which the Iron Guard is eventually to come to strength and power. " The unit of measurement is established : the tomb ! " The losses of the movement down to that time being estimated at ten ' tombs ', Codreanu considers that the quantity of sacrifice necessary to victory is 200 tombs. As translated, the relevant passage is sometimes interpreted to mean that the Iron Guard would have to commit 200 assassinations ; but though it is tempting to see in this evidence of the terrorist activities which undoubtedly were carried on, it appears that this particular sentence refers to the martyrdoms to be suffered by Iron Guardists, and that the 200 tombs are those of Iron Guard casualties.

The other topic, also somewhat obscurely discussed, is the relationship between the student members of the organization and the Jews. Members ought not to vote for political parties which contained Jews ; but if such parties were in power, they might fraternize with them, and continue to take such financial support from them as might be forthcoming. The more, indeed, they could get out of them, the better : presumably upon the principle of spoiling the Egyptians.

The foreign policy of the Iron Guard was naturally the aspect which most interested British observers. As expounded in a speech of Codreanu shortly before the 1937 elections it was refreshingly simple and clear-cut.

" I am against the great democracies of the West. I am against the Little Entente, and I have not the slightest sympathy for the League of Nations, in which I do not believe. I am in favour of a foreign policy attached to the Rome-Berlin Axis and of an alliance with the revolutionary Nationalist Powers directed against Bolshevism. Forty-eight hours after the victory of our organization we shall have an alliance with Rome and Berlin."

From the death of Codreanu almost until the abdication of Carol, the Iron Guard was in effect completely illegal and suppressed. There were times when policemen were instructed to shoot Guardists at sight, and there were times, as for example some weeks before the abdication, when Carol tried to woo Guardist support by having unimportant members of the party, and even for a time Horia Sima, the leader, in his Cabinet. Horia Sima had the proverbial nine lives of a cat throughout the whole period of suppression and illegality. He hid, disguised himself, and narrowly avoided death on many occasions. He organized meetings, circulated leaflets, arranged for the collection of party subscriptions, and, as his secretary told me, actually increased the membership of the party from 80,000 to 400,000. Although I strongly disbelieve these figures, there is little doubt that his organizing ability, so far as illegal movements were concerned, rivalled only that of the Communists. He was, of course, well supplied with funds from Germany, and believed that he could at any moment rely on German support if he considered the time ripe for a *coup d'état* in Bucharest.

His supporters consisted very largely of half-educated young men unable to obtain white-collar jobs. They considered themselves too good to return to till the soil of a peasant holding, and were using up all their energy in propagating the Iron Guard. Their food was supplied when ' on duty ' by the Guardists, and their pocket-money—much smaller than any wage—was given them according to the success they achieved in distributing leaflets and obtaining new members, or even in terrorizing non-supporters. They were young men of no political knowledge or experience ; maybe a few of them spoke two or three hundred words of French, but for the most part they had neither foreign languages nor contact with any foreigners, and had they been offered a good job in the Post Office or on the railways they would quite soon have forgotten the Iron Guard. These were Horia Sima's principal supporters. Only one of them, Cosmavici, later to become a cabinet minister, was of good bourgeois family. Another section of the Guardists whom Horia Sima could not antagonize was not led by any particular person but consisted of what had been the extreme Socialist and Communist elements of the Bucharest tramways and larger factories. After the breakdown of political parties many of them were influenced to join the Guardist movement largely by the idea of getting something done. If they had produced a leader they would certainly have been the strongest element in the whole movement, but as it was they merely caused Horia Sima considerable sleeplessness, and never worked in the party in a united manner.

But the most dangerous section was led by Codreanu's father. He was certainly mad, his particular form of insanity consisting in a pagan mysticism woven round his son's life and introduced into the policy and doctrine of the Iron Guard Party. There is little doubt that the old man thought he ought to have been chosen as leader. He was always willing to see representatives of the foreign Press, even though very much opposed to his views. It was, regrettably, impossible ever to publish an interview with him, as he never uttered a single coherent sentence, but rushed frantically round the room screaming : " My God, my son, leaders of my time, St. Michael and all Angels," etc. It was suggested by those who set themselves out to understand something of what he said that he maintained that his son, who until this event had been a perfectly normal youth, went one day to the chapel of St. Michael on the Archangel's feast-day. Kneeling in front of the altar he had a vision, in which the saint appeared before him begging him to rise up and lead an Iron Guard party similar to the Nazi party in Germany. That St. Michael was ever so indiscreet I do not believe, but I do believe that the mad mystic Codreanu family thought it true. Throughout the period of their suppression the Guardists met in a village at the base of the Carpathians where there was a chapel to St. Michael. Here at full moon the inner circle cut themselves and exchanged blood from the wounds, after which they drank *tsuica* (the Romanian vodka made of plums) and drew lots to decide who was to carry out the murder of any of their violent oppressors. In this way the murder of Calinescu was planned, and thus, after Carol's abdication, they met to discuss his murder on the way out of Romania ; but this section mixed up God, Hitler and *tsuica* in so curious a manner that they were entirely unpractical, and apart from the assassination never did much damage. However, they always formed a minority inside the party difficult for Horia Sima to control. Horia Sima knew perfectly well that Codreanu was angling for the leadership of the party, and knew too that he would never be capable of leading it for twenty-four hours.

In June 1940 Horia Sima resigned from Carol's Cabinet, and thenceforward, whatever efforts Carol made, the Guardists refused to take office ; but it was not until the time of the abdication that they really showed their strength. Suddenly they all appeared in green shirts, they had their own private police force, they trained, marched and sang from dawn till dusk a monotonous dirge about Codreanu called ' Capitaine '. Its exact words I was never able to discover. During the period of illegality many of them had worn tunics with a green tie or green socks, while the girls had worn green scarves, but when the Iron Guard Party, suddenly calling itself the Legionnaires, came into power or thought they came into power on the abdication of King Carol, it appeared as though everyone in Buchares wore green. Stocks of the blue uniform of the National Renaissance Front were thrown into store, and shops were unable to cope with the demand for green shirts and green goods of all kinds. Cafés and shops, but not so much private houses, put up photographs of Horia Sima ; some even dug up old pictures of Codreanu, and after a time photographs of Horia Sima became indistinguishable from the ' martyred Capitaine '. It was a clever photographic trick, supported by a black and white etching which achieved tremendous popularity at the time. No name was attached, and I believe Horia Sima would have said that it was of himself, but it was probably made from one of Codreanu's photographs. Every village had in it one or two Guardists who immediately after Carol's abdication blackmailed the local Orthodox priest to incorporate the Legionnaire doctrine with Christianity. While motoring round among villages I saw a priest conducting a service before a sacred effigy in a little roadside town which had been decorated with green, and the local Greenshirt in uniform was addressing the crowd, obviously supported by the priest.

In this way the Legionary movement, after it assumed some sort of power, achieved tremendous support amongst the ignorant and superstitious peasantry. They did not have to talk about agriculture, which is the lot of most other would-be politicians when talking to countrymen. They merely called God in on their side, and if the priest, who was often little more intelligent than the peasant, refused to comply with the wishes of the Legionnaire, there was always a revolver which quickly brought compliance, for the priest knew that the Greenshirt would use it if he wished, and at that time (September 1940) no policeman in Romania would have dared to arrest a Legionnaire.

The relationship between General Antonescu, as leader of the State after the abdication of the King, and Horia Sima is one of the most interesting and mysterious questions in modern Romanian history. Antonescu, having told the Germans when he assumed office that he would stand by the Vienna Diktat, was supported by Berlin, but he knew that he could not rule Romania without Guardist support. He feared with truth that

about a fifth of the army and even a larger proportion of the
officers had become converts to this movement. This unquestionably distressed Antonescu a good deal, as he had imagined he
would have the support of the whole army. Antonescu had his
stopgap Cabinet, meant to last until the occupation of Transylvania by Hungary had been completed. He was being well
backed by the German Press as a man ' of silence '—a merciless
dictator " who never smiles and whose will and nerves are made
of iron ". But on September 15, the eve of St. Cornelius' Day,
a day of great moment to the Legionnaires, the name-day of
the martyred Codreanu and the day on which, some said, he
first experienced his vision of St. Michael, 400,000 Legionnaires
were supposed to come in from the country. This was a typical
Iron Guard lie, and in fact rather less than 40,000 came into
the capital. Some of these did take part in a lengthy and tedious
procession, but most of the Greenshirts who marched through
the streets came from the slums of Bucharest itself and nearby
villages, which had carefully trained men for the honour of
spending the day marching through the streets and singing
' Capitaine '. At 5 o'clock in the morning contingents from the
villages began to arrive at the Green House, the headquarters
of the party. At 9 the procession started. Practically all those
who took part, men and women, marched well and in formation,
and wore green shirts with dark blue or black trousers. The
first four in each section were generally good-looking youths
of medium height, but the physical fitness trailed off until the
last four in each section were undersized, pimply youths who
looked as though they had never eaten a good hearty meal.
They reminded me very much of the Fascist processions I used
unwillingly to watch on Sunday afternoons while waiting for a
bus in King's Road, Chelsea. In Bucharest as in Chelsea,
the longer the procession, the pimplier the youths.

I watched for a time from the street. The crowd was surprisingly small, but those who were watching were for the most
part enthusiastic. Yet I noticed, when I got bored and went
to watch the great events from my flat terrace, that the people
of non-Guardist sympathies in the flats were more interested

in the rare contingents of peasants wearing picturesque costumes. They marched to a large square in the centre of the town where a stand had been built to accommodate the Axis-supporting diplomats, and near it a huge dais from which Antonescu and Horia Sima both addressed the crowd. The young king took no part in these proceedings; in fact, I believe he even went to his country house at Sinaia for the week-end. The dais and the stand were backed by enormous green banners on which a picture of either Codreanu or Horia Sima was appliquéd in black. From one end of the stand the swastika flew, and from the other the Romanian flag. Professionally I was most annoyed, as all the other special correspondents, including the British, had been invited to attend, although with one exception they failed to do so. But I was not invited, and when friendly colleagues attempted to ascertain the reason for missing me out, the head of the Press Bureau said: " We know she is very Left, and we thought she might cause trouble."

Antonescu was the news of the day; for the first time he wore a green shirt, which caused an exaggeration of the permanent question: " Was Antonescu going to rule the Greenshirts, or the Greenshirts Antonescu ? " Horia Sima's speech consisted of an amplification of the theme that the Legionary proclamation of September 15 had blown away the last hopes of ' plutocratic Judæo-masonry '. Every one was surprised, especially the Guardists themselves, that the day passed without serious incident. It was thought that the unruly elements would get out of hand and shoot up a few of their old enemies. The leaders were not unnaturally worried because they knew that the unruly elements were aware of the hiding-places where large quantities of ammunition, most of it from Germany, was stored. It would not have concerned any of them if a few Jews had been beaten up, but there was always the danger that the Codreanu group might turn on the Sima group and Codreanu père, rather conspicuously, had not attended the procession and demonstration. In all probability this was from pique at not having been asked, as on the day after the abdication Codreanu père led the cheering and was the centre of attraction for the crowd outside the royal

7

palace. In the afternoon I drove along the main Great North Road of Romania which leads through the oilfields across the Carpathians to Hungary and saw the Guardists quietly walking back to their villages.

I was on occasion in a rather difficult position myself, and I tell these stories of my adventures as typical of what happened to English people at the time. When I arrived in Romania I was given a permit to stay for a fortnight; this was generally renewed by a three months' permit. After making my formal application through the Press Bureau several times I was told that it would never be granted. In spite of the very helpful backing of the British Legation I remained without legal papers authorizing me to stay in the country. Strangely enough on several occasions I managed to obtain a permit to leave the country and enter again; this was just like Romanian administrative offices, which never by any remote chance co-operated one with another. On the morning of October 1, three days after the arrest of the five British subjects from Ploesti, two policemen plus a Legionnaire with a nasty-looking plain-clothes man arrived, stating that they had come to take me to the Prefecture of Police. I knew only too well what happened to English people who went there; they were tortured, and frequently made to confess sins which had never been committed. I knew, too, that the only real objection the Romanians could have against me, apart from the fact that I was English and of the Left, was that I had fairly consistently, sometimes subtly and sometimes quite openly, avoided the Romanian censorship for two months. It would not have been difficult for the Press Bureau to have produced a copy of my daily story for the *Daily Express* which had passed the censor, along with a gramophone record of the actual story I had dictated over the telephone to Geneva, the two being in no way the same. Had they done this, I suppose they would have been technically justified in expelling me; but as the censorship was entirely anti-British and pro-German, one would have thought they would wish to avoid making such a conspicuous gesture as to expel an Anglo-Saxon reporter. They refused to give the reason for my expulsion. The Legation rose to the occasion nobly, and I was given every possible support and assistance, and in the end my visa to stay was prolonged for seven days.

From this time on for six weeks it was prolonged again and again, for being ill, for having a motor accident, for having lost my passport, until I could think of no more excuses, and the Romanians said that under no circumstances whatever would they allow me to stay any longer. So I wandered round, staying one night in one friend's flat, another night in my own, until the Greek War began and my paper ordered me to the front. At this point the Romanians refused to give me an exit visa, and kept me waiting for five days, while the Legation again pressed my claims.

There were several awkward moments. One evening I arrived about midnight at the entrance to the block of flats where I lived. Two Guardists put their hands on my arms and asked me if I were Miss Hollingworth. Fortunately I jerked myself away, jumped into my car, and drove madly off in the direction of Giurgiu, spending the night quite comfortably sleeping in my Ford on a by-road a few miles outside the city. On another occasion I had dinner with *The Times* correspondent, Archie Gibson, who took me out for a stroll after dinner. On this occasion he was arrested most brutally by five men at his own gate. They refused to allow him to go into the house to fetch his papers, even though he had his Press card with him. After this *The Times* correspondent was made Assistant Press Attaché.

Anti-Semitism has always been a Romanian characteristic. It was allowed full play during the short Fascist régime of Goga. The fact that Madame Lupescu was a Jewess certainly did the Jewish cause no good. The Jews formed a problem similar to that of the Jews in Poland. They held the trade of the country entirely in their hands, with the exception of that part which was monopolized by foreigners. They controlled industries from behind the scenes, they filled the medical and legal professions, they were very good at finding excuses to avoid military service, and in the small towns they formed a very high proportion of the shopkeeper class, sometimes as much as 95 per cent. Anti-Semitism being the chief plank of the non-constructive Legionnaire programme, many of the Jews, fearing either that the Germans would conquer Romania or that the Guardists would obtain power, had managed to transfer some of their capital abroad by means of judicious use of the Black Bourse. When the time came for them to leave their homeland and follow their money to England or America it was quite impossible for them to do so. Probably the Romanians would have given them exit visas and passports, as they were genuinely anxious to rid the country of Jews. But they would most certainly have made it difficult for them to obtain these documents, and without doubt much money would have been necessary in bribes. But the Romanian citizen was excluded from obtaining any kind of visa. He could not go to England after the war had begun—that is only reasonable—and he could not go to America on a visitor's visa unless he had a return visa to his own country. This no Jew could obtain. German Jews had put the State Department wise to any trick of buying South American visas. The South American countries were themselves reluctant to issue genuine visas, though large numbers of faked ones were stamped on passports. Even if the poor unfortunate Jew fleeing from future torment could manage to obtain a visa, it would be impossible for him to get a transit visa through either Bulgaria or Turkey, still less Germany, to enable him to begin his journey to the New World. The local correspondent of the *New York Times* is one of the few exceptions, and he was undoubtedly assisted by heavy influence in Washington. A few managed to procure visas, but they were very few, and they made the mistake of attempting to take money or jewellery out of the country. They were then arrested, and no one ever knew quite what happened to them. Probably they were killed in the Iron Guard activities which followed.

Decrees were issued in rapid succession forbidding Jews to practise as lawyers, to practise as doctors, or to treat Christians— although there was a clause providing that if a Christian demanded the services of a Jew in the middle of the night, the Jew might not refuse to get up and do whatever was necessary. All Jews were thrown out of the railway administration, hotels, restaurants, and Government offices, and no more than a small percentage were allowed to remain as employees in shops and banks. This caused tremendous havoc, as what efficiency there was in Romania suddenly disappeared and the confusion in the Ministries is impossible to describe. All the administrative buildings in Bucharest were packed from morning till night with hundreds of people mostly trying to find out what the new law meant; some were trying to pay taxes, but invariably the reply was the same : " I do not know, you will have to come again. I do not know who is responsible ; certainly I am not." It was well reflected in the Press Office, where everyone was sacked, the Guardists who were appointed knowing nothing of the Press and being fortunately unable to read English. Occasionally they thought it a good idea to censor a whole story, and not until the Legations abroad cabled back the appallingly anti-Legionnaire stories which were appearing in the British and American Press did they re-engage the English-speaking staff, who were as well able to be pro-Legionnaire as they had been pro-Carol and pro-Antonescu, or as they were to be in a few months' time violently anti-Legionnaire.

All the young men who surrounded Horia Sima demanded jobs. At first they were given them to replace Jews who had been sacked, but this did not use up anything like the large number of hooligan youths who were ready to turn on the leader if no jobs were found. Men and women were therefore sacked without reference to their abilities and replaced by Guardists who, never having done any work before apart from causing trouble, were incapable of performing the most simple clerical duties. In the past one had thought it impossible to increase the confusion in Romania, but the Iron Guard did it only too easily. Here and there Antonescu managed to have a person overlooking the activities of the Guardists, although the overseer would always be technically the man's junior. At the Custom House and at the frontier Guardists merely added an extra passport examination and an extra customs difficulty after the usual officials had finished their own. They exercised their authority none too pleasantly, and prevented many people from leaving the country. I was always surprised that the Germans did not interfere and demand a better administration by threatening to take over themselves unless more efficiency was shown. Perhaps they did not mind the confusion so long as it in no way affected the export of oil or the internal production of agricultural goods.

On November 10 Nature interfered still further, and after a few preliminary shocks a violent earthquake took place. At that moment I was sitting in the waiting-room of a station in Greece in the blackout. Everything rattled, and the lid of the stove fell off. I wondered whether it was another earthquake in Romania. The first reports were excellent news, stating that the oilfields had been destroyed. This seemed too good to be true, and I wished that I had not left for the Greek front, especially as I had been in Romania for all the other excitements.

Many friends have described it to me. At 3.45 the people were awakened by violent shaking, falling plaster, and the noise of cracking masonry. All the English people to whom I have spoken, many of whom were in bombing raids in Poland and Greece, admit that they were terrified. People rushed from one bedroom to another and were generally too frightened to go back to bed, but went out into the drizzle to see what had happened. The largest block of flats, built over a cinema and a row of shops, collapsed entirely. The rubble completely blocked one of the main streets, and posters 200 yards away were unreadable owing to the dust of mortar. The debris of this building, known as the Carlton, was nowhere higher than 6 feet. It was immediately opposite the flat I had lived in, and when the earthquake took place my successor rushed on to his balcony and saw the Carlton building fall. One miracle happened. A fireman who was standing on the roof heard the preliminary noise, put on his helmet, and slid down with the roof over the rest of the building, landing a second or so later dirty and shaken, but quite unharmed, in the middle of the street.

The crowd of frightened people who went out into the streets to see what had happened soon heard that the Carlton was down, and hundreds of cars collected there. Ten minutes later there was no cordon to keep the crowds away from the rubble and the fifty-odd people who were entombed in the basement. Any other nation could have got them out quickly, but it was too much for the Iron Guard administration. Mechanical excavators arrived on the scene two days later after all the people were dead. Everyone ran around, but no one started digging to get them out. Their screams could be heard by the crowd, and later they actually got into telephonic communication with friends. Some were burnt alive from the oil which is used for heating in every big block of flats in Romania, and others were drowned by the water which was used in attempts to put out the fire.

The earthquake left an inheritance of cracks, generally about an inch wide, in every single house in Romania. Builders and architects did a wonderful trade, and a conscientious British architect who went to look at the Legation said that few houses would stand another such shock. In the poorer quarters of the town many of the buildings just crumbled to the floor, but even in the main shopping street, the Calea Victoriei, at least every other house was covered with scaffolding two months later. The British Legation was badly cracked and unsafe. The Minister, Lady Hoare and their guests had to bring their bedding down to sleep in the Chancellery, which was at the back of the residential part and had not been so badly battered. After scaffolding was put up the ceilings fell in and the Minister was forced to move to a small villa on the outskirts of the town. The Legation building remained in scaffolding, upstairs rooms emptied, floors grey with plaster, as all the plaster had been pulled down. Few of my friends who were in Bucharest slept comfortably for weeks afterwards, and the rents of top-floor flats in large buildings fell to nothing, as continual odd jolts and shakes continued until as late as December 1.

The unfortunate reality was that the earthquake had done very little damage either to the petroleum fields or the refineries. Transport was not affected; no fires were started. All the early news of the danger to Germany's expansion in the Balkans through her future inability to obtain petrol was completely unreliable. Telephonic communication with Bulgaria and Hungary was interrupted, and immediately afterwards the Germans began work on overhead cables of an extremely strong variety guaranteed to withstand any known earth tremor.

In the confusion which followed the earthquake, members of the different sections of the Iron Guard began to shoot at one another in the street. In early November there was an attempt to kidnap Horia Sima himself, without doubt organized by the unruly Greenshirts. The attempt failed, as a junior German diplomat told an American friend of mine, only because one of the German agents obtained possession of the plans. To avoid further trouble Sima was invited to dinner with the German Minister on the night he should have been kidnapped. The most popular activity of the unruly Greenshirts during mid-November was to visit the houses of rich Jews (sometimes even rich Christians) and by using a revolver freely to remove all the goods and money. In the case of Jews a few Guardists stopped to torture or beat the householder whilst the thieving took place. The police could not or dared not take action. In any case many of them were new to their jobs, and were themselves Guardists who felt that their positions might easily be lost should they interfere with the actions of other members of the party. The more sober sections of the Guardist movement were delighted to accept the loot collected by the wild young men in green shirts. Huge stores of loot were collected in many Legionary centres.

The economy of the country went to pieces. The Jews, who often knew their jobs, were turned out. The Greenshirts who replaced them were always inexperienced. Gradually the unruly elements came more and more to the fore. They urged that Horia Sima should make a clean sweep of all " corrupt and unclean elements " in the Government and former régime. Without the consent of Sima, or for that matter of any of the leaders, they broke out on November 27 and murdered sixty political prisoners in the Jilava prison. This place was only a few kilometres outside Bucharest, just off the main road to Giurgiu. All the Greenshirts taking part in the outrage stole cars and drove down there. They were well supplied with ammunition, but having overcome the warders they murdered most of the inmates by slow and unpleasant methods. Two of the elder statesmen imprisoned there, M. Madgrearu and Professor Iorga, were well known outside Romania, and the death of the latter especially aroused much adverse comment in the world Press. Antonescu would have liked at this point to suppress the Legionary police, but he found he was not strong enough to do so. He tried hard to change the Head Prefect of Police in Bucharest and several of the other towns, but failed. The only success Antonescu had was in preventing a large number of other assassinations.

Antonescu's desire to have some control in the country and his inability to acquire it became more and more apparent. Christmas brought no relief. The cost of living continued to increase at an alarming rate, and only the Guardists who had recently acquired jobs in the service of the State had their salaries increased as prices rose. Both Antonescu and Sima made many speeches and wrote many appeals, generally on the lines of that made by Antonescu on January 3, in which he condemned all hatred and disrespect for life and property and said : " It is my duty to assure your future and that of the country by concentrating all the forces of the State. Horia Sima, commander of the Legionaries, will be at my side in this struggle to organize your movement."

## CHAPTER VII

## ROMANIA—PETROLEUM, PENETRATION, ARRESTS

PEOPLE who had never been to Romania and who were totally uninterested in Balkan politics always knew that Romania has the largest petroleum fields in Europe outside Russia, as well as a king who keeps a mistress. Oil is of prime importance in normal peace-time Romanian economy. In 1937 petroleum products accounted for 40 per cent. of Romanian exports, supplying 22 per cent. of her total railway receipts and 15 per cent. of her total budget receipts. It seems surprising that oil directly employs less than 25,000 workers, of whom 7000 work in the refineries.

A large part of the development of the oil production has been by foreign companies. In 1938, 90 per cent. was extracted by foreign capital, and the Romanian Government made it quite clear that they would prefer local companies to have a bigger share. Most of the important posts, both administrative and technical, were held by western Europeans, with Englishmen greatly in the majority. Before the war the Germans had no interest worth mentioning in the large oil combines.

Ploesti is the principal town in the petroleum district, and it is here that all the large refineries are situated. A distinct smell of oil permeates the whole town, and petrol at the pump costs 1d. a gallon less than in the rest of Romania (this does not apply to diplomatic petrol, which never cost much, and for the last few months that British diplomats lived in Romania averaged a penny farthing a gallon).

The wells themselves are scattered along the foothills of the Carpathian mountains. They are often only twenty or thirty feet away from one another, and from the air they look like a thin forest of posts. The older ones, especially round Targoviste, have wooden superstructures ; the newer ones are made of steel. Pipes carrying the crude oil to the refineries are often seen at the side of lanes. I was surprised to find that after a picnic

near a monastery in the Targoviste area my clothes were black
with oil.  In some places there are pools of black oil an inch or
two deep lying about on the surface of the ground.

Soon after Hitler came into power the Germans made great
efforts to buy their oil from Romania in order to avoid paying
for oil with free currency.  In other words, Romanian oil was
part of the exchange account, and if Romania did not like the
aspirins and cameras she received in exchange, that was just too
bad for Romania !  Germany could not get lubricating oil from
this source, as Romania's lubricating oil is of poor quality ;  for
example, I respected my Ford far too much to use anything in
her but American lubricating oil whilst I was in Romania.  The
Germans bought their aviation spirit also from other places.
Schacht and Clodius did their work well.

But war added untold material as well as political and
strategic value to the Romanian petroleum fields.  Germany,
despite her own synthetic-oil-manufacturing centres, was anxious
to buy as much oil as possible from Romania.  In 1938 she imported, including what was sent to Czechoslovakia and Austria,
909,000 tons.  This was carried to Germany by means of
Danubian barges loaded by a pipeline running from Ploesti to
Giurgiu, and by sea tankers going through the Mediterranean
and North Sea to Hamburg.  These were loaded by a pipeline
running to Constanza from the oilfields, and at Constanza
were enormous storage tanks capable of containing 750,000
tons.

The British and the French at the beginning of the war
bought as much Romanian oil as possible in order to prevent
the Germans from obtaining it.  In this way the average monthly
deliveries of oil to Germany for the first eight months worked
out at less than half the quantity of oil she had received during
the preceding three months.  After the breakdown of France,
when the difficulties of transport to the United Kingdom became
so great, the German figures began to rise.  The Germans
began, too, to demand political control in the oil areas ; they
were terrified of British sabotage.  It is true that the British
and Romanian Governments had jointly agreed to sabotage the

petroleum fields should the danger of German conquest arise. These plans fell through when the soldiers and politicians who had helped in drawing up the plans were bought by the Germans. They felt that as Germany was going to be the winning horse they had better back her. Oil was constantly in the news, but it was difficult to obtain reliable information. One little man who worked in a small company was quite capable of proving to you that it was physically impossible for Germany to take more oil out of the country than she was doing, while another would tell you that Germany had no need of Romanian oil at all.

The success of British policy in diverting oil supplies from Germany during the first eight months of the war was largely due to the work of one man and his able staff, who formulated the policy which the Government followed, and organized the buying of oil for the United Kingdom and its shipment from Constanza through the Mediterranean to France. The brilliant stroke of forming a British company to purchase or charter all available neutral tank barges on the Danube made German trade very much more difficult. Even after Italy came into the war and the Mediterranean was closed in June 1940, so that no more Romanian oil could be exported to the United Kingdom, Germany was having considerable difficulties in finding the means to transport oil from Romania. The number of rail tank cars was not high enough seriously to affect the exports ; road transport was not to be considered, and the United Kingdom held the charter of the neutral barges. Some of these barges are now lying idle in the Bosphorus, having been brought away during calm weather from the Danube in order to avoid German confiscation.

Germany first got her nose thoroughly into the capital of the Romanian oil business when the company which was a Dutch subsidiary of Shell was taken over by the Germans on the ground that the head office was in The Hague. After this Germany put enormous pressure on Romania to squeeze out British workers from the petroleum fields. I remember going to the British Legation on July 6, to find the garden full of workers who remained there sheltering from the police in order to avoid arrest. Among them was Ted Masterson, manager of one of the largest British-owned companies, who had worked in Romania from the time Europe's large oilfield was only a hole in the ground. They had been given twelve hours to leave the country, and the British Minister had with great difficulty obtained a forty-eight hours' reprieve for all these men who had made Romania's wealth. As a gesture of defiance Sir Reginald gave a farewell luncheon party at ' Cina ', one of the most fashionable restaurants in the city, opposite to the King's palace. The Romanians, however, had their come-back, and arrested all the available workers who had not again taken sanctuary in the garden of the British Legation after their meal. Frantic efforts by the British Minister to get in touch with the Prime Minister and other high officials were fruitless. Only in the late evening did Mr. Robin Hankey, First Secretary of the Legation, manage to arrange for their release. The censorship at the time refused to allow the word " release ", and insisted on " freedom from police supervision ". I only hope readers of daily newspapers are able to translate such quaint phrases into their true meaning. American diplomats in Bucharest were greatly alarmed lest the attack against the British personnel, obviously to please German and Iron Guard interests, should end in the expulsion of all foreigners from the fields and the jeopardizing of American as well as Allied capital. American interests were only about one-third as large as British interests.

A fortnight after the expulsion of the workers a Romanian Commissar, to whom all questions of policy and administration had to be referred, took his stool in the offices of Astra Romana (Shell), Romania's largest oil company. This was the first step towards the company's becoming entirely State-controlled. Technically, the Romanians were in the right. Under the law passed on January 17, 1939, the Government might ask for any information. They also had a right to put in a commissar to run the company if it was not being administered in a way approved by the oil commissioners ; in fact the Ministry of National Economy was supported and controlled by the German

Economic Mission which had just arrived. No other company was subject to this special control, and it seemed that the Ministry of National Economy were keeping a close watch on the Dutch-owned capital. The Romanians were themselves surprised at this rather hasty action. One of those who was working in the fields said to me : " They have only a right to ask for information. They demanded geological data from us which we could easily have obtained from our office in Ploesti in a matter of three days, but before we had time to write and ask for it the commissar was installed." The Astra Romana had a great reputation even in Romania for being honestly and well administered. The commissar was a man from the Ministry of National Economy who knew nothing whatever about oil. At the same time a decree was issued putting all petrol-carrying vehicles under the control of the State on the same terms as the rail tank cars of the State-owned railways. In other words, should Germany have needed them all for her own use, there would have been no difficulty whatever in taking them. There was no further hope of saving British capital, at least for the period of the war.

About this time the Romanian Government refused to release fourteen barges which the British badly needed for use in the Middle East. Barges were never romantic enough objects to become news. Had they been endowed with a little sex-appeal they would have hit the front page for many weeks, as our diplomats very rightly gave a great deal of time and trouble to trying to obtain the release of these barges. Later we were generous enough to release the Romanian ship *Bucegi* which had been held in custody by the British authorities at Alexandria. When the Navy discovered too late that the Romanians were not going to keep their word and release our barges, they dragged the ship into custody a second time at Haifa. Later in August they seized fifty-three ships of the British Danube petrol fleet ; these were never released, and presumably have been long in use by the Germans.

Romania fully understood the true significance of the Regensburg air raids carried out with so much courage by the

R.A.F. on their long-distance night flights. It is in the docks of Regensburg that the rich oil from Romania is unloaded from Danube barges, and stored for distribution over Germany. River transport was not only cheaper and more convenient, owing to the lack of rail trucks, but in view of the transfer of territory and other troubles in Central Europe, it was by far the safest way for the valuable liquid to reach Germany.

Germany and Italy quarrelled for many months over Romania's oil supplies. Italy was in dire need of petroleum, which before the war she had obtained by sea. Her plan to conquer Greece and the eventual war beginning at the end of October prevented her obtaining for home consumption all the oil she was bringing from Albania. This oil, which was of poor quality, has, since she entered the war, made up half of her total imports. While Italy was screaming for oil the Germans allowed the Romanians to slow down production and fill the stores at Constanza with 750,000 tons, which was at that time virtually useless. Some of it was even pumped back by pipeline to Ploesti. Turkey was the only country taking oil by sea from Constanza, and Turkey in her odd way was buying as little as possible because Romania demanded from her payment in dollars, having, quite reasonably, no desire to import any Turkish products except cotton. Italy made daily attempts to get her hands on some of this surplus oil. She sent commissions to Bucharest. They were wined and dined by the Ministry of National Economy and told they could have what oil they wanted. The law which put all oil-carrying vehicles under State control prevented Italy from obtaining any means of transport, as the Germans refused to allow the Ministry of National Economy to release any for Italy's use. On one occasion when 200 Romanian rail tank cars were available and Italy had hired them, the German Legation stepped in and forbade the Romanians from carrying out the agreement, although the oil, which could have been rushed quickly to Italy by the Simplon-Orient route, would have considerably helped Italy's war effort. As the British had chartered all the available barges Italy could do nothing.

On September 26 four British and one American worker

from the petroleum fields suddenly disappeared in the late afternoon. Two of these people had been called on during the morning by Iron Guard police on a charge of suspected sabotage. The manager at the works telephoned through to the police asking their intervention, but the police said : " We cannot do anything for you ; the Iron Guard can arrest whomsoever they please." On the same afternoon as these two men Mr. and Mrs. Tracy also disappeared. Tracy was a fairly humble Canadian engineer. Neighbours saw Mrs. Tracy being taken away in her nightdress. They were accused of attempted sabotage. Two or three weeks previously this same middle-aged English-woman had been the victim of a bomb outrage, when a band of Iron Guard hooligans threw one bomb into the kitchen and another into the bedroom window of their bungalow in the suburbs of Ploesti. I called on Mrs. Tracy at the time. She was completely unperturbed, and struck me as a very sensible woman who, unlike many of the foolish women who go out to Romania, continued with her English life. She cooked her own dinner, a job few Romanian women outside the peasant class ever did. She was cheerful and bright and insisted on giving me tea and cookies, though it was a most inconvenient hour. This motherly woman herself cultivated a charming flower garden.

For several days after she disappeared all the efforts—and they were great—made by the British Legation could not ascertain the whereabouts of any of the persons who were arrested. They had been unable to communicate with the British Consul, which meant that a long-established international custom was broken. All foreigners should be allowed to communicate with their Consul immediately on arrest. No word of the whereabouts of these people had ever been heard by any British official. All the police and Government authorities in Bucharest and Ploesti denied any knowledge of the arrests or of the whereabouts of the persons concerned. The police and the Guardist police in Ploesti and the surrounding villages denied any knowledge as to who had made the arrests. Rumours were wild. It was commonly thought that they had all been abducted to Germany. The prisoners were eventually known to be in the Prefecture of

Police. They were all together in one room, and Mrs. Tracy was still in her nightdress. They had not been allowed to speak to anyone, they had not sufficient food or place to sleep and of course there was no washing accommodation. The British Consul, Mr. Norman Mayers, had great difficulty in seeing even three of the men ; the circumstances were most difficult. The prisoners were brought into a room and told they could speak only in Romanian. Mr. Mayers' Romanian was not brilliant. He asked them if they were all right, and they smiled falsely and said yes. Mayers, however, was bright enough to observe that the shoulder of one man had been dislocated, while the face of another had obviously been banged about. The third could hardly speak or stand owing to the after-effects of continuous beating. A great deal of feeling was most unjustly aroused against the British Legation when the American, whose name was Freeman, was released after a protest by the American Minister, whilst the British stayed on in prison.

The Government was extremely angry, for their position was a difficult one. The British had little more to lose in Romania ; the Germans would have been delighted for us to break off diplomatic relations and depart. We had no chance of blackmail, no strong card to play. We could not break off relations, which was our biggest threat, and leave the men to await almost certain death in a Romanian prison. The charges were gradually revealed. They were largely of a fantastic nature, accusing the victims of sabotage and espionage. After they had been arrested some bright Guardists had put lead filings and a bomb or two into their flats, and these were produced as evidence.

The Romanians in answer to British pressure said that they had a law by which persons who were arrested could be interrogated by the authorities for five days without having legal advice. This law was invented only at the time of the arrests. Although everyone in Romania knew of the arrests, not one word about them had ever appeared in the local newspapers.

Before this situation had in any way been solved, another mysterious arrest was made. Mr. Percy Clark, owner of the

8

cable factory which supplies cable for the wells and refineries, visited Bucharest on business. He stayed at the Hotel Athenée Palace. This was a fairly carefree place, and when during the afternoon two men went up the stairs to see him in his room the management took no notice. He was brought down from his room as a prisoner and put into a car outside without attracting attention at the desk of the receptionists which he had to pass. At the time I entirely failed to understand why he did not scream, but I afterwards heard that he had two revolvers stuck into his ribs and was told that there would be a nasty noise if he screamed.

Percy Clark was not a young man. He refused to make any statement to the police. His arms were twisted behind him. When I saw him two months later he had still no use in his right arm. Percy Clark never said a word. As a man fond of the good things of life and female company, he probably suffered more from the lack of food, alcohol and tobacco, coupled with the tortures, than the others. No specific charge was brought against him, but he was generally believed by the Romanians to be with the others in their sabotage activities.

Scarcely was the news of Percy Clark's arrest confirmed when an important Englishman in the Astra Romana, Mr. A. Miller, was arrested at the Snagove sports pavilion of his company. He was talking to the secretary when the telephone bell rang. The secretary told me : " I went over to my office to answer it. There were four rather rough armed men, not in uniform, who asked for Mr. Miller. As they refused to allow me to go over and fetch him, I used the house telephone and asked him to come over. One of the men then held me in a corner of the room at the point of a revolver. Miller walked in. Three men surrounded him at once. One of them said, ' Are you Mr. Miller ? If so, I arrest you.' Mr. Miller then asked for the documents authorizing his arrest. One of the men produced a paper, which he read, then shrugging his shoulders allowed himself to be taken away to a waiting car. There is no doubt that he believed himself to be arrested by some responsible authority."

British subjects began to feel alarmed ; how many more were going to disappear in this mysterious manner ? It was generally believed that Miller was in some secret prison of the Iron Guard, but every police station and the secret police denied any knowledge as to his whereabouts. No one would take any responsibility. The right hand of the administration had not the least idea what the left hand was doing. The unruly elements, particularly in the provinces, of the Iron Guard would in England have worked out their youthful gangsterism on such harmless occupations as Hyde Park meetings and May Day demonstrations in Trafalgar Square.

On the day Miller was arrested an important Romanian merchant was arrested by the hooligan Iron Guards. By a rather able method of playing for time he was able to telephone to the German Minister, Fabricius, whom he knew. The Romanian told Fabricius himself that he had asked the Green-shirts to leave him and they refused. He then said : " The German Minister is on the line. Would you like him to speak to you ? " The Greenshirts just laughed, and after a few seconds one of them picked up the receiver, thinking it was a joke. Fabricius then told them there was nothing against the Romanian and they were to release him at once. After this the Greenshirts departed. This was some evidence that the unruly elements of the Iron Guard were very much under German influence. There can be no doubt whatsoever that they were in German pay.

The British Military Attaché, Colonel Geoffrey Macnab (unfortunately later taken prisoner in Crete), a man of courage and perseverance, well liked by the Romanians, could not get to see the prisoners, nor could the Consul after his first short interview. The Romanians were at this time beginning to apologize to the British Minister when he made his daily vigorous protests at the treatment the prisoners were receiving. Suddenly the Minister was told that Miller had written and signed a lengthy confession. He did, in fact, write a long piece of quite good fiction, which did not prevent him from being tortured. He was seen by accident by three British officials when they made their daily attempt at the Prefecture and the Sigurantza (Headquarters of the Secret Police) to see all the prisoners. While they were waiting in one room they saw Miller in another. Mr. Le Rougetel, Counsellor of the Legation, told me afterwards : " He was sitting on a form in a pretty filthy room with his head in his hands. They had made him take off his collar and tie, and as he had not shaved for several days he looked rather grim, but when he saw me, and his guard were not looking, he smiled and put his thumbs up, after which the door between us was locked. I was surprised they did not arrest us all, so persistent were we and so determined were they that we should not see anyone."

The real reason why the Romanians kept the prisoners away from officials was that they were afraid of the Press, particularly the American Press. If the story of how they were being treated leaked out, which it certainly would have done if the bleeding and bruised prisoners were seen by British officials, public opinion, especially in America, would have been violently affected.

Not only were the Romanians telling the Minister a different story each day, but the prisoners themselves seemed to do unaccountable things. Mrs. Tracy was released before her husband, and I gathered that she had promised him and the other prisoners not to say a word about their life in prison to anyone outside. At the time very responsible people, such as the American Minister, who was after all a friend of Antonescu, felt that if she were to tell the true story and have it printed in the American Press, the Germans would ask the Romanians to release the prisoners immediately. I think he was right. Another queer act was the letter written by Miller to a Romanian friend saying that he was all right and that certain valuable papers were to be given to the bearer. This was sent before Miller's whereabouts had been ascertained by the Legation.

Quite suddenly it was announced that there would be a trial, and that General Antonescu's nephew, who was a lawyer, would be in charge of it. The trial never took place, as world opinion became so strong that the Romanians had to stop their highly enjoyable mediaeval torture and the prisoners were one by one released.  Percy Clark spent a month in hospital in Romania before proceeding to Istanbul, where three months later he was still receiving treatment, while Tracy was taken straight to the American hospital in Istanbul.  My own view, which has no real official confirmation, is that the Germans genuinely believed that one or all of these men was in possession of useful information and they used it as an excuse to employ the wild undisciplined Guardists.  In this way they saw some return for their money and kept the Guardists occupied, preventing them from indulging in occupations more harmful to the German war machine.

The freeing of the British oil engineers was probably one of the strokes of diplomacy most astutely handled by Sir Reginald Hoare.  In retrospect, when I consider how badly the prisoners were handled, together with the knowledge that all the other engineers were already thrown out and the fact that at the time no one believed there was the least chance of any of these men seeing freedom before the end of the war, I have not the least idea how Sir Reginald did it.  I know we threatened to hold up Romanian shipping, but as there was so little they did not care. What threats or cajoleries were used would be worth recording in any handbook for ambitious young third secretaries to read, to teach them how to handle a difficult situation when everything is against you and you have nothing with which to bargain. What a pity more Balkan Ministers did not think up some such means.

Mr. Miller was released first and Percy Clark later.  I was on the Greek front when the remaining few were quietly sent down to Istanbul.  I very much regret that the Press were never given the full story of the lives these men had led in prison ; indeed, no statement was made concerning their release. This would, in my opinion, have been wonderful publicity in America.

Before the Germans actually sent their army into Romania they were using as their headquarters for the petroleum fields the Petrol Block Company which they had bought up during

1940. They and not the British were carrying out illegal acts against the Romanian State. Rail tank cars returning empty to Ploesti across the Romanian frontier were rarely scrutinized by customs officials. It was in these empty rail cars that considerable quantities of machine-guns, rifles and ammunition were brought into Romania by night, transferred to ordinary road petrol tanks and from there distributed to the German minority in Transylvania just on the far side of the Carpathians. Road cars also brought in ammunition.

There is every year considerable speculation as to when the Danube will freeze and for how long it will remain frozen. Naturally this does not mean that the river has to be solid ice on which one could roast an ox as used to be done on the Thames. The Danube is declared unfit for navigation when blocks of floating ice coming down from the more shallow reaches in the north make its passage difficult. These blocks often pile up owing to some minor obstruction and reach a height of forty or even fifty feet. The whole Danube when frozen gives the impression of low rocky hills. It would be extremely difficult, if not impossible, to walk on it, and I saw no smooth patches where one might skate.

While navigation was impossible during the early part of 1941 the Germans were building 200 new barges to convey oil from the mouth of the pipeline at the Danubian port of Giurgiu up the river to Regensburg, where the oil is transferred to storage tanks and from there distributed throughout Germany. In addition to building barges, there were gangs of soldiers in uniform working in the snow on the building of two new pipelines. The road was continually being blocked by snow, and the supplies and equipment for the gangs of workers were delayed owing to the inefficiency of the Romanian sweepers until the Germans took charge of sweeping the roads themselves. The Romanians had never thought of putting up fences to prevent snowdrifts on the roads. This the Germans did, and it must be admitted that the speed with which they cleared the road after heavy falls of snow was remarkable. The German soldiers wore over their uniform huge leather coats lined with wool, and underneath their hats, scarves which they tied round their chins, leaving only their eyes visible.

I was surprised that the pipeline was in many places actually running above the surface of the ground. All the storage tanks were filled, including the one at Constanza which holds 750,000 tons, and the output of petroleum had to be lessened owing to the inability of the Germans to transport the oil. Experts estimate that the production in Romania now (September 1941) is about 300,000 tons per month. No other country is able to buy the oil. Turkey would dearly like to do so, and she offered to pay for it in dollars. These the Romanians would not accept, demanding Swiss francs. The Turks, unable to produce any Swiss francs, are now extremely short of petrol. Buses are few and far between. There have been no private cars for a year, and even the rations to diplomats are severely restricted.

Soon after these incidents, with the knowledge that so far as the British were concerned Romania was a lost country, all the service attachés and a considerable part of the Legation staff left Romania. Two or three days later, about October 15, the British subjects left or were supposed to leave. All British subjects had been constantly warned by the painstaking Consul that the wisest course was to leave Romania as quickly as possible, but they all stayed on in the hope that His Majesty's Government would eventually pay for their evacuation. He knew, poor man, that if the Germans suddenly declared a protectorate he would be unable to get them out. Even after continual warnings and offers of free passage, many of them stayed on saying : " As long as the Legation stays we shall stay."

At the beginning of October the special correspondents left, for unless one was willing to take the risk of getting uncensored stories out of the country it was impractical from the point of view of newspaper men to stay on. The Romanian censorship was by this time (German troops having entered on October 12) entirely controlled by Herr Hofmann, previously Press Attaché at the German Legation. The only stories allowed out of the country officially were those which had a strong pro-German slant.

I stayed until the beginning of November, spending a few nights in one flat and a few nights in another. The most amusing place I lived in was one of King Carol's flats which he had used as a hide-away from Madame Lupescu. It was on the sixteenth floor of a skyscraper in the centre of the town ; the passage to the lift was dim and generally full of people. He had spared no expense in the furnishings, which was just what I should have imagined in any flat owned by Carol. There was a cocktail bar, and enormous plate-glass French windows opening on to a roof garden which had a small pool. There was inadequate kitchen accommodation, as the flat was not meant for serious eating. The whole place was furnished like a yacht. The rails at the edge of the garden were like the rails on a ship, the lighting was pseudo-searchlights, the beds super-luxury bunks, the stairs transplanted from a ship. The pictures were all poor ones of nude women in compromising attitudes. In the bathroom was a slimming machine which the servants told me the King used regularly.

When I wanted to leave Romania finally, the Romanians, having refused to give me a permit to stay in their country for months, refused me a permit to leave it. This the Legation finally obtained, and rather sadly, with my car full of suitcases, I drove down to Giurgiu. The harbour zone was forbidden to any traffic except what was crossing on the Danube ferry to Bulgaria. I showed my pass to the German sentries and they let me through. For a mile I drove through a German military camp, where the soldiers were preparing their evening meal. They were mostly anti-aircraft, I think. Here and there I saw A.A. guns, some covered and some being greased with their camouflaged covers off. The Germans in the customs shed only made a fuss about the car leaving the country ; everything else went quite smoothly, and it was nearly dark when I drove my car on a zigzag course over a few hundred yards between German A.A. guns until I reached the boards over which one had to drive in the dark. There was a blackout. I felt a little embarrassed that German soldiers should help to guide me. On the ferry itself the Iron Guard police arrested three Poles, after they thought they were safely outside Romania. We protested, but could do nothing. Crossing the Danube from the dark hidden port of Giurgiu to the brilliantly lighted town of Rustchuk on the other side I little thought that within ten weeks I should return again to Romania.

CHAPTER VIII

## GREECE—THE SHADOW AND THE BLOW

I ARRIVED in Greece on November 13 to cover the war which had broken out a fortnight previously and which was already swinging the Italian troops back into Albania. It was my first visit to Athens since the previous August, when I had spent a week there and in Salonika at the time of the torpedoing of the *Helle*. On this occasion my journey from Istanbul took me nine days. I could not help contrasting it with the journey by air from Bucharest, one of the pleasantest I have ever made. On that occasion I had breakfasted in the Romanian capital, was in Salonika by eleven and at Athens in time for lunch. The last stage of the journey, with its constantly changing views of coastal scenery, the impressive cloud-capped heights of Olympus and the open fertile plains of Thessaly and Boeotia, provides a variety unequalled in Europe. One discovers that one has already become a philhellene by the time that the plane reaches Tatoi aerodrome.

The *Helle* sinking had made Greece front-page news. In retrospect, one can see how closely co-ordinated was Axis strategy at this stage of the war. The attack on Greece, to which this was to have been an immediate preliminary, was timed to coincide with the Battle of Britain, already working up to a climax. The conquest of Greece was to form merely a part of the great convergent assault on the whole British position in the Middle East, an assault of which the Italian Press rather unwisely allowed itself to speak at this time. When the history of the war is written in terms of grand strategy, writers will devote much attention to the pincer movement against Suez, which has formed so integral a part of the German strategic plan and which, always on the point of realization, has been frustrated again and again when it seemed perilously near to achievement. The moves on this great European chessboard will be fascinating to follow, with Hitler forcing the game through Vienna, through Munich, through Prague; Britain and France replying with the guarantees to Turkey, Romania and Greece, guarantees which became perilous liabilities when the French debacle revolutionized the whole position in the Mediterranean.

During that dreadful week in June which began with the Italian declaration of war and ended with the first French appeal for an armistice the centre of gravity of the war shifted from the western battlefields to the whole area between the Danube and the Nile. It was clear that for months Britain could not hope to do more than play a waiting game, holding off the attack upon Suez until such time as sufficient reinforcements should have arrived in the Middle East to enable her to safeguard the Canal zone and ultimately to take the offensive. Germany, with the prestige of continuous victory and with the advantage of immensely shorter lines of communication, and Italy, in a position to strike directly across the desert into Egypt and from her advanced base in Albania into the Balkans, seemed to have every card in their hands. The tide of the general advance across the Balkan Peninsula was sweeping on, by conquest (Albania), military infiltration and disintegration (Romania) and economic penetration and encirclement (Yugoslavia). It came sharply up against the resistance of the Greek people, was stemmed, and then thrown back. Ultimately, though the German wave overwhelmed Greece just as it had overwhelmed every small country that had stood in its way, the delay to the Axis time-table which was imposed by the Greek resistance had a major effect upon the whole course of the Greek war. The Greek campaign is an epic, despite the sad anti-climax in which it ended. In all probability, no effort by Britain could have materially affected the issue. That British policy might have done much more to unite Greece and to present a genuinely democratic front against the enemy I firmly believe. The failure to do so certainly contributed to the weakening of Greek resistance in the face of the German invasion in April 1941.

Throughout the years 1936–40, but more especially perhaps during the latter part of this period, British policy in Greece had shown an attachment to the Metaxas dictatorship which, I feel, was in the best interests neither of Britain nor of Greece. It is of course the duty of a Legation to make itself acceptable to the Government to which it is accredited.  But this does not imply that the importance of opposition elements should be ignored, particularly when the opposition, though politically suppressed, was so numerous and so Anglophile in sentiment as was the Venizelist Party in Greece.  Liberal and democratic in politics, the Venizelists were staunch, even uncritical, admirers of England and of English institutions.  They represented, over a long period of years, fully fifty per cent. of the electorate and a decidedly larger proportion of the cultured classes and the intelligentsia.  A young Englishman of Leftish sympathies once described the opponents of the Venizelist Party as being composed of " either stick-in-the-muds or thugs ".  This of course was an overstatement, but one was extremely conscious that in Greece the Venizelists represented that element which understood and sympathized with the principles for which Britain was fighting. Harold Nicolson's *Why Britain is at War*, for instance, was widely read and created a most favourable impression in Athens ; the same could not be said, I am afraid, of Sir Nevile Henderson's *Failure of a Mission.*

The apparent attachment of Britain to the Metaxas dictatorship, while it could not alienate the sympathies of these people, did much to sow doubt and confusion in their minds with regard to the issues at stake in the war.  Articles in praise of the dictatorship in English papers such as *The Times* created a very bad impression.  How, it was asked, can Britain condone in Greece what she condemns in Germany or Italy ?  Here you have all the essential features of Nazi tyranny, the suppression of Parliamentary institutions, of freedom of speech and of the Press ; you have the dragooning of the nation by means of a large secret police force ; you have the banishment of political opponents of the régime ;  you have the beating up of numbers of more obscure people, men and women, on the elastic charge of ' Communism ', a convenient term employed to cover practically all forms of liberal thought.  How do you reconcile your condonation of this set of values in one part of Europe with your struggle to the death with them in another ?

Such was, broadly, the line of argument of the many friends of Britain in Greece, and though it may seem to some to take no account of the compromises in matters of high policy which war imposes, there is little doubt that the failure of the British representatives in Greece to modify the policy of the dictatorship, more particularly after Greece had become involved in the war on the side of Britain, alienated some and deeply discouraged many more.

The personal dictatorship of General Metaxas had been established on August 4, 1936, little more than a fortnight after the outbreak of the Fascist rebellion in Spain. For some months, following the deaths in rapid succession of four ex-Prime Ministers — Venizelos himself, Kondylis who had been responsible for the restoration of King George, Tsaldaris and Demerdjis, there had been an almost complete political deadlock between the two leading parties, the Conservative (Royalist) led by Theotokis and the Liberal (Venizelist) led by Sophoulis. In the summer of 1936 Metaxas, whose following, the very incongruously named " Party of Free Thought ", consisted of only four members in the Chamber, was Prime Minister at the head of a ' Service ' Cabinet. (A ' Service ' Cabinet is a solution employed from time to time during Greece's frequent political crises and deadlocks. A group leader, not necessarily commanding a majority or even a large following, is summoned to take office and to avoid, so far as possible, all controversial issues. Such Cabinets, which are usually somewhat colourless in composition, jog along for two or three months until a change in the political grouping renders them no longer essential.)

The dictatorship was proclaimed by Metaxas on the ground of the necessity of meeting the danger of a Communist revolution. There had been a good deal of unrest among the tobacco workers of the north, a one-day protest General Strike was threatened, and there was the example of Spain where General Franco's rebellion was still gathering momentum. Metaxas knew that his task would be easier in Greece since he was already the Government, although his "Party of Free Thought" consisted of only four members in the Chamber.

The political parties had become aware of the danger, but, as was so continually the case during the "decade of disappointments and lost opportunities", they acted too late. The leaders of the two great parties had come together and agreed on a coalition, the Speaker had been chosen, the principal members of the Cabinet named. But Metaxas forestalled them. He obtained the King's consent to suspend the Constitution, dissolved the Chamber, and established a personal dictatorship responsible only to the Crown.

The régime differed in no essential respect, save only in the absence of Jew-baiting, from the other Corporate States which were becoming so fashionable during these years. The German model was in most respects closely followed, which was not surprising, since Metaxas had received most of his military training in Germany and was known as a strong Germanophile in the last war, being one of the very small group which was banished from Greece for inveterate pro-Germanism when Venizelos returned to power, after the abdication of King Constantine, and brought his country into the war on the side of the Allies.

I met Metaxas on several occasions during my visits to Greece. He started with the great disadvantage, for a dictator, of being physically most unprepossessing. He had none of the carefully cultivated Napoleonic appearance of Mussolini, nor even the cheap kitchen-maid postcard appeal which I suppose exists in Hitler, in spite of the pop-eyes. Metaxas looked like a tubby little elderly professor. He was obviously efficient, and an admirer of efficiency. I should say that the conception of liberty as an absolute political value never entered his head. Like so many political tyrants he was in private life exceptionally courteous, and he possessed charming manners. He did not see many journalists, but when he did he heard them with patience and gave the impression of being a reasonable man. I remember the pains he took to explain to me the strategy leading up to the victory of Koritza, which he always regarded as his particular child. Though probably one of the most distinguished Generals in Europe he never wore uniform. This was not, I believe, due to any desire to play down the military nature of his rule, as was sometimes said, but because his squat, stubby figure looked frankly ridiculous in ' regimentals '. He was one of those men who seem to have been born in a bowler hat and short black coat.

The régime was a tyranny in the strictest sense of the word. Criticism was stifled. Leaders of the Constitutional parties were banished to islands, where, if they suffered no actual ill-treatment, the conditions of living were calculated to, and in fact did, shorten the lives of some of the more elderly politicians. On the other hand, I have heard cases of exiles who were allowed to return to Athens, under strict police supervision, for medical treatment. Special Committees of Safety were formed through-out Greece to try political prisoners against whom no charges could be laid by the ordinary processes of law. These resembled to some extent the Star Chamber in England during the seventeenth century. Large numbers of quite humble people were severely beaten up and, in some fully authenticated cases, tortured. Metaxas himself did not strike me as deliberately cruel—one could even imagine him as a kindly father—so much as ruthless and wholly insensitive to the means which he adopted to secure his ends.

At no time, even during its last months when by standing up to the Italian attack it interpreted the wishes of a united nation, did the dictatorship prove popular. Most of the time it was bitterly hated. It was neatly put to me by one of the more objective Greek politicians that before the Metaxas régime Greece was divided on a fifty-fifty basis between Royalists and Venizelists ; after the establishment of the dictatorship ninety per cent. were united against Metaxas with a dubious ten per cent. in favour. This was an over-simplification, but it was essentially true. It was extraordinarily hard to meet supporters of the dictatorship in any class of society. The suppression of free criticism and the rigid censorship of the Press cut right across the instincts of the most politically minded people in

Europe. Whereas a group of men in an English pub may be safely presumed to be discussing football over their mild and bitter, their counterparts in Greece—keen-eyed eager little men chattering hard and fast before little cups of thick black Turkish coffee—are certain to be discussing politics.

The Greek is an admirable talker, but I should not call him a good conversationalist. He is far too anxious to expound his own views to listen to those of his companion, and a political discussion between a number of Greeks resembles a round game in which one orator holds the floor until he pauses for breath, whereupon another snaps in and has ' la parole ' in a flash. Much of these political arguments, in which no one listens to anyone else, deal with abstractions, because the Greek generally prefers to discuss Liberty and Authority, Democracy and Dictatorship rather than drainage schemes, compulsory inoculation or the supply of boots for the army. I remember one discussion with perhaps the most extreme Anglophile in Athens. It was at the time of the Battle of Britain, and knowing him to be reputed an intelligent man I looked forward to a discussion of the technicalities of air warfare. For the sake of argument I advanced the technical aspects of the battle which seemed favourable to Germany. At my first pause he nipped in with " England will conquer because she has the greater nobility of spirit ". And then he proceeded to develop the theme of English nobility of spirit. I found his uncritical admiration of my country highly flattering, but a trifle embarrassing.

The dictatorship could not hope to be popular in a country where every man is a politician and thinks himself as well able to form a cabinet and direct a policy as the man who has actually been appointed for the work. In the same way the rigid control of the Press is bound to be unpopular. It has turned Greek newspapers, once distinguished for their variety of opinion and freedom of expression, into the dullest in Europe—mere factual records, with not so many facts at that. The Greeks are voracious newspaper readers, but they read very few books. In this they differ to a remarkable extent from Romanians, who are voracious novel readers, most catholic in their tastes. I remember travelling once from Galatz to Bucharest in the same carriage as a young Romanian officer who divided his attention between Florence Barclay's *The Rosary*, Dostoievsky's *The Idiot*, and the most hard-boiled of all Somerset Maugham's novels.

The Greek likes his newspapers numerous and their articles short and preferably well charged with rhetoric. Christopher Buckley, who edited the English weekly paper in Athens, once told me that the most regular items in his mailbag bore such titles as " Ode to the United Glory of England and Greece ", and that even the death of Metaxas brought forth from one source a poem beginning

" Farewell, thou noblest of the human race ! "

Similarly, every Greek sees himself as an editor. I do not know if everyone that one meets has at some time or another really owned or edited a newspaper. I can merely say that it appears to be the case. How many conversations do I not remember in which my companion, after lamenting the political decadence of the day, was accustomed to break off with the sigh : " Ah ! when I had my paper . . .", leaving one to assume that a Junius or a Delane had been lost to the world.

Metaxas' handling of the Press struck me as crude and unimaginative. Just as his portrait, usually though by no means invariably accompanied by that of the King, was to be seen in every shop and office—his successor, Korizis, to his credit, dropped all that nonsense—so the Press had daily to be filled with praise of the régime. Even such positive achievements as the social legislation of the Fourth of August Government, the draining and irrigation, the improved roads (WHY do dictators always concentrate on roads ?), the improvement of the amenities of Athens, lost much of their effect owing to the degree of *réclame* which he exacted from the Press. For practically a month preceding the anniversary of the establishment of his rule the newspapers were compelled to carry, day after day, fulsome articles in praise of the work of the last four years. His taste for the sycophantic led him to inspire articles comparing him to Pericles or to the great Byzantine Emperors. It was customary for such articles to speak of " John Metaxas, Founder of the Third Greek Civilization ". 'Obligatory articles' of this sort became a characteristic feature of the Athens Press. Such fulsome adulation did him more harm than good ; for the keen-witted and hypercritical Greeks are the last people to be taken in by that type of blather, which indeed merely provided matter for ridicule. Equally inept were his attempts to interfere with the cultural tradition of Greece. He refused to allow public performances of *Antigone* unless the 'un-authoritarian' passages in the text were cut, and banned Pericles' Funeral Oration from use in schools on the ground that this speech, the high spot, perhaps, of the whole of Thucydides, was politically subversive, being in praise of democracy. Metaxas was perhaps the 'brainiest' of all the dictators ; he was very far from being the best psychologist.

Another unpopular feature of the régime was the Youth Movement, known as the Neolaia. There is a good deal to be said both for and against such movements, but I could not feel that the Neolaia represented anything but an essentially Fascist organization, closely modelled on the Hitler Youth and the Italian Balilla. They performed a certain amount of social service, though not nearly so much as the Straja Tarii of Romania, which was a far more attractive and less political organization. Membership was compulsory in all schools, and while a large sum was set aside for the organization from the national budget, 'pressure' was exerted on industrialists and merchants to compel them to contribute. Their main occupation appeared to be innumerable parades, much marching up and down the streets on days of public rejoicing, and Sunday outings in lorries. One felt, correctly I believe, that a generation was being trained up in the Fascist outlook and Fascist interpretation of the ideas of 'leadership' and 'authority'. Members took an oath of allegiance to the head of the Government, a fact which strengthened the conviction that Metaxas aimed at building up a personal Praetorian guard. There was also a good deal of Fascist ruffianism in the higher ranks. It is certain that the organization was extremely costly and that it was widely felt, not in military circles alone, that the army was being starved to provide uniforms and outings for the Neolaia. I know of at least one case where money raised by public subscription to provide aircraft for national defence was simply turned over to the Neolaia. It was partly owing to such misappropriations as these that Greece was able to dispose of no more than sixty military aircraft at the opening of the Italian war.

This régime, in so many ways antipathetic to the whole trend of Greek genius, could not have been maintained without the support of a large force of secret police, who for brutality and efficiency probably surpassed any similar organization anywhere in the Balkans. They were Gestapo-modelled and many of their chiefs were Gestapo-trained : another evidence of the way in which the dictatorship took its tone from Germany. They were under the direct control of the sinister Manyadakis, Minister of Public Security, the *éminence grise* behind the régime.

No figure is more closely associated in Greek eyes with the Metaxas dictatorship than Constantine Manyadakis. Physically, he is almost fascinating in his unattractiveness. I have sometimes thought that he deliberately cultivated an unshaven and even gangsterish appearance as a means of enhancing his reputation as the Himmler of the régime. A large portrait of the chief of the Gestapo did in fact hang at one period on the wall of his study. He had a somewhat disconcerting habit of toying with a revolver while giving an interview. Such interviews were granted only with difficulty, and usually took place in the presence of two agents of police who remained in the room throughout the proceedings. Access to the Minister could be obtained most easily through the agency of Thomas Bowman, the exceedingly able British Vice-Consul in Athens, who certainly knew Greece better than any other Englishman and was probably the most influential British subject in the country.

It was singular that Manyadakis, all of whose instincts were sympathetic towards the Totalitarian system, should in fact have been among those Ministers who leaned towards Britain. This was certainly not due to any ideological affinities, but to the shrewd calculation that Britain would be the eventual victor.

He had no interest in the ideals for which Britain was, or was supposedly, fighting. He had all the distrust of the half-educated for non-materialist values. He speaks only Greek and Albanian, which is very rare among Greeks of the educated classes, and his cultural interests are precisely nil. The arguments of humanitarian liberalism, the commonplaces of Britain and America, simply do not concern him. It is not so much that he opposes them with counter-arguments as that he simply disregards their existence. It was he who controlled the highly efficient secret police and who extended the charge of Communism to cover all expressions of Left-Wing political sentiment. The arrest, flogging, exile or torture of political opponents was the work of his agents. Yet Manyadakis was in his way a fascinating figure. He possessed a grim, Goering-like humour, manifested in such remarks as his description of the régime in Greece not as a dictatorship but as a 'controlled democracy', or in his reply to an enthusiastic American journalist who had praised to him the heroism of the Greek soldiers on the Albanian front : " After the war, it will be my business to arrest the heroes." Another American correspondent, who had been received by the King of Greece, had been authorized by the Sovereign to publish a statement expressing the latter's general sympathy with democratic principles. This statement of the King was seized on with gusto by a well-known Greek Liberal journalist and published in the *Eleutheron Bema*, the leading Greek daily paper. The journalist was arrested and banished to an island. Manyadakis was heard to remark publicly : " If there are any more indiscretions of that sort I shall have to arrest the King."

A tremendous worker, though uncultured and uneducated, his one relaxation was the little court which he held late at night in the lounge of the King George Hotel. Here, with a group of some half-dozen intimates, he sat and listened to the gossip of the day. The composition of this circle never varied greatly. There was a certain Greek journalist, sub-editor of an important daily paper, whose conversation Manyadakis found amusing and refreshing, whom he expected to be in nightly attendance as a sort of Court Jester. On one occasion this unfortunate creature, during a period of exceptional pressure on his paper, absented himself for two successive nights from the gathering. Manyadakis' reaction was swift and characteristic. On the third evening a police agent arrived at the office of the newspaper with orders to arrest the defaulter. It was typical of the Minister that the arrest should have been timed to coincide with the rush hour on the paper. The unfortunate young journalist, after spending a night cooling his heels in gaol, was never again known to absent himself from the ' Court '.

Yet Manyadakis admired cheek of a certain sort. Early in the Italian war an American journalist, recently arrived in Athens, whose flair for getting hold of the key-men of the administration was certainly greater than his command of the Greek language, decided, quite correctly, that a pass signed by Manyadakis was an Open Sesame ! throughout Greece. He laboriously committed a single sentence of Greek to memory, and with the aid of this thrust his way into the official presence, where, brandishing a sheet of notepaper, he greeted the Minister with the words, accompanied by a wealth of transatlantic gesture : " Thelo ena megalo Manyadakis ! " (" I want a great big Manyadakis ! " *i.e.* signature). He obtained his request.

I cannot say that, apart from Manyadakis and Metaxas himself, the personnel of the Greek Government inspired me with any great respect. " Old decayed serving-men and tapsters " would perhaps be an unfair description, but it was emphatically a scratch team, united only in their dependence on the ruthless driving power of the Premier. The Minister of Press had run an obscure and unsuccessful paper with a negligible circulation. It had, however, supported Metaxas at a time when the entire Athens Press was hostile to, or neglectful of, the General. He had his reward. The Permanent Under-Secretary for Foreign Affairs was an ex-Venizelist, an old man, tired and cynical, the last person to take a strong stand on matters of foreign policy. Some of the younger men, such as Ziphos, the Minister of Shipping, a sincere Anglophile, owed their inclusion to their personal devotion to Metaxas.

The Fourth of August celebrations occurred on a Sunday that year. Venizelists as in previous years ostentatiously absented themselves, many taking the opportunity to visit the country or the seaside. It is ironical to reflect that the two foreign Governments which addressed public messages of congratulation to General Metaxas on this, the fourth anniversary of his dictatorship, were those of Germany and Italy.

After that things developed rapidly. Axis strategy was unrolling the map of aggression, and it was the turn of Greece to face the test. It might have been supposed that the Nazis felt sure of Metaxas. His German training, his sympathies in the last war, the nature of his régime (" The old parliamentary system has vanished for ever ") should have made him *persona gratissima* at Berlin. It is significant that, whereas the British guarantee to Greece in April 1939 was very much played down and Greek Government spokesmen were instructed to call attention to its unilateral nature to foreign correspondents, every prominence was given to the obviously worthless Italian ' scrap of paper ' guarantee in June 1940. Since the beginning of the war Metaxas had repudiated positive Germanophile sentiments. " I am not pro-German, I am not pro-English, I am pro-Greek," said he ; and then, with an access of candour : " I am not pro-German, but it is a question of finding a market for our tobacco crop." As in the case of the other Balkan countries, Greek economic dependence on Germany had increased throughout the 'thirties, exports to the latter country rising from about 20 per cent. (1929) to about 33 per cent. (1938), and imports from 10 per cent. (1929) to 23 per cent. (1937). Greece tumbled willy-nilly into Schacht's economic net. The manufactured goods (typewriters, sewing-machines and all the rest of it) with which Germany repaid Greek produce were often valued at as high a rate as 25 per cent. above that asked by other countries. Germany had outbid the United States for Greek produce, and she now turned the clearing system to her advantage. This accounts for the fact that a large section of the business element in Greece could not be indifferent to the effects of a war with Germany on the whole structure of

Greek commerce. But that did not imply that they were ideologically Germanophile or failed to realize that with the victory of the Axis Greece would be reduced to a state of political and economic vassalage to one or other of the Fascist dictators.

Nevertheless, the Germans were taking no risks. Metaxas, with all his faults, though a spiritual Nazi, was a patriot, and Berlin wanted an entirely pliable tool. It hoped to find this in Kodzias, Minister-Governor of Athens, who at that time was being heavily played up by the Germans. Kodzias did not strike me as essentially Germanophile. A large, vain, genial, talkative man, he appeared neither profound nor discreet, but in no sense dangerous. Had it not been for the manner in which his pride had been wounded when he was taken up and subsequently dropped by the former British Minister, Sir Sydney Waterlow, it is improbable that the Germans, who note all such things, would have taken the trouble to play with him. However, he had subsequently visited Germany, had made the acquaintance of Goebbels, had been photographed driving in a car with Goering, and his wounded self-esteem had been healed. But he was never a big enough figure for the part for which he was cast.

It will never be quite certain how far the plot actually went during the ten days between the Fourth of August celebrations and the torpedoing of the *Helle*. With the moral support of Germany it was intended that Kodzias should declare himself Prime Minister, and effect some sort of *coup d'état* with the assistance of Skylakakis, a former Minister of the Interior under Metaxas, of Platys, Deputy Chief of the General Staff, Logothetopoulos and Louvaris, professors at Athens University, who were to divide between them the principal portfolios of the Government. It is interesting to note that two at least of these have received appointments under the quisling Tsolakoglou régime.

Then occurred the torpedoing of the *Helle*. I suspect that the plot was timed to synchronize with this incident, and that the intriguers miscalculated the vigorous Greek reaction to the outrage. An alternative theory, for which there is a good deal to be said, is that Mussolini, after ineffectively watching Hitler steal the limelight for so long, acted on his own initiative in an endeavour to heighten his value as an ally. This would account for the absence of vigorous German diplomatic support for Italy during these days. In any case, it would appear that the Axis, or at any rate Italy, miscalculated then, as they miscalculated on October 28, in supposing that the fact that the Metaxas régime was unpopular with the bulk of the country meant that it would be unsupported in any stand which it might attempt to make against the aggressor. Grazzi appears to have been genuinely under the impression that internal revolution would break out. He made the same mistake in October. It was a singular misreading of psychology to suppose that in order to settle scores with their own Fascist ruler the Greeks would play the game of Italian Fascism, thereby helping to ensure the victory of international Fascism in the general struggle. Threatened aggression from Italy or Germany, indeed, was the one way of rallying these people to a Government which they intensely resented and which they regarded with well-justified suspicion. I do not think that the disinterested part which they played received sufficient credit from British official quarters either then or subsequently.

Metaxas stood his ground against Italian threats. While studiously avoiding 'provocation' to Italy he notified the Italians that force would be met by force if any military action were taken against Greece. Under the circumstances it was a bold decision to take. Greece was quite unready to face an attack. Her armed forces were unmobilized, inadequate and scandalously under-equipped. Britain, at that time fighting for sheer existence against the great air attacks which were to have been the preliminary to invasion, could scarcely have given even nominal support; she had just been compelled to withdraw from British Somaliland through lack of man-power, and she was holding Egypt and the Sudan with forces ridiculously outnumbered in men and material by the Italian armies in Libya and East Africa. But Hitler seems to have given no encouragement to his junior partner, and Mussolini probably considered that, given a few weeks more of psychological preparation and war of nerves, the prize would drop into his lap like over-ripe fruit. Everyone in Greece knew that the sinking of the *Helle* had been the work of an Italian submarine, but the newspapers were only allowed to speak of a " submarine of unknown nationality ", even though it was an open secret within a day or two that splintered fragments of the torpedo had been recovered and had been proved to be of Italian origin. The most that foreign correspondents could imply was to give as much prominence as possible to Greek acceptance of British assurances that none of our submarines had been in the neighbourhood of Tenos at the time of the outrage.

Meanwhile Metaxas was dealing firmly with the timorous plotters within his own household. At a cabinet meeting within a few days of the *Helle* incident, passing his eye all round his assembled colleagues, he spoke as follows : " I have heard reports that my health is failing and that I shall soon no longer be equal to the fulfilment of my public duties. If there is any-one here who has been responsible for the spreading of these reports let me take this opportunity of assuring him that I have never felt better in my life. I have heard reports that I am about to give place to someone whose foreign policy will be more completely in accord with Germany. I have no intention of doing this, nor of permitting this country to become in any way a protectorate of Germany. I say this the more emphatically as I am in a position to state that the attack on Britain may be regarded as having failed."

Three members of the cabinet—I believe Mavroudis, Kyriakos and Ziphos, but I do not know for certain—here interrupted with applause. Metaxas seemed surprised and even a little put out. Then he continued :

" If there is anyone here who thinks that he is in a position to take my place, let me tell him that I shall not send him into exile on an island. No ! but I shall send him to an island ; I shall send him to Daphne ! " The best known lunatic asylum in Greece is at Daphne.

A day or two later, though the cabinet was continuing to meet regularly in Athens, Kodzias withdrew to the country resort at Kephissia, some miles distant. This was widely regarded as an indication that he had fallen under the Premier's displeasure. For some days there was talk of his dismissal from the Government, but ultimately some sort of reconciliation was patched up through the agency of Prince Paul, the Heir Presumptive. Kodzias returned to Athens, was present in the company of Metaxas at a public meeting at Peiraeus, and was generally understood to have been received back into favour, though I have heard that he was not invariably summoned to meetings of the Cabinet during the weeks that followed. In any case, the plot had clearly miscarried, and his usefulness to the Axis was at an end. He was still regarded with a good deal of suspicion, probably quite unjustly, in pro-British circles. One has only to meet the man to realize that he is not the stuff of which Nazi plotters are made. He must still have felt uneasy about his position and repute, for a day or two after the beginning of the Italian war he found it necessary to issue to the Press a public denial that he had opposed in a cabinet meeting the Premier's decision to reject the Italian ultimatum and to defend the country against invasion. After that he became quite innocuous, and by the time he reached Egypt after the close of the Greek campaign he was a declared Anglophile.

The torpedoing of the *Helle* was not the only, or indeed the first, provocation which Greece had to endure from Italy during August–October 1940. Italy, having seized Albania by naked aggression without any shadow of extenuating circumstance in 1939, had become, by a pleasing metamorphosis, the most devoted champion of Albanian nationalism and an advocate of a Greater Albania, still of course under the ' protection ' of Italy. The Italian and the Italian-controlled Albanian Press carried on a vigorous campaign against Greek rule in Southern Epirus. A bandit named Daout Hoggia, who had disappeared under somewhat mysterious circumstances, was represented as a noble-minded patriot done to death by the Greeks. When this obscure ruffian proved a damp squib so far as provoking an extension of the World War was concerned, other nebulous frontiersmen of the most dubious antecedents were painstakingly resurrected. The Greek and Albanian Press fenced with one another over the bodies of these undistinguished Patrocluses, whom Albanian papers asserted to have been murdered in the past few weeks by the Greeks as part of a systematic campaign of terrorization of the Albanian minority, and whom the Greeks discovered either to be still living or to have died peacefully in their beds in 1912. The whole period of assertion and counter-assertion reminded one of a scene before a drop-curtain in an Elizabethan play. The sets were being shifted and the leading characters were assembling in the wings for the big scene that was to follow; meanwhile the funny men were being put up to do their stuff.

Early in October an Italian plane dropped three bombs on Greek territory between Thebes and Livadia. This further act of provocation, though fairly widely known, was almost success-fully hushed up by the Greek censorship, as the Government was leaning over backwards in its attempts to avoid anything which might be interpreted as 'provocation' of the Fascist Power.

Everyone was discussing the forthcoming attack, yet as the weeks passed it had seemed harder and harder to believe in it. Even as late as October 23, Metaxas, in conversation with Botosakis, the ' armament king ' of Greece, scoffed at the idea of an immediate attack. This may have been bluff for internal consumption. Greece, which had been quite unprepared in August, was disposing her scanty resources to the best of her ability. Her army, partly mobilized, was awaiting the attack on the Albanian frontier. Metaxas told his Cabinet that the troops would be kept with the colours until the threat to Greek independence was definitely past, but that the cost of this con-tinued state of semi-mobilization was appalling and he could not begin to consider how it was going to be met. Kodzias is said to have cried out in genial tones: "Never mind! the English will pay."

October 17 had been fixed by many of the pundits as ' zero hour ', and when that date passed there was a certain relaxation of tension. People who knew nothing of the terrain on which the war would be fought and less than nothing of the technicalities of military transport were to be heard talking learnedly of the effect of autumn floods and winter snows in rendering an attack impossible. Some of the best critics on the spot, who were well aware of the determination of Italy to pick a quarrel, were yet inclined to believe that, having let slip her opportunity in August, Italy would hold her hand until the spring. By that time, it was assumed, very accurately as events proved, Germany would have come down through the Bulgarian passes and her troops would be on the Thracian and Macedonian frontier. A simultaneous attack from north-east and north-west, or the mere threat of one, would, it was believed, rapidly compel the Greek Government to accept the German terms. The spirit of the Greek troops would have been depressed by a winter of inaction in totally inadequate bivouacs on the snowy mountains of the Pindus. It would be the 'Maginot winter' of 1939–40 over again. Very early on the morning of October 28 a British correspondent, after exhaustively discussing the pros and cons in relation to an immediate attack, was heard to sum up : "We have just four months more." At that moment Grazzi was preparing to deliver his ultimatum. The four months proved just four hours.

This line of argument would have been perfectly sound had Mussolini not so blatantly underestimated his opponents. Grazzi, his Minister in Athens, completely misinformed him about the true sentiments of the Greek people. He confused the unpopularity of the Government, and the profound mistrust with which it was regarded, with a reluctance to fight if circumstances should force Greece into war with a Fascist Power. The picture that I have seen painted of Metaxas rallying the nation behind him in defence of the fatherland is a most pernicious misinterpretation of the true facts. It was not Metaxas who brought Greece into the war on the side of Britain ; Mussolini did that. He did not rally the country behind him. Force of circumstances placed him in a position in which he could not avoid interpreting the overwhelming popular sentiment in favour of resistance to Fascist Imperialism.

I am very conscious of the fact that successful popular risings are virtually a thing of the past in these days of tank and bombing aeroplane. Spontaneous mass risings like those of the workers of Paris in 1830 or 1848 have little chance of success now. The days of the barricades are over; people cannot pile up the paving-stones where there is now only tarmac. Nevertheless I believe that had Metaxas accepted Grazzi's ultimatum he would have been swept from office by a popular rising in forty-eight hours. There have been more revolutions than I can readily count in Greece in the twenty years since the last war, and not all the protagonists of the last Liberal revolution were in exile. Metaxas knew that he must reject the ultimatum, and as a soldier and, according to his lights, a patriot I do not think he would have wished it otherwise. But the opening words of his address to the newspaper owners of Athens on the very first day of the war are significant. " Gentlemen," he began, " I had no alternative. The Axis asked me to co-operate. I asked what were the conditions of co-operation. I was told that I must surrender the Tchamouria region of Northern Epirus to Italy and allow Bulgaria an outlet to the Aegean Sea. This was in addition to economic co-operation. Had I made these concessions, I should have divided Greece into three parts—one part ruled by the Axis, a second remaining to us, and Crete, which would certainly have been promptly seized by the British. Gentlemen, I had no alternative."

Grazzi's ultimatum had been delivered at the burglar's hour of 3 a.m. on October 28. It followed a dinner at the Italian Legation at which several leading figures of the August the Fourth régime were present. As the guests departed each of them was handed a leaflet containing the following appeal : " Greeks ! do not be misled and allow yourselves to become the tools of British Imperialism. The Italian nation wishes you nothing but well, and the Italian army is at hand to free you from your oppressors. Resistance is unnecessary and will be unavailing. Place yourselves under the protection of the great Italian State."

A little later Grazzi stole out on his errand.

The terms of the Italian ultimatum were clearly incompatible with the continued existence of Greece as an independent nation. The Greek Government was accused of having weighted its neutrality heavily in favour of Britain—a charge calculated to make any British Press correspondent smile wryly, recalling the 'stop' imposed upon telling the barest truth about Axis activities in Greece. The Government was specifically charged with having allowed the use of her naval and air bases to the British Fleet and to British aircraft. Italy demanded the right of immediate occupation of unspecified strategic points in Greece. A three-hour time-limit was given for acceptance of the ultimatum.

It was, of course, not meant to be accepted. Even before the close of the brief period allowed, Italian troops were moving forward in the frontier districts. Documents later discovered showed that every detail of the attack had been prepared. Acceptance of the ultimatum would have made not the slightest difference. Italian troops would have moved forward just the same at the same hour. Probably Mussolini preferred that the Greeks should put up at least some semblance of resistance. His prestige needed some victories to set against the sweep of Napoleonic triumphs of Nazi Germany. It goes hard for Fascist Italy that she is compelled to include Guadalajara among her battle honours.

By the time I arrived in Greece the tide was already swinging back against the invader. I write these lines in Cairo many months later, at a time when memories of the Greek resistance and counter-attack, though they can never be forgotten, are in danger of being dimmed by the anti-climax of the later months— the gradual slowing down of the Greek offensive, the weeks when the Albanian front remained virtually winter-bound while the armies of the Reich were gathering in Bulgaria, the German assault sweeping away Greek resistance and the handful of British and Imperial troops who could be spared from the African battlefields, the sad epilogue of the Battle of Crete, fought and lost while I was tossing at sea in an open caique between Mersin and Alexandria.

Among the exiled Greeks in Egypt there is something of the atmosphere of a Jacobite Court. Greek quarrels with Greek —though that is nothing new ; and mutual recriminations take the place of the comradeship and unity that, superficially at least, were so striking a feature of the early weeks of the war. But when that has been admitted, the Greek resistance must surely stand among the highest achievements of the war. It did not prove decisive strategically, for it imposed only a delay ; it did not ultimately prevent the enemy conquest of the Balkans. It was a delay, however, which proved of incalculable value in enabling us to strengthen our position in the whole Middle Eastern theatre where we had been so perilously weak during the previous summer. But in any case it proved decisive psychologically. Just as the bubble of German invincibility had been pricked by our air victories in the Battle of Britain during August and September, so the true value of Mussolini's modern Roman Legionaries was exposed on the Pindus and above Koritza. Admittedly, no one had taken the Italians very seriously as a military force either in England or elsewhere, but the fact remains that the bubble had not yet been pricked. British forces had in fact retired before the Italians in Somaliland, in Kenya, in the Sudan, in the Western Desert. These retreats were rendered necessary by our extreme weakness in men and material ; they proved absolutely justified strategically, and a few weeks later we were to demonstrate our military superiority to the Italians in the succession of operations from Sidi Barrani to Benghazi. But until the battle of the Pindus the vast Italian bluff had not been called, and if the Italians ran fast and far in the course of some of the first actions, they fought hard in the series of counter-attacks in the early months of the following year. Both in attack and defence the Greek army proved superior to them, yet this superiority was certainly not expected when the campaign opened. It is believed that the General Staff themselves shared the view of their opposite numbers in the Italian army that a week would see the end of it all. It was commonly believed that Mussolini had in fact fixed November 4 as the day on which the Italian forces were to enter in triumph; quick going, but not impossible for a vanguard, given a total Greek collapse.

Military experts have assured me that the Italian plan of campaign was perfectly sound. It was its execution that was faulty. The road into Greece which appeared to offer the best prospects of speedy success was that from Koritza to Florina and thence to Salonika. It was here that the main attack was generally expected, and here that the bulk of the Greek forces were concentrated. It seemed by no means improbable that the Italians would endeavour to turn the whole Greek position here by a violation of Yugoslav territory, entering through Struga or possibly through the gap between Lakes Okhrida and Prespa, cutting swiftly across to Monastir, and entering Greece in the rear of her defences. A somewhat similar strategy was adopted by Germany in April from the opposite direction of Bulgaria. Whether the Yugoslav Government could have accepted this violation of its territory and still remained in power is extremely doubtful. They did in fact close their eyes to the dropping of bombs on Monastir on two occasions, but a flagrant violation of this nature would almost certainly have brought the Cvetkovič Government down and the Revolution of March 27 would have been anticipated in the previous November. Nevertheless there was much talk among foreign correspondents, during those early days, of the ' Monastir Gap ', and the correspondent of one famous English paper went so far as to condemn the war as ' phoney ' as early as 9 p.m. on the first evening because the Italians had not already entered Yugoslavia by this route.

An alternative route for the invasion seemed to lie along the coast of Epirus towards the Greek naval base of Preveza. This gave no prospect of such immediate strategical result, but would help to isolate Corfu and the Ionian islands.

Actually the main Italian thrust followed neither of these routes. While troops advanced in the direction of Florina in the north and the Kalamas River in the south, the principal attack was launched in the centre across the wooded country of the Pindus towards Janina and, still more, Metsovo.

Metsovo was an admirable objective. It lies on the main lateral road, parallel to the frontier, from Janina to Salonika, and possession of it would paralyse communications between the two parts of the Greek front. Moreover, from Metsovo another road runs to Trikkala and into the plain of Thessaly. If Metsovo were taken in the first day or two there might be a clear run through to the road junctions at Larissa and Lamia and thence to Athens.

The Italians got very near their objective. They took Konitsa, penetrated almost to the outskirts of Janina, and came within a few kilometres of Metsovo, so near that their aviators dropped food supplies on the town under the impression that it was already in the hands of their infantry. The Greeks were desperately under-equipped and under-munitioned—inexcusably so, considering the length of time that the Government had had to prepare—but they managed to bring up reinforcements, and the British rushed across a number of Bren-gun carriers which went straight into action. The picturesque incident of the women of the Pindus villages dragging the guns up the mountain paths is no legend, in spite of having so powerfully caught public imagination, and it certainly played its part in deciding the issue.

After ten days the force of the Italian attack was spent. The invaders were in a desperately difficult position, and the Greek Government had hopes of a spectacular haul of prisoners amounting to at least a whole division. But the greatest portion of the force appears to have extricated itself, and the actual number of prisoners taken was comparatively small. In its general lines the battle followed the model of Cannae or Tannenberg on a tiny scale. If the forces engaged were not large, the moral effect was tremendous. It was the first defeat which the Axis had suffered on land since the beginning of the war, and it helped to throw the whole time-table out of gear. On the Greeks it had an immense influence. Internal quarrels were forgotten, and the whole nation was whipped up to a state of enthusiasm. The nearest parallel I can find is that of Baylen in the Napoleonic Wars, when Spanish guerillas, after their

Government had tamely accepted French control, surrounded and annihilated a corps of the hitherto invincible French army in the mountains of Andalusia. All Spain rose in arms, and although within five months a French army, led by Napoleon in person, had swept down into the peninsula, scattered the Spanish levies like chaff and overrun almost the whole country, the rising was the signal for the despatch of British forces (" Any country which finds itself attacked by the French Empire automatically becomes our ally and has a right to appeal to Britain for assistance," said Canning, in a declaration which has a strangely contemporary ring). It led also to the adoption of persistent guerilla tactics by the Spaniards, which Napoleon, busy with campaigns first in Austria and then in Russia, was never able to suppress. I need not labour the parallel.

Meanwhile the Greeks had at an early stage taken the offensive on the northern sector. As early as October 31 they were on Albanian soil, they had taken Biklichta, the first village on the road to Koritza, by November 2, and they continued during the succeeding days to extend their grip along the mountain ridge of Morava to the south-east of the town, avoiding descent into the lower ground where Koritza stands, where the mechanized forces of the enemy would have put the lightly-armed Greeks, fighting with rifle and bayonet, at a disadvantage.

The Italian forces in the centre fell back in disorder from the Pindus, and the Greeks following them up took Erseka, lying on the main lateral road inside the Albanian frontier. In the south, where the Italians seem to have concentrated fewer troops and where it appears that a mainly subsidiary action had been intended, the invasion had, in a modest way, been relatively more successful. The Kalamas River, something of an obstacle at its mouth at this season, had been reached and crossed in the first two or three days, and Goumenitza, a little way to the south, had been taken. But the collapse in the centre and the acute threat to Koritza in the north rendered a general retreat inevitable. The Italians fell back all along the line and by November 18 the last of their troops had left Greek soil.

## CHAPTER IX

## ATHENS—ALBANIAN FRONT—ATHENS

WHEN I arrived at the Greek frontier at 5.30 one dark cold November morning I left the comfortable express train on which I had been travelling, walked across the frontier (I had been warned to expect this and had only a rucksack in my possession) and found myself in the god-forsaken frontier station of Pythion. Exhaustive inquiries revealed the fact that there would be no train before a military one which was leaving at 7.30 that evening, on which I should be very lucky to obtain a seat or a permit to use a seat. I knew I should obtain both. The day was awful. Although the Greek frontier was hardly guarded at all at this point, it was forbidden to walk outside the station platform. There were four or five cottages near the village, none of which provided so much as a boiled egg. There was no comfortable chair, not even a warm spot where I could sit and read. Actually, as I am able to go to sleep on a stone floor, I fared less badly than my companion, Sam Brewer of the Chicago *Herald-Tribune*. I drank red wine every time I woke up, both then and later, on the interminable railway journey.

At half-past seven the shuttle train arrived. I had obtained some kind of bogus pass to get to Alexandroupolis, which was reached by following the river Maritza (the frontier between Greece and Turkey) to its mouth. Here soldiers wet and cold crowded in at every wayside station. The blackout was rigidly observed. We arrived in Alexandroupolis as one always does arrive at the wrong station. There was a war on; there were no taxis; there were no porters; but we found our way across the town to the other station, which was a mile and a half away. Stumbling in and out of puddles, the rain running down my neck, I clung to my typewriter, feeling that the rain must surely penetrate its outer covering.

At the station we were told there was a train going to

Salonika at 2.30, but that police permits must be obtained to get on it. We traversed the town once more to the police station, which was by the sea-coast. I have never felt the sea so un-attractive. I shook three sleeping policemen, but none of them could be made to understand what I wanted. Extremely hungry, I then found the best restaurant in the town, and saw at one table a crowd of heavily braided gentlemen whom I took to be senior officers. I went up to their table and said, " Forgive me, but do any of you gentlemen speak English ? " Immediately the reply came : " Yes. Won't you sit down and have a drink and tell us what you want ? " On any other occasion I would most gladly have done so, but I was in a hurry to reach Athens. Editors in London naturally cannot understand how difficult and how lengthy journeys become in war-time. So I merely told the Greek captain that I wanted a permit to go on the troop train that night to Salonika. He was kind, and telephoned about the town to find a colonel, but came back with a hopeless look on his face, saying, " Only the colonel can give the permit, and he is out this evening." I understood from this that the worthy colonel was endeavouring to forget the war in the arms of his local girl-friend.

I wandered back to the police station, and thence back again to the railway station. Thank God I never catch cold, as I was quite soaked to the skin. The Greek ticket-office man allowed me to sit in his room, where it was too dark to read, and await the train which had already been stated to be two hours late—the train for which in any case I had no permit. Sam Brewer, who had meanwhile gone to an hotel, came along to the station to see if there was any hope of getting away that night. The ticket-collector was so sorry for us that he made out a paper, covered it with stamps and pushed us on to the train.

The train was of the variety often seen in France—Hommes 40, Chevaux 8 ; the men were all hungry and thirsty, dirty and verminous. There was no possibility of obtaining food down the line. The rate at which the train moved would have won any slow bicycle race at a public school. Why, at a time of national stress and danger, when mobilization should have been speeded up, the speed of trains should be reduced to walking pace is more than I can imagine. That the train had to stop at every station to pick up fresh recruits I fully realized, but why crawl between stations ?

We took fifty-six hours to reach Salonika. I slept, there being nothing else to do, and the period of blackout being interminably long. Occasionally we passed trains full of cheering troops who, lucky devils, were going to the front, which was where I wanted to get. Had I transferred myself and my ruck-sack from one train to the other I could easily have got there, but of course, as on all major occasions of my life, I lacked the guts.

We arrived at Salonika just before dawn. There were no taxis or porters, and the railway station is at least two miles from the town. After waiting in the cold and wet for about an hour, an old car came along which with many creaks and groans took us to an hotel. Even at this time the inhabitants of Salonika were very suspicious. There was no coffee, they were most unwilling to produce any food, and I felt a definitely hostile air, though not half so hostile as I was to feel later. The regulations for registering with the police were past belief. Having registered myself in two offices I felt it was time I began my work as a journalist and wrote a story about Salonika. So I walked round and looked at the Mediterranean Palace, the hotel which was more or less destroyed, and at a few bomb-holes in the road. The damage was really very slight, except in one slum street where the houses had been so badly built that they just fell down. Whilst I was doing this an air-raid siren hurt my ear-drums. Hysterical screams, cries, and a stampede of what seemed to be the entire population carried me with it into an underground shelter. Here, sitting on benches, or standing with bowed heads, as the roof was very low, the Greeks waited for an hour and a half while three Italian bombers flew around, doing no damage whatever. Women crossed themselves ; men wept ; I felt as if I were in a submarine, and that at any moment the oxygen would give out. I staggered over the sweaty and exhausted bodies to the door to try to get out. But it was locked from the outside. When the 'All Clear' went I rushed to the bank above. No sooner was I free than the damned siren went again. This time I took excellent care not to be carried along by the crowd. I rushed outside into the open air, but every restaurant was closed and all the shops shut.

What I really complained of at Salonika was that during an air raid the whole life of the town closed down. At length I was able to get to my typewriter and write a few words describing what little actual damage had been done by repeated Italian attacks. I took this to the censor. Hardly a word of it would be allowed. I begged, stormed, tried every trick, but not one word except a brief statement saying that I was in Salonika would he allow. By means of bribing his assistant I got a telephone call to my own 'string man' in Belgrade in order that my paper should know I was alive. He, of course, had not the wit to realize that it was the pernicious censorship which made it impossible for me to get out further stories.

I went to the British Consulate. The Greek Military were trying to bully me to obtain further permits. The Consul, as might be expected, was at home, not in his office. I spoke to him on the telephone. He told me he would be in his office at five o'clock. As it was then three I went myself to the military to get my permit. With some difficulty I found a room. Five hundred German passports were being stamped with a permit to go anywhere and do anything, and it was with great difficulty that I, an Englishwoman, could obtain a permit to stay in Salonika for a few days and then proceed by train to Athens. The Germans were very much the favoured folk, even after the war with Italy began, especially in the north of Greece.

Finding our Consul completely ineffective, uninterested in the war, and having a fierce hatred of the diplomatic staff in Athens, some of whom were friends of mine, I decided to quit Salonika, as my paper paid me to send news, and this the censor would not allow. Months later I heard from a most reliable American diplomat that the obstructive and unpleasant censor in Salonika was a member of the Fifth Column. It was his job to see that no news favourable to Greece or the Allies got out of the country. He was well paid for his services and given a good post in the administration when the Germans conquered Salonika in April. He now is one of the few Greeks there who is the proud possessor of a motor-car.

The journey to Athens was similar to that to Salonika; slow, uncomfortable and dreary. Every station seemed to want a permit to allow one on to the next. We arrived in Athens about four o'clock in the morning, and thanks to the help of a senior Greek officer I was allowed out of the station quickly instead of waiting for hours to be examined by the police. I actually found a taxi and drove to the King George Hotel, the Grande Bretagne having become the headquarters of the British Military Mission and the Greek General Staff. It is interesting to note that as, in the last war, the French made the British pay rent for the trenches they occupied, so the British were made to pay full hotel rates for the rooms the mission occupied in the Grande Bretagne.

Even with a war on, Athens was a delightful place to be in. The climate was enchanting, warm and sunny. In the square in front of the hotel oranges were ripening on the trees, and every morning, although it was mid-November, I had my breakfast outside on the terrace. I had taken up my abode at the King George. Most of the journalists were staying there. The first person I met, who greeted me with such sincere warmth that I knew I should enjoy some part of my stay in Greece, was Ralph Barnes, only a few days later to be killed in returning from a bombing raid over Italy. I knew him well in Bucharest, where he spent some weeks after his expulsion from Germany. Ralph was never brilliant, but so conscientious and hard-working that he never sent a story (as I fear most American reporters do) until he had confirmed it. I told him of my difficulties with the censor in Salonika. He laughed and told me that they were as bad in Athens. He even jokingly said that he would like to go back to Germany where they were clever enough not to have censors except for military matters.

All the journalists were fighting to be allowed to go up to the front, and the Greek authorities, though their country was doing well, had not the gumption to realize what wonderful publicity it would be for their cause to allow reporters there. On my first evening in Athens I attended the Press Conference. The man who sat next to me was Christopher Buckley. He was working for the *Daily Telegraph*. His solid and basic knowledge of history placed him head and shoulders above the other correspondents, most of whom were only aware that there had been some boring people one learnt about at school who lived in Greece. These people as a rule added to their general knowledge, or lack of it, by not knowing whether Italy was east or west of Greece. American newspapers often sent out reporters who had been good at enlivening funerals in Chicago or company meetings in New York, but whose talents were not great enough to be allowed full play at a big race meeting.

As a rule I do not attend Press Conferences. They remind me of staff meetings at a girls' school. At these intensely unexciting gatherings there is seldom any news of great moment, and if there is all one's colleagues get it at the same time as oneself, so that the only way one can hope to boost oneself is by the superior presentation of one's material. And it was just in this respect that the Athens censorship proved so impossible. Its attempt to compel distinguished foreign correspondents to confine their messages rigidly along the lines of official communiqués and hand-outs were so entirely childish that one began to suspect that one was up against not merely the stupidity of the unemployed journalist, or the ex-schoolboy with blue pencil in hand for the first time, but against positive Fifth Column elements as in Salonika. The censorship did not even allow us to speak of ' The Axis ' or in any way to refer to Germany. The German Legation still functioned. The D.N.B. man sometimes sat next to me at Press Conferences, and one had the feeling then that if the British had not been financing the war and if the Greeks had not been extremely lucky during the first week or two of it the resistance would have faded out.

The Director of Foreign Press, George Seferiades, a man of high culture, an intellectual and poet, translator of the poems of T. S. Eliot into modern Greek, did his best, but the difficulties of the position were too much for him. Of Colonel Melas, the chief military censor, I can only say that if he was not a Fifth Columnist he handled the foreign Press in a way indistinguishable from that which a German agent would have adopted. At a time when it was important for the sake of Greece herself to 'play up' her military successes to the outside world, Colonel Melas conceived it to be his duty to suppress all objective treatment of the military situation, even when that treatment reflected particular credit on the Greek troops or General Staff.

Colonel Melas was deaf, a powerful weapon in the hands of an obstructive censor, as one gets tired of shouting arguments into his ear, to be answered after five minutes' slow and careful exposition of one's case with, " Eh ! what's that ?  I couldn't hear you." One then gives up in despair and goes off to have a drink and grouse with one's colleagues who have received equally scurvy treatment. Most of the foreign correspondents in Athens at the time were sincere philhellenes (I except some of the American agency men who would have murdered their own mothers in order to 'scoop' a story), but they received little encouragement to remain so. I do not know what happened to Colonel Melas at the time of the collapse, but I have heard that he stayed behind in Athens. I can only hope that he is proving as obstructive and unhelpful to the Germans as he certainly was to us, but I fear that they will not provide him with the same opportunities.

There were only two alternatives to be followed. Either, like Patrick Maitland of *The Times* or Christopher Buckley, one deliberately 'played down' the news and established one's personal boycott on the mention of some of the favourite themes of the régime (*e.g.* the Neolaia) or, as in my own case, shortly after my return from visiting the front, one simply quitted the country. It was simply no use remaining in a country where the Ministry of Press and the General Staff stultified their own propaganda by treating allied journalists with, to say the least, such reserve. It drove one sometimes beyond even anger. I well remember one of the toughest of all the little American agency men crying out in despair, after his story had been hacked to ribbons by the censor, " Mr. Zarifis, I'm not gonna be angry ! I'm not gonna lose my temper ! I'm not even gonna complain ! I'm just kinda hurt."

General Gambier-Parry had been appointed temporary head of the British Military Mission and flown over from Cairo some days before I arrived. Were he not so good a soldier I should most certainly suggest that he had missed his vocation as a diplomat. He was in the extraordinary position in Greece of being both liked and trusted by all sides. The King said : " Thank God for a British soldier who can appreciate Bach." Metaxas said : " Parry's advice and suggestions in the campaign leading to the taking of Koritza were invaluable. His brain saved us many lives and at least one day in capturing the town." He got on well with the Greek General Staff. Prince Peter, chief liaison officer, became a firm personal friend. The Venizelists were attracted equally by his personality and by his efficiency, and the Legation all liked him immediately. But even Parry could not persuade the Greeks to allow any British officer or any British or American reporter up to the front. Everyone was pulling their own private strings to get there. So great was the delay and so poor the quality of news which the censor allowed to pass that my paper ordered me away, but supported by the British Legation I persuaded them to let me stay on.

In theory, everyone was to go up together. But the whole excursion was badly organized by Public Relations in Athens. I found myself in a car, not too happily, with Henry Stokes of Reuters and his little ' string man ' in Athens, who was reporting all our movements to the Greek Secret Police.

Henry Stokes is smaller than I am, and one would expect him to be tough. We had a pretty gruelling journey from Athens, spending the first night in Lamia, then travelling through beautiful mountain passes to Larissa, where we had to report to the General at the Base Camp from whom we were to obtain our papers before we were allowed to proceed to Kotzani. The General, like most senior officers, was charming. He had one blue eye and one brown, and even though his brother was Greek Minister in Berlin I felt by the stories he told me of Fifth Column activities that he was staunch and reliable. He told me the raids on Larissa had not been serious, but the population had been rather disturbed, as there were no shelters, no anti-aircraft, and everyone knew that Larissa was the junction from which all the soldiers went to the front. He said I could go to whichever part of the front I chose. I explained to him my object, which was to see as much fighting as possible and then get back as quickly as I could to send my story from Athens.

He advised me to go north to the Koritza sector, where he thought the Italians were still putting up some resistance, though the town itself had fallen about two days previously. I took his advice. He gave me my papers, and some cigarettes to take to the troops, and I departed.

There was tremendous effort to get away before anyone else. The drive to Kozani across the river Haliacmon passed through the small village of Servia, originally inhabited by Serbian colonists who immigrated to this fertile plain, it is believed, about the time of Dushan II. To our right were the heights of Olympus, and on our left mountains, gradually increasing in size towards the Pindus range. We spent the night at Kozani, a Greek town which has nothing to recommend it. The beds were damp, and although bugs do not worry me very much there were too many to kill or to allow me to sleep peacefully.

I was glad to make an early start, but annoyed to see Henry Stokes dressed as though he were out for a walk in Hyde Park in the early spring. I made no pretence at washing. We crossed a small range of mountains ; the road is not marked on any map, but it was being used by all military transport going up to the northern front. Suddenly I saw Kastoria. What a pity, I felt, that being a reporter I must hurry. How I should have loved to dally in this heavenly town situated on a narrow peninsula which extends into a beautiful lake. The inhabitants in medieval times must have been very free from the raids of Macedonian Terrorists. Here I met the first troops who had been to the front. They were a fine crowd. They gave me Albanian money, changed Albanian for English cigarettes (they certainly got the best of the bargain), and supplied me with vivid descriptions of the rapidly retreating Italians. I asked the party standing round my car :

" Were any of you in Koritza ? "

" Yes," said one young corporal whose mother had been in America. " We only arrived back half an hour ago. We had a hell of a strafing coming through the narrow pass between Albania and Greece."

I asked him if they had taken many prisoners.

" Hundreds," he said. " They gave themselves up faster than we could take them."

The house beside which we stood had been partially destroyed by an extremely accurate Italian bomb. As it was only a farmhouse in the fields some miles away from the town I imagine it must have been the Fifth Column who informed the Italians that this particular building was being used as the local headquarters.

The road from Kastoria to Koritza is appalling. There is only the one mountain pass, and if the weather were really bad it would be impossible to go through by car. We only just managed it, and on two occasions had to be pulled out by bullocks. Soon after the pass began to descend we went by the old Greek and Albanian frontier post, long since deserted. It could never have been a very popular frontier for tourists. Immediately afterwards, I saw long and deep tank traps stretching from one side of the valley to the other—barbed-wire entanglements running up the side of the hills, which were crowned with pill-boxes. The Italians cannot have been very thoughtful before they began the war if they really thought the Greeks were going to get tanks as far as that through the narrow pass. The roads were pretty deserted. Here and there I saw the white skeleton of a horse or donkey which, probably owing to lameness, had been shot by one of the soldiers. They had then cut every particle of meat from the bones. The entrails generally stank at the side.

We soon arrived at the first village inside Albania, Biklichta— largely destroyed by the Italian artillery. Here and there the four walls of a house remained. In one such place a dazed-looking old woman sat. Thinking she had been there throughout the whole bombardment I went up to her offering brandy, only to find she was dead. Few people, however, had attempted to stay in the village during the bombardment. The advance-guard of those who were returning had begun to arrive. Women were already dumping bedding by the most sheltered wall and putting children to sleep. Much ammunition which had been left behind by the Italians was being brought into the village by a constant stream of donkeys, and stored in the local slaughter-house. There were Mills bombs, hand-grenades, machine-gun ammunition, camp beds, uniforms, blankets and cooking apparatus. I suggested to the officer that the blankets should be given to the refugees who were returning to their destroyed homes. He shook his head, and said :

" The army will need them."

I went into several of the destroyed houses in order to see how badly they had been looted. In one I found a large pile of copies of the *Evening Standard* three years old. I never solved the mystery of how they got there, or who in that remote village could read sufficient English to collect the *Evening Standard* each day. Perhaps the Accounts Department of the *Evening Standard* will find a subscriber who once lived on the Greek-Albanian frontier ! The village, like so many villages in Albania, bore obvious signs of Italian tyranny. Names had been covered over, but could be seen through the newly painted Italian version. Outside the village I began to see large quantities of Greek troops. They were in the fields, many of them, cutting cabbages, munching hard, and putting what they could not get in their mouths under their coats.

The nearer we drove to Koritza the more transport we passed—motor transport which was supplying the mule and donkey transport which did the real mountain fighting. In order to prevent ourselves being arrested, and also because I had done it in Germany on the day before the war, we had the Union Jack flying from the left mudguard of the car.

I entered Koritza, the first British subject to step on Axis territory. The Greeks cheered the car and I waved back. We passed the airfield at Koritza and saw about eleven ruined Italian planes, including one enormous passenger liner which had been turned into a troop-carrier. The seats had been removed, and wooden forms, very narrow, run from end to end of the plane. Half the occupants had to stand. It must have carried about fifty troops.

British bombing, despite the difficulties of the narrow valley, had been extremely accurate, and the airport was badly knocked about. The Italians had made poor efforts to destroy the aircraft on the ground (I cannot think why they had not tried to fly them away). Some of the planes were already in the workshops with Greek mechanics endeavouring to make them again serviceable. A large petrol tank had not been destroyed, and this was proving extremely useful to the Greeks.

We drove on into the town. There were plenty of air-raid shelters, sandbags and the usual impedimenta of war, but not one house could I find which had been damaged by a British bomb. The town was as packed with people as Mile End Road on a Saturday night. All the shops were open and doing a roaring trade with the Greek soldiers. The town was still under military discipline, and we had some difficulty in finding the local headquarters, which were hidden by the one de luxe block of flats in the place. One inquirer informed me in answer to a question about the locality of Headquarters : " There's a bath in every flat, and central heating just as they have in New York." This building, which is so much the pride and joy of the local inhabitants, had been erected by the National Bank of Albania. The Colonel, when we found him—as yet no Generals had penetrated to Koritza—fell on our necks when we offered him Greek cigarettes. In return, he gave me a huge Italian flag (which I regret to say I left in my hotel in Athens), as many Fascist caps and badges as we wanted, Albanian cigarettes, and—most important of all—a permit for me to stay in Koritza and go up to the front as much as I liked. Rather mistakenly, having got so much out of him, I invited him to come and have dinner in the hotel, but first I walked round the town to look for some Wellington boots to wear on the following day when visiting the front. I like towns in which the cobbler makes his own boots and the baker his own bread, but especially I liked it in Koritza, because one member of the family which owned each of the principal shops had at some time visited that Mecca of the Balkans—America.

"You English girl! I Albanian boy! I live Chicago—bootblack—five years. What do you want?"

I explained that I wanted a pair of Wellington boots or riding boots. They showed me some truly magnificent riding boots which had been made for the wife of some Italian General, who had left too hurriedly to collect them. The Albanian money was changed greatly to the disadvantage of the Greeks at the pre-war rate of exchange (7 drachmas=1 lek). This made everything absurdly expensive. A night in the hotel in Koritza cost as much as at the best hotel in Athens, and the price of my badly needed boots was completely Bond Street. They worked out at about £20.

Koritza, compared with other Albanian towns I visited, is a very bourgeois place. I saw typewriters for sale in one shop window and the latest shade of Elizabeth Arden lipstick. I would have bought the latter, unsuitable though it was to the costume I was then wearing for the front, but the price was exorbitant. However, when I went into the bookshop I lost my head and bought an enormous map of Albania which cost £3, and which I had to give up with a patriotic smile when I returned to Athens, as the British Military Mission found it to be the newest Italian map of Albania that had been produced. I deeply regretted this, as I have a passion for maps and always do my best work in a room lined with them.

There were many pleasant villas with gardens of their own, generally occupied by ex-Chicago bootblacks who, having made a fortune of a few thousand dollars, had returned to live in retirement in the place of their birth. The Albanian flag flew beside the Greek one opposite to our hotel. Having rushed about so much since morning I was very hungry, and overjoyed to see the large quantities of good Chianti which the Italians had obligingly left behind.

My Colonel arrived. He was duller than I had thought, so I pretended my German was even worse than it is—and that is pretty bad—and devoted myself to the unadulterated joy of eating macaroni swilled down with Chianti and large quantities of crisp white bread such as I had not seen since leaving Romania and which was totally unobtainable in Greece throughout the war. Much to my joy, Arthur Merton, affectionately known to his colleagues as " General Sir Arthur ", arrived with his followers, Dimbleby of the B.B.C., and Ted Gennock, a Press photographer, accompanied by a Conducting Officer, but Merton was emphatically conducting the party himself, and did not intend to have any criticism or suggestions from Mr. Stokes of Reuter's, who wished to prevent the party from starting out at too early an hour on the following day.

Next morning at half past five I put on all the woolly sweaters I could muster and stumbled out into the dark streets to find somewhere where I could buy a cup of coffee. The shops were not open, but at last I found a wooden tavern where the soldiers were having their early morning meal. I waited around for the chauffeurs to bring the cars. As always on these occasions there were endless delays, but at length two carloads of us set out for the front.

As it grew lighter we saw naked corpses at the side of the road, many of whom had been shot in the back while endeavouring to escape from their deep trenches as the Greeks advanced. Corpses on battlefields are always naked, as the advancing army, whatever its nationality, rapidly relieves them not only of watch and rings but of warm coat, vests and trousers. The photographer got busy on the corpses. I merely looked at them, saw they were young Italians, and felt rather pacifist-minded.

There were surprisingly few signs of battle along land which had seen the retreat of the Italians and the advance of the Greeks. Certainly, little fighting took place. The most important was in the trenches which had been dug some miles outside the airport of Koritza to defend it. Here between sixty and seventy

Italians had been killed, and Albanians were already beginning to dig a grave for them.

We drove by car as far as possible to the base of the Morava mountains where fighting was still going on. Those who had been in the early part of the battle had already returned to their base camps. One in five of the donkeys had died on the mountains. It was impossible to find out the death-rate through exposure amongst the men, but it must have been high. After the orange groves of Athens one has to be pretty tough to spend nights in the mist and sleet of a mountain without any cover, without a hot drink, with only a handful of olives and a loaf of bread as food for three days. I was told by the Publicity Department that only peasants from the mountainous part of Greece were sent up to the mountains. This was untrue. Although I was dressed in Wellingtons and a long sheepskin coat and padded with as many scarves and woollen sweaters as I could find, the men thought I was something pretty odd when I suddenly appeared at their base camp. They were all most friendly, without being in the least forward or unpleasant. They embarrassed me by offering me bits of dirty food. The only time my life was really in danger was when I produced a packet of cigarettes in front of about fifty men. They had not seen any for days. I could only throw them into the air and let them fight for them. Several were from Salonika and had been educated by French nuns there, and although brigandly looking soldiers of the roughest type they spoke French. I asked them :

" How long were you up on the mountain ? "

One giant about six foot six with no teeth and tattoo marks of a villainous nature over the exposed part of his neck and hands replied in delicate Parisian drawing-room French :

" I was up there for six days."

" Did you do much fighting ? "

" No, we could never find the Wops to fight them. It was very difficult up there. We were generally above the cloud line. They fired wildly, killing very few Greek soldiers. But we couldn't be sure how many were hidden behind the huge boulders up there."

II

" Wasn't there any real scrap at all ? "

" Oh yes, on a plateau ; they are fighting there still. But my bright officer wouldn't let me stay. Thought I was too delicate to stand the mountain air much longer."

My friend then proceeded to demonstrate his strength by knocking down a few of the smaller soldiers who were standing round him listening to him speaking a foreign language, so I withdrew before any more of the Greek army should be knocked out and nosed round the base camp myself. There was no sleeping accommodation for the men, nor stabling for the horses or donkeys. They all lay about on the wet ground in what had been the orchard of a pleasant largish mountain farmstead. The farmhouse, which had been fitted up with extremely inadequate field telephones, was occupied by four Staff officers. I asked them if I might borrow a horse. They said they had not got one even for their own use, but they could probably find a donkey that was not lame if I really wanted to go up the mountain. They were obviously in a tremendous muddle, moving some units to an advanced position without having any means of giving orders to the commanding officers except by pigeons, which only work over special terrain, and runners, which over the muddy mountain passes were a contradiction in terms. Had it not been for the blessed supplies of macaroni which the Italians left behind, one officer told me, the Greeks would have been unable to continue fighting, as their supplies, all of which had to come through the narrow pass I have already described, were simply not arriving. This, the commanding officer said, was largely due to lack of planning by G.H.Q. in Athens. The lack of petrol on the Greek side of the Albanian frontier, as well as of motor transport, had directly caused many deaths. We had passed the first convoy of ambulances miles behind. The wounded, so my friend told me, had not a hope. They just died. Had there been any serious fighting instead of a hurried run of Italians it would have been difficult to maintain strict discipline amongst the troops.

I asked what they thought of the Italian soldiers. The officer said : " Absolutely nothing ! They run at the sound of a shot, unless there are bayonets behind them. All over these hills you will find small tanks, guns, even aeroplanes, that have been left in order that the Wops might run more quickly."

He asked me if I would like to see some prisoners, and took me to the stables, where ten Italians grinning from ear to ear and eating some of their own macaroni from tin plates stood as we entered.

" Can anyone speak English ? " I said.

" Rather ! " said one. " I'm a cockney, I am. My father had a little restaurant in Soho, but when I was five we moved back to Trieste, as my mother didn't like the English climate. But I still remember my English."

" Why are you fighting now ? " I asked.

" No choice," he said, " for the likes of me. We were just given our orders and had to obey them. I hate these bleeding hills and I want to go back to Trieste, but it's better to be a prisoner than scrambling about rocks all day. I wasn't born to be a mountain deer."

" What do you think about Mussolini ? " I asked.

" I used to think him a silly old bastard, trying to make us all prompt, hardworking and unnatural-like. But since he sent me to this bleeding place I know he's the devil incarnate. Why, the man needs seventy people to take him to the water-closet. Otherwise somebody would put a bullet through his block."

" Aren't you rather disloyal, speaking of your own country like this ? "

" Perhaps I am disloyal," he said, " but me and my pals didn't want to fight, and now we are taken prisoner we are not going to pretend we love the old bastard."

" What do you think of the King ? "

" Oh ! he's all right," said the young man rather contemptuously.

" What sort of Government would you like in Italy ? "

" I don't care about Governments," he said. " All I want is to live with my wife and children, keep a little restaurant and sit and look at the ships coming into Trieste harbour."

" How do your mates feel ? " I asked.

"Oh, less than I do. They aren't educated like me. They can't speak any English."

"What were they before they joined up?"

"Dock labourers. They're all beef and no brains. That's why they was sent to haul guns about these slopes."

"What are you going to do with yourselves now you are prisoners?"

"Oh, we've got a pack of cards and I expect we shall soon enough be given some work to do. I don't care where they send me to work so long as they send me away from these wet hills."

With this I departed, suggesting that he might try and educate his fellow-prisoners by teaching them a bit of English.

A single file of slowly-moving donkeys and mules was arriving from the mountains. Men and animals were exhausted and frequently lame. One donkey or mule carried the equipment, such as it was, for three soldiers who were far tougher than the animals. The men had not shaved or washed for about ten days. They looked tough, and despite the low temperature made a bee-line for the water supply. Unlike Englishmen under similar conditions they failed to consider the animals at all, and only after they had eaten, slept and drunk did they think of watering the donkeys. What really amounted to grim cruelty was the way no donkey was ever relieved of its burden. The saddles, night and day, were never removed at all. Such unspeakable cruelty throws an unfavourable light on the Greek character, but I must admit that the Turks behave equally badly to their animals, and probably any Balkan people in a state of war would not have been much better.

I started to ascend the slopes in a car, but it soon stuck in the mud, and it had obviously got to be footwork or nothing. So I began walking. It was heavy going; the mud was often more than eight inches deep, and I had to walk at the edge of the path to make way for the transport which was coming down. Every twenty yards was an open box containing Mills bombs, and by its side a full one. Strewn all over the track were empty tins of Italian foodstuffs which had been taken by the Greeks from the corpses or prisoners and eaten. Walking through a deep ravine with bloodstained water flowing at the side I saw an Italian hut built of wood to house five or six officers. Everything had been removed from inside but the dog who piteously awaited his master's return. I took him up the mountain with me, feeding him on biscuits, and had no difficulty in finding a Greek soldier to adopt him.

The troops coming down were armed with pre-1914 rifles ; not one of them had any ammunition left. Having heard gunfire for some time, I at last arrived on the plain where the fighting was taking place. The Italians must have had some heavy artillery, but they were shooting wildly as they retreated, and many of the soldiers were giving themselves up. I had been at the front in Poland and seen the German attack crush Silesia. My views now had to change. This was no front of blazing guns, of well-uniformed marching men. In the Polish campaign and the worst part of the retreat I saw more formal order amongst the Poles than amongst the Greeks who were under enemy fire. It was not that the Greeks were not brave. Mountain warfare is obviously unsuited to modern methods, and the people taking part in it revert almost automatically to the methods of a century ago. This was a doll's house battle-field compared with Poland. The continual rifle firing, when one could see through the mist the men who were firing the shots, showed the Greeks at their best rounding up pockets of Italians, many of whom were still at large on the rugged heights above us. Several times as I walked, unaccountable bits of slate slipped down on to my path, which made me finger my revolver, for, as the mountaineer well knows, there must have been people above me on the rocks—Italians, getting desperate for food, who must sooner or later give themselves up, but who, until they did so, would shoot a person for a packet of cigarettes or a blanket.

The Greeks were very active in rushing to the dead, when the mist cleared exposing any new corpses, to relieve them of their uniforms. I am superstitious about this, and never actually take anything from a dead body, but my morals on the matter are unsound, as I gladly accepted a beautiful green cloak from a dead Italian officer offered to me by a Greek. There seemed very little to see; there was no man-to-man fighting at all, and the opposing units, with the exception of the Italians who would sooner or later be rounded up, were half a mile away. Never could they see one another, owing to clouds and mist. Several tanks, of Italian origin, were scattered among the Greek forces, who were not taking advantage of the fact that they appeared to be in good working order, three parts full of petrol, and unharmed by enemy fire. The Italians had just walked off and left them; but how they managed to get the tanks on to the mountains in the first place I entirely fail to understand. Tramping about in mud in the clouds, not really being able to see much of what is going on—in fact finding that not much *was* going on—seemed to me an unprofitable occupation. So I descended to the valley to find in a majestic-looking car which had once belonged to Venizelos " General Sir Arthur " surrounded by buckets, camp beds, everything one could ever need at the front. He said to me : " I decided not to get my boots dirty. You must be cold. What will you have to drink ? Tea or coffee or perhaps a little drop of brandy ? "

I chose the coffee.

" Now, what kind of sandwich would you like ? Chicken, *foie gras* or sardine ? "

I chose the sardine, and was given a large block of milk chocolate to round off my meal. I always think affectionately of " General Sir Arthur " when I see a picnic basket. As one of the senior officers in the British mechanized division which took Benghazi said to me : " Any bloody fool can be uncomfortable in a war. But it takes a clever and experienced man to be well provided."

" General Sir Arthur " was just as well provided and just as munificent at the time of the evacuation from Greece a few months later. Christopher Buckley, who left Greece with him, told me that he was then travelling with ten days' supply of food. A large part of this he deposited at the Legation for the use of Legation clerks and cipherers who were being hastily evacuated ;

with the remainder he contrived to feed a considerable number of the ship's passengers during the voyage to Alexandria.

I was all in favour of going to another part of the front to see whether one could find more activity, but the men were tired. So being a minority of one, I had to return to Koritza.

We got back to Koritza about dusk. Italian bombers were trying to hit the new Greek headquarters. I visited Café Munich, the local brothel, now deserted, which had housed fifty Italian women. It was divided into two sections, one for officers and one for other ranks. In the latter department the men bought tickets from a woman behind a glass window as at a cinema. The equivalent of 2s. 6d. enabled them to enjoy the company of an Italian lady for twenty minutes. On the officers' side the price was more than double, but as far as I could gather the time was unlimited. I walked through the passages and looked into many of the deserted rooms. They were cleaner than I had expected, devoid of the pink lighting effects so noticeable in the brothels in Romania. The women must have left in enormous haste. There were underclothes lying about, which no woman would willingly have left behind, and I saw two fur coats. I looked at the gramophones which seemed to be an essential part of the furniture in each room ; I cannot quite think why. I was amused to notice amongst records of Italian Grand Opera, records in English of " Tea for Two ", " Sing to Me, Gipsy " and " The Maid of the Mountains ". An air of staleness, of male sweat, of lipstick stains made me feel hot and uncomfortable. The bathroom surprised me. It was large and airy, tiled, and with every kind of modern American douching gadget, and with two large white couches, perfectly clean. I can only assume that this was prepared for the defeated Italian commander-in-chief to forget his sorrows in the company of the lady of his choice. In the ' Other Ranks ' part, the partitions between each couch were only about five feet high, and as the couches were not provided with sheets I felt that this section of the State-run brothel was not as free from the propagation of venereal diseases as it should have been. Suddenly I felt the need for air and rushed into the street.

I met a young Albanian woman and asked her why she was crying. She said :

" Before the war I had a house, a husband and a baby."

" Where are they now ? " I asked.

" My mother took my baby to Elbasan on the last bus, and I have not heard from her since. My husband was taken away with all the other young men in the village when the Italian soldiers forced our Albanian men to join the army."

" Why don't you go back to your house, now the fighting is over ? " I asked.

" I think it's been destroyed, and anyway I couldn't see it again after what happened there."

" What did happen there ? "

" After my husband had gone the Italians organized a drunken orgy in the local café two days before the war began. They refused to pay for any of the wine they drank, and when they were all full of wine, roaring and singing, they ran into the streets, and forced their way into many of the houses as they did into mine."

They had raped the woman and stolen her few pieces of treasured jewellery.

I was picking up Italian uniform belts, Fascist badges and tin hats, some in the hope that they would be useful and others merely to take back to my friends in Athens, when a well-dressed man passed me. He was the local chemist, and so proud of his American passport that it always showed from his waistcoat pocket. I asked him, pure Albanian though he was, how the Italians had fought.

He laughed and said :

" The Italian officers used the Palace Hotel restaurant " (which was where I fed) " almost as a mess. I was there with them, having a cocktail before lunch one day, when we heard the sound of heavy artillery coming pretty close. Previously we had heard only the distant rumble of guns. The senior officer jumped up, leaving behind him his belt—which, madam, is why you are able to pick up so many—shouting : ' The Greeks are coming. Run quickly ! ' He got into his car outside the door and drove away in a cloud of smoke, only stopping at the Café Munich to pick up his favourite girl. The other officers left their posts and fled, mostly in cars."

I asked him about the local politics in Albania, as I had been there before the war, studying the problem of the Minorities around Lake Okhrida. I asked him whether they wanted King Zog to return. He shook his head.

" Does anyone want Zog to come back ? " I said.

" Perhaps ten per cent. of the people, most of them those to whom he gave jobs, but the great mass disliked him."

" Well, surely you don't want Wilhelm of Wied, who is still painstakingly learning Albanian somewhere in Germany ? His son I met quite recently staying with Alphonso Merry del Val, Spanish Chargé d'Affaires in Bucharest. He's a poor specimen."

" No, we don't want that lot. In fact, these Albanians don't know how they want to be governed. Now, we Americans . . ." (and he proceeded to give me a lecture on the American Constitution, which he had undoubtedly learnt up in order to take his Citizenship Exam.).

In the surrounding villages hundreds of refugees were returning to their partially destroyed homes, after having spent days hiding themselves and their animals for safety amongst the mountains. There were few men amongst them. The poorest ones carried a bundle of bedding on their backs, with perhaps a chicken or two in their arms, the children being pulled along by whatever arm the mother could spare at the moment. Next in rank of prosperity were those who had saved a donkey from being commandeered by the army. The donkey had taken all the possessions to the woods. Returning, they looked disillusioned, tired and hungry, and one knew that in nine cases out of ten worse disillusionment awaited them when they saw their homes. What they had left had generally been destroyed, or more probably looted. Even if their house had escaped bombs and artillery they had no food for the remainder of the winter, no chairs and no bedding. The livestock which had not been taken to the hills had certainly been killed in order to feed hungry soldiers. The lucky ones had tiny carts made of wood and without springs. In these everything of value belonging to the family had been put—the chickens, the calf, the blankets—but granny and the babies invariably walked with the horse. It reminded me so much of Poland, where one frequently saw a really old lady holding an umbrella up over the head of a cow, human life being of so much less value than animal life. Little did I realize that all these people would barely get settled into their houses again when the Italians would retake Koritza.

On our return journey to Athens, when crossing the Larissa plain, an air-raid alarm sounded. Troops dispersed rapidly, and the inhabitants of a small village through which we were passing became so alarmed that the old women literally buried their heads in a large ditch. The planes flew around at about five hundred feet and bombed Larissa, doing little damage. The familiar sound of the bombs whistling through the air frightened Drossos, Reuter's local Athens man, rather badly and he wanted to take cover and to waste hours of our precious time in hiding from a few Italian bombers who, however low they were flying, never managed to bomb accurately. I resisted. It was very important to me to get my story off before the other correspondents who were in the car behind. Naturally it was impossible for us at this time to telephone our stories to local men in Athens, but Drossos telephoned by the simple method of producing his card from Manyadakis and was able to slip messages and stories through for Reuter's. This only really aroused my fury when I found that the head of the British Military Mission, General Gambier-Parry, was himself unable to get an important military call to the General in Larissa. One had the feeling the whole time that there was an internal war going on between the army and the secret police. Before one got up to the front line the credentials of Mr. Drossos brought bows and scrapes from the local officials. As soon as we got to the front the attitude changed, and one felt an under-current of, " Now we are the bosses up here, and you damned secret policemen had better watch your step ". When Drossos tried to throw his weight about at the front he was given less facilities than foreigners, but on the return journey he came into his own again.

When I returned to Athens, General Haywood, who was to take General Gambier-Parry's place as head of the Mission, had just been flown out from England. Both Generals were anxious to know what I had seen at the front. So on the first night of my return I had dinner with them both. On the following day Parry was himself leaving for the front. I had many hints to give him about the clothes he should take. I made him buy Wellington boots to protect his beautiful General's uniform from the mud. Unfortunately, he was later taken prisoner in Libya, accompanied by two other Generals, Neame and O'Connor. I know nothing of the rights and wrongs of whether they should have avoided being taken prisoners or not. I only know that I have heard about fifteen different versions of the story. After his capture there was much tendency in ill-informed quarters to make him the scapegoat for the reverses in Greece, Crete and Libya, as he was the one person unable to reply from his prison camp to the criticisms which were so ignorantly made. One example arose out of the fact that General Haywood did not have an easy time in replacing him, as the King would barely accept him and everyone else without exception would have preferred Parry to stay. His enemies blamed him for this and suggested that, although it was his job to make himself charming to the Greeks, he should never have made himself as charming as he did.

For reasons I have given I did not remain long in Athens after my return to the front. Had the Greek authorities shown a more co-operative spirit towards Allied journalists, there is no doubt that far more of them would have stayed in the country, thereby building up in the world Press a greater knowledge and appreciation of the effort of the Greek people, which in turn would have reflected itself in more material forms. But the wretched creatures who controlled or miscontrolled Greek policy in these matters could not or would not see this. By the end of the year there was a general thinning out of the journalists, particularly after the beginning of Wavell's Libyan offensive, which naturally drew off some of the war correspondents who had large areas to cover, such as " General Sir Arthur ".

I left Athens early in December. My journey back to Istanbul was obviously going to be boring, so I was delighted to find that Lord Glenconner would be travelling at the same time. Christopher Glenconner still has the air of a playboy about him. Tall, slim, handsome and amusing, he hides the serious student of economics, the devoted husband and adoring father. From the British point of view perhaps even more important, he hid the astute business man. At this time he was head of the United Kingdom Commercial Corporation in Turkey and had been down to Athens to explore the possibilities of developing this business organization in Greece.

We were told that we must be at the station promptly at a quarter to five. There was only one train a day, and on the previous day, when we had thought of going and the compartment had been specially reserved, the train was held for an hour and a half for the " English milord ". We collected in the smelly lounge of the hotel. Last night's dirty glasses were still about and no one had as yet begun sweeping. I gulped down a cup of poor coffee and got into one of the taxis, which had been most difficult to obtain. The train was of the normal kind and quite comfortable, but I could say every hour or so to Christopher Glenconner how right I was, as he had sworn on the authority of Cook's that there would be a dining-car on the train. I knew better. He was extremely glad to eat large chunks of salami with brown bread washed down with the red retsina, the *vin du table* of the Greek household or taverna, which most visitors to Greece begin by abominating on account of its strong resinous flavour but end by adoring. It was fantastically cheap—about three-halfpence a carafe—and I never taste it without a feeling of nostalgia for the little tavernas in town or country where I have sat sipping it and eating plateful after plateful of *mezze* (a sort of *hors d'œuvre* usually composed of sardine, anchovy, red caviare, which is very plentiful in Greece, and hard-boiled egg), while some eager and of course talkative Greek discoursed on " the glory of your so noble country which lights a torch throughout the world" and the iniquities of his own Government, punctuated with "Ah, when I had my newspaper . . ."

Our good fortune in having a proper coach came to an end at Larissa, where we had to transfer to an unheated wooden truck. Glenconner remained in very good spirits through that night and the following day. He was wonderful at jumping out of the train to fill our bottles with water, buying oranges, and on one occasion even tiny bits of meat grilled over a charcoal fire and stuck on a skewer. They were delicious. Glenconner's secretary was not nearly so used to roughing it. He was miserable, but sensibly drank a large quantity of wine and went to sleep on one side of the carriage while Glenconner and I told one another the stories (I have no doubt with large omissions on both sides) of our lives. It was impossible owing to the joltings of the train, the frequent stops and the fights I had, to keep lice-covered soldiers from swarming into the carriage, as we already had three Greek officers in our not over-commodious truck.

We arrived in Salonika about four o'clock in the morning and I took the party to the Hotel Luxe, where the Glenconner charm, exercised to its full extent, produced a meal of coffee, toast, marmalade, butter and boiled eggs. There are few things in life I enjoy more than having my breakfast before I go to bed, though I rarely do so, as, much as I like dancing for an hour or two, there are few things more boring than sitting about in a night-club all night unless news of world-shaking importance is expected.

At 7 o'clock Glenconner and I met in an old-fashioned telephone booth in an effort to telephone the British Consulate. War or no war, it was another hour before he answered. We wanted a car to take us as near as possible to the Turkish frontier, certainly to Alexandroupolis, thus saving at least a day on the trains. But much as the Consul-General cringed to the British peer he did not offer to lend his car (which after all belonged to the Government and not to him), and the other, belonging to the Vice-Consul, had taken a clerk and his girl to Kavalla for the day, contrary to the orders which the British Legation in

Athens had sent by telegram to the Consulate in advance. It was no good raging, although once more I realized that my newspaper would not understand why the journey took so long. Glenconner, with gold, hired an old taxi. I bought some sweets to eat on the way, knowing how partial his Lordship was to chocolate.

We drove past the lakes to the sea at Stavroso and crossed a well-guarded bridge. We drove for miles by the sea and crossed the Struma feeling very pleased with ourselves. We calculated the time we should save. Soon after this our troubles began. The engine boiled ; there was no water with which we could refill it. We walked about the mountain looking for water, and at last found a dirty little pool. We filled our hats with it and carried it to the car, losing a considerable amount on the way. After several journeys we started the car, but it soon passed out on us, and we sat about waiting for the Consular car complete with girl-friend to return from Kavalla. When they appeared, instead of being helpful and offering to take us, stranded as we were, to Kavalla, they offered us chocolates, of which we had already had quite enough, but made it clear that we were to be cast for the role of the man who fell among thieves and they for the parts of priest and Levite. However, Glenconner took a firm line, and I an angry one, which resulted in our being taken, most unwillingly on their part, to Kavalla, where without waiting for food or drink we tried our luck with another taxi.

I experienced a moment of horror at leaving this exquisite town and racing on past the Greek fortifications—the so-called " Metaxas Line "—which were inadequate in the extreme, consisting of tank traps running from the sides of the mountains to the sea without any concrete filling, made in soft earth that could have been filled in a matter of minutes. Here and there was an odd machine-gun nest. I do not think there were many camouflaged ones, and I only saw eight.

Seres is the centre of the tobacco industry and incidentally of pro-German sympathy. The inhabitants feel, for some reason, that they should have been part of Bulgaria rather than Greece. We were ordering a much-needed meal in the local taverna and trying to persuade the proprietor to let us cook it ourselves when the word got round the town that three English people had arrived. Two Americans, working for Chesterfield cigarettes, swooped down on us and took us out to their compound. I think this was one of the most moving experiences in my life. I have never had the sense of being so genuinely welcomed even by my closest friends as I had from those two Americans who had never seen me before and would never see me again. One was young, the other elderly; one a New Englander, the other came from Chicago. Both, I suppose, were doing well, in a material sense, but both were longing to hear the sound of the English language again. We had already eaten at the taverna, but they insisted on our partaking of innumerable " Old Fashioneds " (rye whisky, sugar, orange bitters and mixed fruit). Fortunately I have an extremely strong head, but I can certainly assert that a good time was most emphatically had by all. Later, our hosts became autobiographical and reminiscent; we adjourned to the radio; the old man talked of all he had done in his life, the young man of all he had missed.

They were very anxious that we should stay the night, and both Glenconner and his secretary seemed disposed to agree. Personally I should have liked it, but I felt my editor would not be understanding, so I pulled two very reluctant men out into a temperature well below zero at 2 o'clock in the morning.

Our journey to the frontier exceeded in discomfort anything I have hitherto described. The bomb-broken windows allowed the snow freely to enter our unheated wooden carriage. A false conception of internal security had dictated that the times of trains should be kept secret; this involved a good deal of waiting about on icy station platforms for trains which might or might not materialize. The trains also developed a tendency to stop in places where there was no possible chance of obtaining refreshment. I refused to allow the men to stop for breakfast in Alexandroupolis, even though we were assured it would make no difference to the time at which we should cross the frontier into Turkey, and owing to my anxiety to get on as fast as possible and my unwillingness to take risks, they missed a much-needed morning cup of tea after the whisky of the night before. I felt a little ashamed when I did get them hungry to the frontier to discover that we could quite easily have breakfasted in comfort, come on by a later train and still caught the only available train running into Turkey.

I was sorry to leave Greece. After all, the Greek War was still the biggest story in the Balkans, and I had many friends in the country. I bitterly regretted the stupidity of the people who were, in effect, driving me away. I comforted myself with the thought that after seven weeks I should at last have a change of clothes, having left everything I possessed in a hotel bedroom at the Pera Palace when I left Turkey.

## CHAPTER X

## ROMANIA—CIVIL WAR

DURING the revolution or civil war in Romania I was lucky to be the only British reporter in the country. It was impossible to get information out of the country during the revolt itself by any means whatsoever. All telephone lines were cut off. No cables were allowed to leave. No planes or trains went from the country at all. In the future reporters will be well advised to carry radio sets from which messages may be sent. It seemed to me rather a pity that the Legations, several of which had radio transmission sets, did not allow me to send out simple messages. This would have been in the better interests of the State as, of course, the German journalists were sending out news to Berlin by radio, and all American newspapers were forced to use reports from the German agencies, as there was nothing else available. I managed to send out an account, which, though true, was a gross understatement, as soon as the telephone lines functioned again. But the general run of newspaper men so lacked courage that when I had smuggled a story out to Bulgaria, the local correspondent of my paper dare not telephone or cable it from there for fear of the Germans !

It is some time now since I left Romania, and I have read all the reports that were written at the time. They all appear to me to be untrue. How could correspondents in Belgrade and Istanbul report on a civil war in Romania when they had no idea what was happening ? I have seen accounts of buildings being burnt down which I know are still standing. Men were reported shot who were walking the streets, but the most melodramatic events were missed. I am now reproducing my diary which I wrote up almost hourly during the revolt. I reproduce my interpretation, which has since proved to be in parts incorrect. But all the scenes described I myself saw, and if there be any inaccuracy it is in understatement.

I had too recently seen Jews tortured to write about it at

that time. But it is true that the Guardists during the revolt picked up about five hundred Jews from one of the poorer quarters. They did not choose them—just the first men, women and children that they saw. These people were taken in lorries to the slaughter-houses and killed in the manner in which the Jewish religion demands that cattle should be slaughtered. Middle-aged women were hung up by chains, their throats were cut, and they were allowed to bleed to death whilst the jeering crowd imitated the prayers of the rabbi. After fifty people had been killed in this way the crowd got tired and just shot the rest.

On Monday, January 20, General Antonescu's life was three times threatened by members of the Iron Guard. Early in the morning a man, dressed as a messenger from the Ministry of Foreign Affairs, arrived with an important note which he said he must deliver into the hand of the General. The General came out of his bathroom and saw the so-called messenger draw a revolver from his pocket. He was able to get to his bedroom, where Madame Antonescu gave the alarm. Twice during the evening Iron Guardists, not wearing uniform, tried to enter the house through the kitchen premises, and when arrested were found to have loaded revolvers in their possession. They admitted they were on a mission to save Romania from Antonescu. This followed the dismissal of ten thousand Iron Guard commissars, who since the beginning of the Legionary régime had control of all the leading factories, mines, shops, docks and hotels in Romania. The commissars, who were ignorant members of the party and followers of Horia Sima, had been receiving a salary of fifty thousand lei a month. (A policeman in Bucharest earns fifteen hundred lei a month and the manager of the largest bank thirty thousand lei.) The dissatisfied commissars and other followers of Horia Sima held a meeting at which they said Antonescu was in the hands of the British Intelligence Service and ended with loud shouts of " Down with Antonescu ", " Horia Sima for ever ! " At the same time the students were holding a meeting criticizing Antonescu for having changed the Minister of the Interior after the murder of the German officer, Major Dietrich. The long-awaited internal clash between the Guardists and Antonescu must take place within a few days, if not hours.

This morning there have been several clashes resulting in seven deaths in various parts of the town, and Antonescu, to show his strength, has ordered his crack regiment to march up and down the main boulevards all day, carrying sub-machine-guns. In several alleyways near the Royal Palace and the Green House (headquarters of the Guardist movement) field artillery is visible. No one yet knows whether the Germans will back Horia Sima or Antonescu. Antonescu is himself quite confident that he will receive full German support.

Internal alarm may be the cause of the beginning of the Balkan 'Blitz'. A rapid thaw is now taking place, and soon ordinary motor transport will be possible along the country roads. German circles talk of a swift drive across Bulgaria to Salonika " to save the Italians ". This means it is not likely that the Germans are thinking of Salonika, especially as experts agree that all military preparations here indicate a drive from the Romanian Dobrudja district around Constanza. Every day more German troops are being billeted in the towns and villages to the north of the Danube, in order to put pressure on the Bulgarians. The speech of the Foreign Secretary, Filoff, leaves the Germans in no doubt as to whether they may use Bulgaria as a corridor for armies. But Bulgaria, with only twelve divisions, only eight of which have any degree of efficiency, cannot possibly say no, nor has she murmured about the hundreds of soldiers whom reliable British witnesses know have crossed into Bulgaria in plain clothes every day for the last three weeks. Russia cannot say no either. Germany is perfectly aware of her unpreparedness for a Balkan war. She will do as she did in Poland—pick up a bit of territory; and in this case the bit of territory will be the valuable ground around the Danube delta. Turkey will fight if a German army noisily marches into Bulgaria or if the army percolates through Bulgaria and attacks Turkey. But she will fight against Germany with nothing like the fervour that she would against Russia. It is impossible to mention Russia in any despatch written from Turkey, so nervous are the Turks of the Russians. Should another strong frost take place the drive will be held up, as the pontoons which I have seen at various strategic points along the Danube cannot possibly be used when they would be likely to be broken by ice floes weighing hundreds of tons. Meanwhile there are no passenger trains in Hungary and very few indeed in Romania. The new avalanche of German soldiers is arriving and Romanians all over the country are being forced to house and feed them. This is not producing the hatred and antipathy one would expect. Romanians after the abdication, the loss of Bessarabia, Transylvania and the Dobrudja and the earthquake, appear to be past feeling anything or caring about anything. German sources continue to alarm the population with stories of a Russian invasion as more German troops flood the country.

*Wednesday, January 22.*

The Iron Guard is fighting General Antonescu, and the Civil War, long expected, rages in Romania. On Tuesday morning General Antonescu again paraded a regiment of soldiers, but they made no effort to take key buildings held by the Iron Guards. By the afternoon several isolated incidents, in which about seven people were killed, took place. Their dead bodies surrounded by candles with a picture of Codreanu above them were exhibited in the yard in front of the Prefecture of Police in Bucharest.

The population drank their coffee and crowded out of curiosity into the special streets where traffic was forbidden. But the Guardists were not idle ; the crowds were given hurriedly printed leaflets accusing General Antonescu of being in the power of the British. The Bucharest radio was quiet except for a short and rather weak appeal by the General that order might be restored without loss of life. After his appeal marches of the Iron Guard—the organization he was trying to quell— were played. A curfew was called at 10 p.m. The police guarding the various legations decided life was too dangerous and went home. Odd rifle shots were to be heard throughout the night, and it was impossible to drive from one end of the town to the other, owing to the cordon of tanks round the barracks held by the Legionaries in the residential part of the town and the Ministry of Foreign Affairs, also held by the Legionaries. General Antonescu was confident of German support if necessary, but rumour said that Horia Sima had already gone to Berlin to bid for the support of Hitler.

During the night fights in Ploesti and Giurgiu resulted in those two important towns falling into the hands of the Legionaries. The army, however, said they had taken over the Prefecture of Police in all important towns with the exception of Jassy and Bucharest.

On Wednesday morning no newspapers, no trams, no buses; a few shops were opened, but they kept their shutters down so that they may close at a moment's notice. Taxis become few and far between as they run out of petrol, unable to buy further supplies. In the early afternoon the Iron Guards, who had been parading the streets singing their songs without interruption, set fire to the synagogue, and Romanian officers watched without making any effort to prevent the outrage. At 4 o'clock, following minor efforts during the morning, a determined effort with heavy artillery was made to take the Legionary barracks. Noise of guns and smoke frightened a large part of the population, who retired to their homes.

*7.30 p.m.*

Noise of machine-guns, rifle fire and heavy artillery can be heard all over the town; crowds of enthusiastic Iron Guard supporters rush through the streets shouting, " Up with Horia Sima ". The soldiers are now only managing to hold a few streets in the town. It is impossible to telephone to the Ministry of Foreign Affairs and few private telephone lines are working, although Romanian officers hold the base of the telephone building; all the rooms filled with apparatus are held by Iron Guardists. Only Iron Guard newspapers are on sale in the streets. Everyone feels that the General has lost, as the situation rapidly deteriorates and the noise of the shots increases. No one knows the number of dead or wounded, but the total must now be well on 5000. General Dragalina, in command of the Third Army at Brasov, has gone over to the Guardists and is bringing his men by means of forced marches to Bucharest. The 38th Infantry Regiment at Braila is also marching on Bucharest, and the 4th Army Corps at Jassy have joined the Guardist cause.

Petrol waggons used by the army to barricade streets in Bucharest have been set on fire by the Legionaries. There is a general feeling that the Germans will not allow this state of affairs to last for many more hours, and as it seems unlikely that General Antonescu can re-establish order, the German military mission may take over by to-night. They may form another puppet Romanian Government or establish a protectorate ; they themselves do not yet know.

12.30 *a.m.* (*Thursday*).

General Antonescu received General Hansen and arranged for German support. German troops were stationed during the night outside Bucharest ready to meet any army coming into the capital.

I awoke from my couch in the drawing-room of the British Legation to the sound of heavy artillery. What remains of the British community in Romania had concentrated into two or three houses. Until 10 o'clock shots could be heard in all directions and it was impossible to decide who was shooting at whom from where. At this hour General Antonescu spoke over the radio assuring the nation that he had the army with him, but reminding people that they must defend their own homes against the thieves and odd hooligans who were still at large. " Call in the army to help you," he said. How people were to call in the army when wild armed Guardists were on their doorstep, and no telephones were working, is difficult to say. At 10 o'clock also appeared a statement by Horia Sima, in which he ordered all Legionaries to stop firing and resume their normal life. (This is now known to be bogus.) He said that the continuance of the civil war was against the interests of the Axis, and the Iron Guardists must surrender the buildings that they were holding immediately. Planes dropped pamphlets giving General Antonescu's speech, and planes dropped papers with Horia Sima's declaration. The German planes flying low zoomed ferociously around the town and for a time it seemed that the firing had stopped. General Antonescu issued a communiqué saying that they had control of the entire situation. Large lorries went into the scenes of action, coming out laden with the dead. I myself saw six enormous lorries packed high with corpses.

Before lunch, however, it was apparent that the Civil War was not over ; the Iron Guardists had not given up the buildings they were holding, and firing more furious broke out around the Prefecture and the Foreign Office. This was continued for five or six hours, heavy artillery being brought into play, and the normal life of the town, which had started during the morning, again ceases. At 5 p.m. about fifty German light tanks and fifty German armed motor-cycles and sidecars with attendant camions drove purposefully to the field of action. After two hours many of the streets where the fiercest fighting had taken place, had been cleared. And now at 7.45 p.m. there is still a little fighting for the German army to subdue around the Ministry of Foreign Affairs.

General Antonescu says that it is only the bad elements in the Iron Guard that are disaffected. He makes every excuse for the burning of Jewish shops and the many hundreds of deaths that have been caused. He had rather pointedly throughout the whole course of the Civil War not wished to squash the Guards entirely. The Germans will soon have stopped the fighting and now no one knows whether they will take control of the country or not.

*Friday, January 24.*

To-day is a public holiday in Bucharest, not, however, to celebrate the termination of the Civil War, but one of many years' standing, still cynically celebrating Greater Romania. Shops and factories are all closed. The population has had plenty of time to take stock of the situation and to see the many marks of blood on the dirty snow of the streets. Over 2000 people are reported to have been killed in Bucharest and between 11,000 and 12,000 in the country as a whole. Many of these were innocent onlookers who were shot down by the army's machine-guns in an effort to oust the Guardists. Two sections of the town are still closed to traffic and Romanian tanks are roaring around these areas cleaning up the last pockets of holders-out.

This morning the leader of the Iron Guard student movement, who published the pamphlet specifically stating that the British Intelligence Service had organized the shooting of the German officer, Major Dietrich, was shot. Mystery surrounds Horia Sima ; rumour says he may be shot too. In any case there seems little doubt that he was behind the whole plot. The German officers who took over the Prefecture of Police, which the Romanian army had failed to take from the Legionaries, and the Ministry of Foreign Affairs, are still standing by with tanks and twenty or thirty $4\frac{1}{2}$-inch guns and ten 6-inch guns, but the town is quiet and the shooting has stopped. General Antonescu, having made himself head of the Iron Guard movement, now proposes to form a Government within two days. There is no doubt that the Government will be a military dictatorship and only the Under-Secretaries will be civilians. This Government can last only if the Germans support General Antonescu thoroughly. General Antonescu has not the usual attributes of a dictator, and although a good soldier and an honest man, he has by no means a strong personality. Under German direction he is calling up more recruits in an effort to occupy the younger and more unruly sections of the population.

Walking around the streets of Bucharest looking at the many houses which have been destroyed or badly damaged by gunfire one sees that there is noticeably a stronger anti-British atmosphere than there was before the civil war. The Germans on the other hand are more popular ; those Romanians who resented their presence here now feel that a lengthy and uncomfortable war was stopped by German action. . . .

I had a narrow escape. A stray shot was fired from near

my flat on a company of soldiers in the street. They immediately opened fire. Not a single window in my flat is whole; the walls are potmarked three inches into the brick with machine-gun fire, mirrors broken, bookcases destroyed, curtains hanging in tatters; some shots even went through the wall. Luckily the soldiers soon discovered that there were no Guardists inside the house, and made no effort to enter. As yet no policemen have reappeared in the streets. They were the first to run away at the beginning of the disturbances, and order is still being maintained entirely by the army.

*Monday, January 27.*

During Saturday and Sunday General Antonescu has made many emotional appeals to the Romanian people to be calm and to accept the new order which he is about to inaugurate. The public has, however, been shocked by the extent of the damage during the civil war. Visits to the Jewish quarter revealed the complete wrecking of houses and shops from which all the goods have been looted by Guardists. Many more people were cruelly shot than was at first supposed. Jews were strangled in public outside the burning synagogue, Jewish children were killed by Guardists while their houses were being looted, elderly bearded Jews were slain in the street, and I have seen their bodies lying naked in a yard after the Guardists had stolen their possessions. Others were packed into lorries and taken ten to fifteen kilometres out of the city on the way to Giurgiu, where they were thrown out of the lorries and shot, about a hundred metres from the roadside. A reliable witness describes this horrible scene in which about six hundred people were shot together and the Legionaries going around afterwards shooting with revolvers those who moved. Perhaps 1500 people were killed in this way, and are still lying unburied by the roadside.

A strict curfew is imposed at 10 o'clock, and all restaurants and places of entertainment are closed at 9, but the rioting is not yet over. On Monday morning between 3.30 and 4.10 a.m. Romanian soldiers fired continuously with rifles from a garden below my window, over one of the widest roads in the city.

Where the fiercest fighting took place flags are now being un-
furled and a stand put up on which lie the coffins of those
soldiers who died fighting, covered with wreaths and wrapped
with the Romanian flag.  Meanwhile the public of Bucharest
are being searched and are ordered to show their legitimation
papers every hundred yards.  There is a serious house-to-house
search for arms being made, and no one can go in or out of the
capital, nor may anyone travel, as only military trains are now
running.  General Antonescu is ill, and the new German
Minister, von Killinger, who arrived a few days ago, has not yet
decided what Romanian puppets shall be employed in the new
Government.

News continues to percolate to the capital of what happened
in the countryside.  At Constanza the Iron Guard only surrendered at 1.30 p.m. on Friday to the German Consul and two
German officers.  They firmly refused to surrender to the
Romanian army before that time, even after three ultimatums
had been issued.  The British Consul, Mr. Kendall, throughout
the civil war had a very nasty time.  Although no shots were
fired, there were continuous hostile demonstrations outside the
British Consulate, and a special pamphlet was produced by the
Iron Guard against the British, mentioning Mr. Kendall by
name.  The Romanian army have now disarmed most of the
Iron Guard in Constanza, but the leaders of the whole outrage
are still walking about as free men and proud of themselves.

Mystery still surrounds the fate of Horia Sima, who was
arrested in his house and had in his possession 3,000,000 lei
which had been pilfered from the Jewish shops in the city.
Many arrests have taken place in Bucharest, but the Iron Guard
are by no means smoked out.  Tanks are still being used on
houses containing nests of them.  A part of the German army
remains outside Bucharest to quell any Romanian troops or
Iron Guards who might march on the city.

*Wednesday, January* 29.

Some days ago General Jacobici, Minister for Defence,
gave a dinner party, and had as one of his guests General Hansen,

head of the German military mission in Romania. As the General was leaving he expressed the wish that he might return the invitation to Jacobici in Athens at Easter.

A large quantity of arms has been found in the trams and taxis. I had a curious experience when my taxi was stopped and to my horror the police found a rifle in the back luggage container, but although they examined me and the rest of the car very carefully, they did not arrest the taxi-driver nor make any difficulties for me ; in fact the taxi-driver and the police parted on the best of terms.

Two Americans arriving here from Italy reported that they had seen German troops in Milan and Trieste, but " nothing like as many as in Bucharest ". They believed the Germans there were technical experts. Many of the Germans now arriving in Bucharest have motored through from France and Belgium, and were dissatisfied that some of their colleagues already here were motoring back to Italy. This is a fair grouse, as travelling is still extremely difficult in Romania. The recent snow has entirely blocked the road from Bucharest to Giurgiu, and vast numbers of German soldiers are busy with spades trying to clear it. There is still a cordon around one of the streets at the back of the Foreign Office and the 4th Army Command is still reported to be against the General and with the Legionary movement.

*Saturday, February* 1.

Horia Sima is hiding in the Italian Legation which is heavily guarded by Romanian soldiers. Sima was first given sanctuary in the German Legation until Fabricius left ; then he was transferred by a German army lorry.

Everyone here asks why the Germans, who knew of Sima's plans to throw out Antonescu's Government, gave their support to Antonescu only on the third day of the revolt, and why, after the revolt, they protected the leading Iron Guardists and prevented Antonescu from taking serious measures to suppress them.

An Iron Guardist ex-Minister told me yesterday, " You

cannot have a Nazi State without a Nazi Party. We are the Nazi Party, and in the end the Germans will support us. Only because the wrong section of the Guardists was in power in some districts, allowing the industrial and economic life of the country to go to ruin, thereby endangering the success of Hitler's Balkan blitz, did the Germans come in on the side of the General."

Every decent Romanian feels that he ought to support the General, but many are disgusted by the flattering telegrams he exchanges with Hitler. Maniu has decided not to hinder the General in his efforts to keep order. He has made it clear in a manifesto which, though unpublished, has been widely circulated, that he disapproves most strongly of the foreign policy of the Government, especially of " marching hand in hand with the Axis ".

The Russian Ambassador stated yesterday that the Communists took no part in the revolution.

The revolution is not yet over. On Friday evening a Romanian captain was stabbed at the Gare du Nord by a young woman Guardist. This evening a Colonel and two junior officers were shot, again by women Guardists. As I write a searchlight flashes up and down the road in front of my window, looking for Guardists who are still holding out on some nearby roofs. There are cordons still round large sections of the town, and diplomats of the great Powers have been carefully examined to make sure that they carried no arms when they entered the Foreign Office this morning. I was searched for arms five times within half a mile this evening, and there are three soldiers with loaded rifles every fifty yards in all the main streets.

Germany, having used force to end the revolt in Romania, did not hurry to remove the military equipment in and around Bucharest, which was kept there to remind odd Guardists of what would happen if another revolt broke out. The State funerals of those who had been killed went off quietly enough. Trials began of those who had organized the Civil War or assisted in it in a big way. Romanians and foreigners were equally surprised by the very light sentences which were given to Guardist ringleaders, whilst the corpses from the revolt they had caused were still being removed by special gangs of men during the night from the cellars of houses and shops in the main streets. The curfew was rigidly imposed, although on several occasions, not wanting to spend the evening from 9 o'clock onwards in my flat, I had dinner at the Athenée Palace with colleagues who were staying there and then walked home by myself, a matter of over two miles. The snowy streets were absolutely empty save for the guards walking up and down. Surprisingly enough they never asked me for my pass. My policy was to walk down the centre of the road in order to avoid being shot at by an over-zealous sentry should I suddenly emerge from a shadow. I heard afterwards that all the soldiers had orders to shoot at sight anyone they saw walking in the square in front of the Ministry of Foreign Affairs. I heard this only after I had crossed it at least half a dozen times. In this square were four or five huge searchlights which every night were used after the curfew to help the sentries pick out people walking about the streets or, judging by the way they were used, climbing around house roofs.

There was a noticeable increase in the number of German soldiers ; there were reputed to be altogether eighteen divisions in the country, and it was evident that as soon as the roads thawed Bulgaria was going to be overrun. The social life of the English in Bucharest at that time became rather limited, as few Romanians were any longer brave enough to be seen openly with English people or to entertain them in their houses for fear of wrath to come. I suddenly found myself getting to know English people who had been in Romania as long as I had, but whom I had not previously known at all. There were parties in restaurants for the Legation staff, which were great fun, but they had to stop, as the restaurants were otherwise entirely filled by Germans who, when slightly cheered by good food and drink, were liable to cause incidents. So, although no orders were given, it was generally understood that not more than three or four English people should go together into a restaurant.

At this point the Counsellor, Mr. Le Rougetel, gave two parties in his roomy flat. He imported a Russian band from a night-club which was glad to have some work to do as the club was not allowed to open, and the parties had to go on until 5 o'clock because before that hour no one could go home. It was a curious huddle of English people drinking, dancing, singing Russian songs and being gay together, with a tremendous atmosphere of antagonism outside.

The last of these parties took place two days before we broke off diplomatic relations. Everyone in the room knew it was really a farewell gathering, but on this occasion the discretion of the entire Legation staff in that melodramatic atmosphere was enormous. No look or word betrayed the real situation. When I was dancing with various people I thought : " Poor man, you are far braver than many who will be killed in battle ; you will never get out of this country alive." I was most surprised that the Germans allowed all the Legation staff and its hangers-on to leave Romania without trouble.

I remember going out from one of these parties, driving home through the silent snow-lined streets, and being stopped at a cross-roads. Three machine-guns on stands were immediately turned on the car, whilst the officials looked at the papers of the diplomat in the car who had permission to be out. The soldiers hanging around breathed fire and venom against the British.

The Romanians, owing to their own stupidity and to the cleverness of the German propaganda, really believed that we were going to bomb the petroleum fields at any minute, although it would have seemed obvious to a child of the meanest intelligence that they would not be bombed so long as the diplomatic mission remained in Bucharest. In fact, though no British Government would obviously ever contemplate taking such action, it would have been well worth while to have bombed the refineries at Ploesti whilst the Legation remained, in order to take the Germans by surprise and cause the maximum of damage. It would have meant certain imprisonment and probable death to all the English in Romania. But I think the death of three hundred might have been justified by the nuisance and trouble to the Germans. Critical as I am of all officials, I can find no fault with the conduct of British affairs during those last anxious weeks.

The German invasion of Bulgaria in force took place at the beginning of March, but this represented only the culmination of a long period of infiltration on a scale that was quite unrealized by the public in Britain at that time. It was not possible at any one moment to say that the German army had entered Bulgaria, just as it had not been possible to say at what moment the German army entered Romania. At the beginning of February the penetration had already been a matter of common knowledge in the Legations of Bucharest for some days, but owing to the fact that it was not possible during the disturbed days of the Civil War to obtain a permit to leave the capital or to telephone to frontier towns, the news did not get eye-witness confirmation until February 5. The number of German troops in uniform actually crossing the frontier at this time by train or lorry was not large. Probably it did not yet average more than eight hundred or a thousand a day. But those eight hundred were carrying vast quantities of military equipment. The technique had changed since the days when Hitler's soldiers had marched into Vienna and Prague. Nowadays, first of all the tourists arrive and begin to display their well-known zeal for holiday-making near points of strategic importance; after this come the technical and economic experts, then troops without uniform, and lastly troops in uniform. Exactly the same method was being used in Bulgaria as had been used in Romania. By this time there were eighteen German divisions in Romania and the equivalent of three in plain clothes in Bulgaria. As the Danube was still frozen, all the latter had crossed by the land frontier of the Dobrudja from Constanza.

Meanwhile, in the casino at the mountain resort of Sinaia, once Queen Marie's favourite holiday town, the gilded and red plush roulette tables were now covered with maps and telephones. Sinaia, famous for its luxury hotels (which are very good even by western European standards) had become the headquarters of the German General Staff in Romania. No one but Germans might stay there, however much they might want to ski. The German aim was to conquer the Balkans by bluff rather than by blitz. That had always been Hitler's way—demoralize, and then (if it is still necessary) fight. The plan was clear enough. While the camouflaged invaders continued to enter the country the Germans would delay their main invasion until the ice melted and pontoon bridges could be placed across the Danube.

It was extraordinarily hard to get confirmed news of the troop movements through the Dobrudja into Bulgaria. The Germans had blocked all the roads on both sides of the frontier for a considerable distance, and allowed only peasants who lived in the forbidden area to pass. However, the telephone lines to this part of the country after being closed for some time were opened up, and I did succeed in getting through a call and actually speaking to three peasants who had seen the lorries crossing the frontier. All this time large quantities of anti-aircraft equipment were being shifted across the frontier to guard the new aerodromes which were being built in Bulgaria. In addition, this anti-aircraft equipment was needed in Bulgaria to protect the stores of petrol and food which the German tourists and plain-clothes soldiers had been building up ever since the previous September. Much of this military equipment was French, and it was possible to see, under the newly-painted German labels, the old French signs. I remember seeing at this time a bus-load of German soldiers passing through the main street of Bucharest in a vehicle which carried a board indicating that Brussels was its normal destination. Similarly, all the equipment which was used for the Danube pontoons was of French workmanship, much of it having been built by them for their own use in crossing the Seine after the bridges had been destroyed by German bombers.

Simultaneously, the German units at Constanza were practising hard at embarkation and disembarkation. These units had come across to Romania from Le Havre. Opinion at that time was divided between those who took this as evidence that the Germans had for the moment given up the idea of trying to invade Britain and those who thought that these units had been brought to Romania for the express purpose of making us think that they had given up the idea of invasion. Few in British Legation circles excepting Robin Hankey, even though they knew of the secret war going on in the Danube delta between Russians and Germans, believed that they were rehearsing for an attack upon Russia. Turkey was regarded as a more probable objective, and it was realized also that for the invasion of Bulgaria it would be as easy, if not easier, to transport troops by the Black Sea from Constanza to Varna or Burgas as by rail or road.

Romania had by this time become the auction-room for the sale of large quantities of loot from France. Early in February notices appeared in the streets of Constanza announcing auction sales of valuable goods. At the appointed time, two large German army lorries appeared, packed high with stolen property. Then in the square which forms the centre of the town and where the statue of Ovid stands forlornly miserable recalling his exile here in the days of Augustus, the sale began. Mr. Kendall, the British Consul, saw gold coffee-spoons, silver coffee-pots, silver teapots, made by famous French firms and embellished with the arms of noble French families, sold in the streets. The German soldiers looked on anxiously to see what prices their lots would fetch. But the Romanians were poor and the German sellers looked disappointed at the results of the transactions. Linen sheets embroidered with the crests of Dukes and ex-Premiers were selling for three hundred lei, which at the existing ' black ' rate of exchange was the equivalent of not more tha two shillings. Mink coats which had hardly been worn by their original owners were selling for less than £10.

After the sale, when the auctioneers had taken their percentages, the German soldiers departed to a beerhouse to divide the spoils. The lot was valuable, but they had only obtained a small price for it.

Never until these last weeks in Romania had it been possible to buy in Bucharest French perfume bottled in France. Previously it had always been sent to Romania in bulk and bottled there. But now the shops were full of French-bottled Guerlain, Lanvin Prétexte and Patou Cocktail Dry, and also of

French powders from the more exclusive houses. I asked the owner of one of the largest shops where he bought them and he, thinking I was American, said, "From the German army, of course". Obviously an army organized as the German army is organized had the blessing of Berlin in these dealings. Berlin had reduced their pay whilst they were in Romania, knowing that they could well make up for it by selling French loot.

Romania by this time was a country that had lost its soul. Partition, foreign occupation, earthquake, rebellion, civil war had entirely broken the national morale. Even her few honest leaders like Maniu were ineffective ; they could only wring their hands and bemoan the evils of the age.

One of the ways in which this was manifested was in the treatment of the Polish troops who still remained. A great number had managed to get away from Constanza and other parts of the country, but those who were still in Romania at the beginning of 1941 were simply sent back to occupied Poland in the course of the first five weeks of the year. Subsequently all Polish women refugees were also sent back. There is, I believe, no precedent in history for the sending back of interned soldiers to enemy territory. The Romanians gave the excuse that they needed the food and the accommodation for the steadily increasing number of Germans in the country. British and American protests were of absolutely no avail. The Romanians endeavoured to make many of the Polish sign certificates saying that they wished to return to German-occupied territory. I never heard that any soldier had signed this document.

In these last weeks in Romania, though there were stringent regulations against the carrying of firearms, and the police were continually searching civilians for them, it was not safe to go about without a revolver, as armed bands of hooligans were always liable to attack solitary individuals if there were no German soldiers in sight. It was forbidden for more than three people to walk together, which simply aggravated the evil it was designed to cure. Personally, I had three revolvers, one of them small enough to go in my evening handbag, and I always slept with one under my pillow. After I left Romania when the

Legation evacuated to Turkey, it took me three weeks to get accustomed to going about without one. I was very fortunate in that I never had mine taken from me, though about this time I was shot at in the streets.

Decent Romanians were sick and tired of the disorders, but they saw no way other than a complete and proper German occupation to prevent their children from being beaten up in the streets. The Germans kept the fear of Russia so cleverly to the fore that everyone with a decent suit of clothing feared Communism. They felt relieved, too, that their country would not be the battleground of a new Balkan blitz : it would merely be the base from which the blitz was to be organized. That the country would not be a battlefield was certain, as it was clear to all that the Turks were unlikely to fight until their own frontier was crossed. The tears and emotion so much in evidence before the British left were largely stimulated by the fear of future air raids, a fear which was cleverly played up by the Germans in the Romanian Press and over the radio.

Many Romanians were genuinely sorry that their country had, as they thought, backed the wrong horse when they heard over the B.B.C. of the British successes in Africa. Secret societies sprang up all over the country which listened in to the English news and whose members relieved their feelings by cursing the Germans ; but the Romanians were in far too weak a position militarily, and their morale was too low, for them to dare to breathe a word in public against the Germans so long as the latter remained in control of their country. This was only human. Equally the more sinister secret societies of the Iron Guard flourished despite the many communiqués breathing fire and slaughter against them issued by General Antonescu. Such was the Lewis Carroll atmosphere prevailing at this time that the General was trying to win back the support of the Guardists by avoiding the imposition of the severe punishments which he and his Government were almost daily proclaiming against them.

I was in a position to know. After diplomatic relations were broken off I was asked to help with the transport and evacuation of the Legation staff, and of those members of the British colony who had stayed on until the last minute hoping that His Majesty would pay for their evacuation. Never have I had a piece of work which I enjoyed more. The Legation staff were all working under great pressure and strain, but they were all unfailingly helpful. My lack of knowledge of internal Legation red tape must have been most tedious for them all, but my journalistic language and undiplomatic manner were worse. Only once was I charmingly and gently reminded by the First Secretary that the Ministers of Allied Governments really must not be treated as though they were German Jewish refugees. At the last moment the Belgian Legation staff, a few Dutch, and masses of semi-diplomatic Poles who had been left behind by their Legation, all wanted to come with us. Of course they all expected to have sleepers on our special train and First Class cabins on the ship.

The Belgians were the worst. They produced two babies unexpectedly at the last moment. Few of the staff had time for their personal packing and no time for last-moment purchases. The Americans were splendid. They were taking over British interests, but they also did any odd job to help the British diplomats. What a tremendous send-off they organized ! Our special train was leaving at 10.30 p.m. As the curfew was at 10 p.m., any Romanian who came not only risked imprisonment in the future for being pro-British but immediate arrest.

The station was so heavily guarded with German and Romanian troops that only people who shouted at them in English could get through to the train. What a train it was ! At the last moment I had to put five children in one sleeper (that being all that was available) because an Italian woman, married to an Italian man, arrived at the Consulate late in the afternoon demanding to be evacuated. All her eight children had British passports, having been born in Soho over the small café they ran there. We had to take them. The Consul insisted, as the two eldest boys were of military age. Like so many other British subjects in Romania, they could not speak English.

Princess Elizabeth Bibesco stands out in my mind as the tragic queen of the stage. Though her friends were just leaving her in a land of enemies, she gave everyone a charming parting gift. She stood in the dark station, wearing violets, her white face no longer animated by smart repartee—merely masklike, shrunk and sunken with misery. I had arranged for a dining-car, and having checked everyone on the train, made for the car. Reaction had set in, and as the train speeded through that German-occupied territory the archivists' gramophone played the latest dance tunes. At midnight I went to bed and thanked God I was not a diplomat. Poor devils—they had done nothing but say good-bye in different ways to men they knew to be scoundrels and liars.

When we woke up we were in Constanza station. I dressed and rushed out to give the list of passengers to the Consul. There was no question of leaving the station. Thirty-five German lorries and about six tanks were lined up in the siding. We could see the Turkish ship on which we were to sail, the *Izmir*. It was melodramatic. No one was allowed to leave the train. We sat over breakfast wonderfully lightheartedly, I must say, wondering whether we should return to Bucharest that evening looking rather foolish. Apparently there was a hitch about the Romanians leaving London. There was a pile of ciphered telegrams to be unscrambled at the Consulate. With some difficulty the Minister was allowed to leave the station and go to the Consulate, where he helped with the deciphering. We waited. German troops looked at us over the railings as though we were already interned.

At last the order came that we could embark. We left Constanza, leaving behind one Englishman there who had been arrested by the Germans during the course of the embarkation. As the ship moved, the barriers on to the docks were raised, and hundreds of German soldiers rushed on to the docks. They stood silently watching the ship slide away.

In the midst of the thousands of grey-green uniforms, one

small man in black stood waving a large white handkerchief. He was the American diplomat who came to see us off. We waved until the ship turned out of the harbour. The diplomats were satisfied with the cabins they had, but all the other passengers, especially the Belgians, complained about the accommodation for the single night. We were to make a detour owing to the minefields in the Black Sea. The Minister provided champagne for dinner, which stopped complaints. It was one of the happiest journeys I recollect, and I wished it could last longer. But the beautiful Bosphorus was visible, and my colleague, Derek Patmore, who had left Bucharest the previous October, embarked to mix with the mighty and obtain a thrilling story at second hand.

## CHAPTER XI

## BULGARIA—GERMAN STALKING-HORSE

BULGARIA is always said to be the only truly Balkan country. Greece is Mediterranean, Turkey Asiatic, Romania and Yugoslavia Danubian, but Bulgaria, although the Danube is her northern frontier, can never be considered as anything but Balkan. She was the last country to gain her independence from the Turks ; perhaps for this reason feeling against Turkey is specially strong there, even stronger than in Greece. Bulgaria has no industries, no aristocracy, and only a small and corrupt bourgeoisie. The grandfather of every Bulgarian you meet is a peasant, however much the Bulgarian asserts, as he generally does, that he is a member of the only aristocratic family in the country.

What a charming country it can be ! I arrived there in November—not perhaps the ideal time of year for motoring in the Balkans—and drove from the Danubian ferry at Rustchuk to the old capital at Tirnovo. The roads were bad but passable ; there were even occasional petrol pumps. From Tirnovo I had planned to cross the best-known pass of the Balkan mountains, the Shipka Pass, down to Stara Zagora, in order that I might cross the country and reach Turkey more quickly than would be possible by the roundabout way via Sofia. All along the road peasants were working, bridges were being widened. I saw more steamrollers in that morning journey that I had thought existed in the whole of the Balkan peninsula. They were all made in Germany, and I even heard the driver of one of them speak German.

In the pleasant town at the base of the pass, Gabrovo, I was told that it would not be possible to cross the pass. I laughed and told them my car had special diplomatic papers, I was being accompanied by a diplomat and had a *laissez-passer*, so I thought there could be no difficulty in crossing the pass. But there only a few kilometres outside the town was a second barrier and a stone wall supporting it, so that it was physically impossible to drive the car further.  Here policemen and soldiers bullied, shouted and gesticulated, ordering me back to the town. My papers had no effect.  They said it was forbidden to cross the pass.  I asked why.  One man volunteered the information that the road was being re-made.  This I could see already. Another man, one of the type I love to meet in Balkan villages, who had been in America for a few months, told me that the Germans were making a new aerodrome in the Balkan mountains about ten miles south of Gabrovo.

We were extremely anxious to cross this lovely range of mountains, and we motored to the west of another pass at Troyan in the hope of being able to cross the pass above Troyan and from there motor down to Plovdiv.  Troyan is a charming small town at the foot of the mountains, with a hotel which, considering it is situated in a small town, is extremely comfortable and quite free from bugs—a most refreshing discovery after several nights in Balkan villages.  Here we found the same situation ; no power on earth could get us past the barrier and on to the pass to cross the mountains.  Here too after a certain amount of bullying we heard that an aerodrome was being built. Bulgaria, in November 1940, seemed to be building an uncommon number of aerodromes ; we heard too that Germans were being employed on the work.

But a greater misfortune was to befall me.  When, being driven to take the longer way round to Turkey, I at last arrived in Sofia, I was received most kindly by the British Minister, who entertained me many times and took a great deal of trouble to explain to me what the situation was at that time.  He was genuinely convinced that King Boris was not violently pro-German, that he would in fact remain neutral and emotionally pro-ally.  I felt grateful, though longing to say : " Boris cannot be pro-English when he is allowing the Germans to build aerodromes all over his country."  The Minister was so sincere that it seemed difficult to doubt him, and so kind when he said, " It is perhaps better for you not to write too much about what you consider to be German penetration.  The Bulgarians want encouragement. If we suggest that they have already gone over to the Axis, and we are discontented with them, we shall only move them further away from us."

Out of consideration for the Minister I wrote a ' colour ' story about Bulgaria which I had to telephone to Sofia, after which it was telephoned to Geneva and from there cabled to London. At some point in the transmission the word ' German ' was inserted in an unfortunate place, so that instead of my having been stopped by Bulgarian authorities and so prevented from crossing the mountains, the story had me stopped by German authorities in Bulgaria.

This started a first-class row. The Bulgarian Minister in London complained to the Foreign Office and to the *Daily Express*. Mr. Rendel quite rightly said, " I trusted this woman and entertained her and now she has gone away and written just the things about Bulgaria which I least wanted said ". The Bulgarian newspapers repeated the *Express* story as the lying tale of a British journalist, with a notice that I was expelled from Bulgaria. Actually this was not true, as I left by car of my own free will and drove into Turkey. I was so besieged with angry telegrams from my paper and my friends that it was a relief to go to the Greek front and let people's tempers die down. It must be said in fairness to Mr. Rendel that when he learned the true circumstances he wrote me a charming letter of apology.

Bulgaria had been falling into the Axis camp since the rise of Hitler. After the last war there had been a reaction against Germany in Bulgaria, and a feeling that, having backed the wrong horse twice in previous wars, they must be most careful this time to pick the winner. King Boris had too much German blood to be able to think quite objectively about Germany, and he had married an Italian princess. Bulgaria, like Hungary, always tried to attach herself to the Rome end of the Axis, this being more respectable in her eyes. Dissatisfied powers though both were, they disliked the parvenu quality of Nazi Germany. Bulgaria was a natural supplier of wheat, maize and tobacco for Austria and Germany. The transport could be effected slowly but cheaply by means of the Danube, or quickly by the Simplon-Orient line through Yugoslavia. She had no industries worth mentioning, and it seemed a pity that all her inhabitants were not content to remain agricultural producers ; as farmers and gardeners they are superb, probably the best in Europe, whereas their efforts in industry are catastrophic.

Some years ago the Government organized an exhibition at Varna for all the local manufactured goods. It was called the " Bulgarian Wembley ". The Press Department in Sofia tried to persuade me to go down there and, bribed by a free ticket and the prospect of pleasant bathing in the Black Sea, I went. For three hours I looked around the exhibition and could find nothing worth carrying back to Sofia. One object, however, attracted my attention, a large, beautifully shaped rowing boat. But the man who was taking me round said, " We were going to build an artificial pond to show off that boat, which was built by the Bulgarian navy, but as the wretched thing always overturns when it is put into water, we found it better to show it on dry land ".

The Bulgarians are amongst the best gardeners in the world. All the large estates of Balkan kings and princes are run by Bulgarians, no matter how the races concerned hate one another. They seem to be natural flower producers and market gardeners ; flowers overflow from every little peasant plot, and the restaurants in Sofia are famous not for their food but for the vast banks of flowers between the tables.

An unofficial agreement was reached between Hungary and Bulgaria ; the Hungarians import about fifty market gardeners a year and the Bulgarians about fifty Hungarian cabaret artists a year. At a time when currency restrictions became fashionable the members of both professions were preparing to depart for their home country, as it was impossible for them to send money home to their parents or wives and children. So it was arranged that the money earned by the Hungarian dancing girls in Bulgaria could be used by the wives of the Bulgarian gardeners in Hungary, while the parents of the dancing girls in Budapest should be supported by the wages of the Bulgarian gardeners.

The Bulgarians always maintain that they have been thrown further into the Axis camp than was necessary owing to the bad commercial treatment given them by the United Kingdom. The case of Bulgarian bacon is always quoted. Bulgarian pigs are good. The Bulgarians tried to sell bacon to England, but were unable to do so, as it was not specially cured for the English taste ; but in a desperate effort to start some industries and to trade with the United Kingdom, the Bulgarians built a factory to cure bacon in the manner of Harris' best Wiltshire. They were encouraged by His Majesty's representatives in Sofia, and it was generally understood that a ready market would be found in England. But Baldwin negotiated the Ottawa Agreement almost at the same time the factory was finished. Dominions bacon was given large preferences, and an import tax was put on Bulgarian bacon so heavy that importation was altogether impracticable. This was discouraging to the Bulgarian would-be industrialists.

Meanwhile Schacht toured the Balkans making his famous exchange agreements, which at first were laughed at by all and sundry. There were stories of trainloads of aspirin and photographic equipment and binoculars, which no peasant country could possibly need. Mouth organs or anything Germany chose to supply was sent in exchange for food. The Government had to pay the peasants and was unable to sell the mouth-organs. But this method worked from the German point of view. Trade between Germany and Bulgaria increased from 22 per cent. in 1929 to 61 per cent. in 1936. Had we invested a few million pounds in buying up Bulgarian produce at a greater price than Germany, we could have prevented Germany obtaining the economic stranglehold on which she established her political footing. Professor Zagoroff, who was Minister of Commerce, and the Bulgarian Minister in London both worked very hard to increase the trade between Bulgaria and the United Kingdom.

Zagoroff was a disillusioned man when I last saw him in

Sofia. A highly cultured Bulgarian is rare, and one of liberal views who has been educated at the London School of Economics even rarer. Zagoroff was genuinely Anglophile and a statistician of no mean order. His annual book of statistics on Bulgaria always amused me by the details it gave of the numbers of suicides, what class of society they came from, their sex, and the time of the day the deed was done. One gathered that in Bulgaria few peasants ever committed suicide, whereas a considerable number of young men of intellectual pretensions between the ages of 15 and 25 did so between 5 o'clock and 8 on the morning after a bank holiday.

Zagoroff introduced me to other members of the Bulgarian Cabinet, who seemed as naturally pro-German as he was pro-English. He told me, " It is hopeless. I know I am fighting a losing battle, and I can get no real help from the English, who regard Bulgaria as very unimportant, whereas the Germans seem to think we are the most important country in the world. By the time your excellent Commercial Counsellor and Consul, Brenan, arrived it was far too late to do anything." The Bulgarians had been subjected to orgies of emotion about themselves, entirely unsupported by financial backing, when Sir Edward Boyle, Chairman of the Balkan Committee, paid his periodic visits to the country of his adoption.

Everyone knows how King Boris likes to have tea with his wife and children, like any other middle-class German ; how he loves to drive railway engines and catch butterflies in the palace garden. This outward simplicity hides a really shrewd, selfish and self-seeking man who is able enough to act a double part, politically speaking, without being found out, as in the case of many English people of simple habits who can easily get away with Machiavellian schemes.

When I first visited Sofia there was mud which turned to sand in summer on the road from the station, which is about two miles from the centre of the town, right to the square in which the royal palace is situated. Now everything is very paved and smart, but the King still lives in a hideous yellow villa formerly inhabited by the Turkish governor. The stones of the square in front of it are yellow too, and the best view of the snow-peaked mountains surrounding Sofia has been blotted out by the hideous structure built by the Germans for the National Bank.

Life in Bulgaria was cheap enough, but not nearly so cheap or pleasant as in Romania. The American Minister was Governor George Earle who, it was always suggested, was sent to Sofia to get him out of the United States because after being Governor of Pennsylvania he had developed Presidential ambitions. He was reputed to have inherited at least $40,000,000, and a certain shrewdness enabled him to hang on to his money. He was an amusing man and a friend of Roosevelt, but his fanatical anti-German ideas got him into much hot water and did the Allied cause no good, nor so far as I could make out, was he a great success as a Minister. His most confidential telegrams, copies of which he once showed me, were based on information picked up from journalists which must have arrived in New York at least two days after the stories had appeared in the London Press. It is difficult to understand the curious diplomatic passion for ciphering in general, but for such un-confidential stuff it is a waste of time and the taxpayers' money.

Governor Earle volunteered to resign his job as Minister and join the British Navy, but the President would not release him. His secretaries resented his undiplomatic habits, and the ladies of easy virtue in Sofia complained that he was mean. His hour came when he bribed the band at a night-club to play " Tipperary ". A German rushed up to him preparing to hit him hard over the head when the American Minister deftly picked up a bottle and knocked the German out. It made a front-page story for several days, especially as Earle, a little bit full of himself, knocked out two Germans when he got into the street and thought he saw a group of Storm Troopers ready to attack him. He quarrelled with the Bulgarian Government and with his own colleagues in Romania, especially the noted Germanophile, Major Ratay, but no one was strong enough to get him removed. I noticed when travelling through the country that even wayside shops in small Bulgarian villages

sold tins of the Pennsylvanian oil from which the Earle fortune
had originally sprung.

The Bulgarian army, which consisted of about twelve
divisions, was better trained than the Romanian. The soldiers
gave the impression of being a hardier people and their uniforms
of superior quality to the Romanian or Hungarian, whereas
only two divisions of the Romanian soldiers, which King Carol
kept in Bucharest as his special body-guard, were ever fully
dressed. The Bulgarians rather surprisingly seemed to possess
boots and tunics and caps all of khaki, rarely wearing odd bits
of peasant dress as substitutes for army clothes which had not
been supplied by the Government. From the summer of 1940
onwards the army was mostly stationed on or near the southern
Turkish and Greek frontier, and when fully mobilized there
were eight divisions in the south, two divisions on the Yugoslav
frontier, half a division along the Danube, one division in Sofia
and the remainder along the Black Sea coast. This should have
indicated, however much King Boris might, as he so frequently
did, proclaim Bulgaria's neutrality, that the danger in the eyes
of the Government came from the Turks and Greeks and not
from Germany, which was known to be penetrating Hungary
and Romania at an alarming rate.

Boris had his choice. He was shrewd enough to see, no
matter what he might say, that Germany intended to penetrate
through to the Straits. He knew that the Balkan mountains
were the line of defence against the Germans if they wanted to
take Constantinople. He had the opportunity of taking the
advice of the British Minister, which was hotly supported by
Governor Earle, and trying to bury the hatchet with the Turks
and form an alliance against German penetration. He would,
of course, have had the support of the Greeks, and he might
well have had that of the Yugoslavs. But he undoubtedly
calculated that the German army, which at that time could have
overrun at least the north of his country, occupying Sofia,
might well use Bulgaria as a battlefield and conquer the whole
of the country.

So Boris chose to remain a king with Hitler's blessing rather than risk losing his country and being an exile. Now he must do exactly as his masters in Berlin tell him, and so long as he does so and the population remains comparatively peaceful, he will be allowed to be king. Should the Germans suffer serious reverses in their war with Russia, or should the Germans begin to crack, the population of Bulgaria would quickly rise against the King and his masters.

The bourgeois population of Bulgaria, largely owing to the small amount of industry in the country, is only three per cent. of the total. The Bulgarian peasant is very conscious of his Slavonic race and his cousinship with the Russians ; since the time when Russia gave Bulgaria her independence there has been no doubt about his feelings. These feelings have been enhanced by expert Communist agitators, who easily penetrated the country, travelling by sea illegally from Russia, and by the reverence many of them feel for their own murdered peasant leader, Stambulisky, who though not a member of the Communist Party, was an agrarian of the extreme left. Political parties in Bulgaria are illegal, as in every other Balkan country, but it has been reliably estimated that at least ninety per cent. of the population are at heart agrarians whose natural sympathy, political as well as racial, is with Russia.

The Bulgarians have a brave fearlessness not found in their Romanian neighbours, though the latter are equally blood-thirsty. Soon after the German occupation there were peasant riots in the villages round Varna when the population saw quantities of grain and other foodstuffs being transported towards Germany. These riots are assumed to have been started by Russian agitators, as relations between Germany and Russia were at that time becoming really strained. It was difficult for journalists ever to believe that there was not some-thing wrong in the relations between these two Powers ; the wish was so much father to the thought that many stories were written on these lines through the spring and summer of 1940 whenever there was no ' hard ' news to send. While the Germans and the Russians were outwardly on cordial terms, a minor war in the Danube delta persisted from the date of the arrival of the

German Mission in Romania until the German occupation of Bulgaria.

This private war never received much publicity, owing to the fact that the leaders of the great world Press are completely uninterested in the names of little Danubian towns and villages. It was also impossible, owing to snow and ice, coupled with the great breakdown of the Romanian railway system and the utilization of what transport there was for the movements of German troops and supplies, for journalists to penetrate this little known area. The roads were impassable for motor traffic, many of the telephone lines were broken down, and the Danube was frozen so that even water transport was lacking. For this reason many of the villages in the delta were isolated for weeks on end.

Germany illegally dissolved the European commission which controlled the Lower Danube from Braila to the sea (she also dissolved the International commission controlling the upper waters of that river). This commission, having been set up afresh at the time of the 1919 peace treaty, had on it representatives of the Danubian States and of Great Britain and France. Germany's new commission brought in Russia, because the latter, after the occupation of Bessarabia, considered herself a Danubian Power and was, Germany thought, unlikely to take an active part; in any case she would keep out the Western Powers. Russia, however, was making a desperate effort to control the commission, bullying the representatives of the rump state of Romania. Germany could never agree to such Russian activity, as she thought it would renew Russian control of any supplies or warships entering the Danube. The illegal commission was unable to come to any conclusions and the meeting held in October was adjourned until January 15.

During this period Russia brought more and more troops to the frontier, and the British Consul-General from Galatz when driving along the Romanian side of the river Pruth noticed the building of fortifications. Villages near the frontier on the Russian side were evacuated. The Russians actually took several islands of the delta and at one time were preparing to land on Sulina. In fact, all the rich civilians left Sulina with the mayor and all the important members of the civil service. When they had been away from their native town for two or three days they found that the Russians had quite unaccountably landed only a few troops in Sulina and had rapidly taken them away again.

An almost daily sight was German planes flying over the frontier above Russian territory and Russian planes flying over the delta, where they constantly dropped bombs. I tried to get a story through the censorship, but it was not allowed, and was not of sufficient international value or interest at that time for me to risk being shot in an effort to get it out of the country illegally.

These bombs did no one any harm, but gave the Germans the idea—probably a true one—that the Russians aimed at slipping across the Danube delta and gradually occupying the quadrangle of land which lies between the Black Sea and the Danube over that part of its course where the river flows due north. This low-lying land, protected by the river, which is here at its widest and flanked by difficult marshes, is known as the Dobrudja. A strip at the southern end, approximately thirty miles in depth, which had been taken from Bulgaria after the second Balkan War (1913) had been returned by Romania after lengthy but peaceful negotiations in September 1940. The regaining of the Southern Dobrudja by the Bulgarians excited them far more than it grieved Romania. On the day that the Craiova agreement was signed it had very much second place in my news story from Bucharest. The Bulgarians were allowed to occupy the country along the Black Sea to the north of Varna and along the Danube up to and including the fortress of Silistria. They regained their identical frontier of 1912.

Negotiations between Romania and Bulgaria had been going on for so many weeks that the country had already been virtually evacuated. There was, however, one point of sentimental interest. Queen Marie of Romania's heart was buried in a golden casket at her favourite seaside resort of Balcic. This little graveyard was permanently guarded by Romanian soldiers.

14

Like a small chapel, which was built on a little peninsula here by King Carol, it is now Bulgarian territory. The Bulgarians rather generously offered that the graveyard might remain for ever Romanian soil; Queen Marie as an Englishwoman would probably have preferred that it be considered English, considering the odd way Romanians have behaved during the last year or two. The loss of the Dobrudja from Romania's point of view came after the great excitement which occurred with the loss of Bessarabia and at a time when Transylvania and the abdication were the real items of interest in Romania. The Bulgarians paid a small indemnity of just over 17,000,000 leva for the improvements which had been made in the territory since 1912.

With the Russians thrusting down to the Danube delta and the Bulgarians advancing their frontier to within a few miles of Constanza it may be clearly seen how nearly these two Slav countries were approaching one another, and how easy it would have been geographically, once the Danube had been crossed, for a strong Russian force to march down through the Dobrudja to Bulgaria. There were considerable numbers of Bulgarians scattered about that part of the Dobrudja which remained in Romanian hands, and the Russians possibly hoped that this would facilitate a push through into Bulgaria where, however much the Government might dislike them, the peasants would welcome them. Supported by troops and ammunition from Russia across the Black Sea, the Russians could easily have established themselves in Bulgaria had Germany been, as she was expected to be, heavily occupied with the invasion of England.

The invasion of England did not happen. Russia never saw her moment for occupying Bulgaria; (the Turks were naturally frightened of this, as they feared a common frontier with Russia far more than they feared the prospect of being surrounded by the Germans). Russian control of the straits remains a dream, but the stories written during the summer and autumn of 1940 about Russian and German troops piling up on their 1500-mile frontier have proved to be profoundly true.

The German garrison at Galatz, established nominally to evacuate Germans from Bessarabia, was the beginning of the end of the Russian dream of a common frontier with Bulgaria. The Russians were not materially put off by the Germans at Galatz; they built large gun emplacements and trained them on the Romanian town of Sulina. In these positions the guns controlled the whole Danube mouth. Russian ships landed large numbers of mysterious gentlemen at Varna, where they opened a large Russian Consulate employing about fifteen men who had really nothing to do except on the days when the ship from Odessa berthed there.

Skirmishes between Romanian and Russian troops took place weekly, and there was little doubt in the minds of the people there at the time that the Russian-German quarrel over the Danube delta was symptomatic of the major Balkan quarrel which was gradually ripening between these two countries. Russia placed battleships outside the mouth of the frozen Danube. There seems little doubt that it was to annul Russian pressure and Russian danger in this part of the world that Germany placed her striking force there. Had Russia ever been able to penetrate Bulgaria it is very likely that the peasants would have received the soldiers with open arms, whilst the Government and Court escaped to Germany as refugees. Russia had been sowing seeds to some extent in Yugoslavia, where from June 1940 onwards there was continual propaganda, and many peasants would certainly have preferred an occupation by a Slav race, even if they were Communists, than by a Nordic one.

Germany was not going to risk a stab in the back from any of the Slav countries, as she distrusted the Left Slav element in Yugoslavia, small though it was. The Germans, while the fighting in the Danubian delta was progressing, elaborated their plans for the peaceful penetration of Bulgaria. It would seem doubtful, again owing to an unusually heavy snowfall, which cut off most of the road transport and impeded telephones and telegraphs, whether the Russians knew of the elaborate and detailed steps which the Germans were taking, though one would have supposed that they might have guessed them.

At the beginning of January about eight hundred German troops a day were smuggled into Bulgaria, the Germans choosing the easy flat route by the Black Sea on which Russia had her eye. Half a division of German troops was stationed near Constanza, so that not much notice was taken when every night a train arrived with about eight hundred soldiers. I have stood at the station and seen them detrain in uniform. After detraining they went into the town of Constanza, had a drink and a meal, changed their clothes, and reappeared at the station in mufti three hours later, when they left for Bulgaria. The train went as far as the frontier at Negru Voda, where large numbers of lorries awaited them to take them by night to Bulgaria. These were the experts and technicians preparing the aerodromes, arranging for camping sites, for food, and generally marking out the land. Although I had myself seen the German soldiers in mufti getting into the train with their uniforms in their cases, any rumour that this was happening was hotly denied by both Bulgarians and Romanians.

I had, of course, long anticipated this German advance towards Bulgaria, which was clearly in the direct line of Hitler's drive to the south-east. As early as the summer of 1940 I felt that things would look interesting on the other side of the Danube, and so I paid a short visit to Bulgaria, crossing the Danube from Giurgiu to Rustchuk. The Danube itself looked like an inland German river ; there was an enormous amount of traffic and each barge flew the Swastika. The Germans had managed to obtain control of the port of Giurgiu by means of a Romanian decree which forbade people to go on to the riverside docks. Men who had worked there for thirty years were no longer allowed to enter. Giurgiu is famous only for the pipe line from the oil district of Ploesti which conducts the oil to the riverside barges.

On the Bulgarian side of the river German influence was just as strong, although this was never admitted. Even in June the three extremely bugridden hotels of Rustchuk were crammed with Germans, and I had difficulty in obtaining a room. All the shops were full of German products. There were rumours, some of which I believe were true, of German mechanics and technical experts, probably soldiers, being landed from barges in a backwater up the river from Rustchuk.  The cost of living in Bulgaria, as in Romania and Yugoslavia, was rising by leaps and bounds, and the paraphernalia of visas and certificates to say how much money one had brought into the country and how much one would take out again, was increasing.

As I only wanted to stay in this miserable town one night, I had considerable difficulty, there being no British consul present, in persuading them I was not a spy.  The Germans had built a huge new school, and German labour was supervising the building of a road outside the town and improving the docks on the side of the Danube.  Everyone said they did not like the Germans ; they looked on the Russians with no particular certainty, but at least they regarded them as their great Slav brothers who had helped them in the past.  They hated the Germans, but, like everyone else in that part of Europe, were so impressed by their efficiency and their overwhelming successes that they thought there was nothing else to do but follow the German line.

In Romania the sixteen German divisions spaced themselves out for the occupation which was made difficult only by the crossing of the Danube.  Pontoon bridges were built at Giurgiu and at two other places to the west.  The main body of troops was billeted at Craiova, Caracal and other villages between forty and eighty kilometres to the north of the Danube.  Except for those manning the anti-aircraft guns at Ghiurgiu and the pontoon workers, the number of soldiers stationed by the Danube was small.  The frontiers were well guarded ; the Germans built a line of fortifications from Galatz (where the river Pruth joins the Danube) to Focsani and on to the Carpathians.  Not only had they 60,000 in the arm of Romania to the north of this line of fortifications but they were also most carefully guarding the most precious of the oilfields against any sudden attack from the Russian frontier.

The plan was that at a given moment, when the bell was pushed in Berlin, after the snow had melted and the Danube thawed, the mechanized divisions stationed in these towns fifty kilometres or so to the north of the Danube should dash down and cross on the pontoons which the river station troops had set up, and thereafter occupy Bulgaria. The politically conscious, as well as those trained as military observers, could not get away from the very strong atmosphere created by vast numbers of German lorries and other mechanized equipment racing round the country. The Turkish Legations in Sofia and in Bucharest wrongly affirmed that when German troops reached the Bulgarian-Turkish frontier Turkey would fight.

## CHAPTER XII

## GREECE—CRUMBLING DICTATORSHIP

FROM the other Balkan capitals I followed closely the sad anti-climax that succeeded the brilliant Greek victories of the early part of the war. I had seen enough during my weeks in Greece to deduce what was likely to happen when the spring came, particularly if no means were found of stemming the German infiltration into Bulgaria. It was clear to me that with German troops lining the Thracian and Macedonian frontiers of Greece the latent Fifth Column elements, many of them so close to the core of the Fourth of August régime, would gather strength. Few of these were genuine sympathizers with the Nazi ideology—for the German mentality is almost as antipathetic to the modern as to the classical Greek outlook—but many professional men had been trained in Germany. Far more numerous than the German sympathizers were those who had a very natural awe of the German army and German military achievements. The Germans of course took the opportunity of showing their film " Victory in the West " to a carefully selected audience in Athens in February. Essentially, then, there was an active defeatist element playing on the war-weariness and awe of a considerably larger body.

This defeatism, to call it by its mildest name, began at the core of the Government. It was natural enough that it should. The Government was Fascist ; the Opposition was democratic. The Government had been involved in war against the Axis by force of circumstances, not by ideological conviction ; the Opposition was whole-heartedly devoted to England, though not perhaps the England represented by Lord Londonderry or Sir Horace Wilson. There was in fact plenty of admiration for England in every class of Greek society. It all depended *which* England.

Naturally one has every sympathy with the Government of a nation as small in population and military strength as Greece in its efforts to avoid a clash with the greatest military power in the world. But where one quarrelled with the Greek Government, apart from its deplorable internal policy, was in its unintelligent attachment to the 'non-provocation' fallacy. If only, the argument ran, we do nothing whatever to provoke Germany or Italy, if only we avoid not merely provocation but the very appearance of giving provocation, if only we refuse to recognize deliberate provocation directed against ourselves, if only we deny to our friends and allies the privileges and facilities they have a right to expect from us . . . why then, perhaps, we shall be left in peace, and asked for nothing further than some degree of economic collaboration.

So ran the argument. Obviously any line of policy which can spare a small nation the horrors of a Blitzkrieg deserves to be carefully studied, though it must be remembered that every nation which practises 'non-provocation' helps to facilitate the triumph of aggression in Europe. But, in point of fact 'non-provocation' simply does not work. The corpses of Norway and Holland—to name but two countries which consistently practised 'non-provocation'—are a witness to the consequences of this policy. The smaller nations have learnt, at what a cost it is needless to record, that they could no more afford to be 'non-provocative' than Britain and France could afford to be 'non-interventionist' in the Spanish war.

Metaxas himself, German-trained and German in his sympathies during the last war, cannot escape responsibility for fathering this policy. From the first he was obsessed by the fear that Germany would come down through the Balkans, where she was at that time engaged in the process of absorbing Romania, upon Greece. In this anticipation he was, as we now know, entirely correct, and those—and they were numerous and well-informed—who expected an attack upon Turkey in the spring proved mistaken.

Clearly the best way of preventing this was to allow the R.A.F. the use of air bases in northern Greece and to establish adequate military defensive positions. Actually, Metaxas consistently refused to allow the British the use of the air base at Salonika, because to do so would constitute provocation to

Germany. Work was begun on a big air base in the Thessalian plain to the north of Larissa. It was to take long-distance bombers capable of reaching the Ploesti oilfields. But an entirely inaccurate and misleading report was put about with regard to the scale of the base and the amount of labour being employed on it. Meanwhile Salonika had to pay for its lack of air defence with a series of savage raids. But the effects went far deeper, for the lack of any British air bases in Northern Greece certainly contributed to the German advance into Bulgaria in the early spring of the following year.

Another fault for which Metaxas must be held responsible was his inconsistent attitude with regard to the fortification of the Doiran-Ghevgeli gap. The map of Greece shows that the defence of Western Macedonia and Thrace presents peculiar difficulties in face of an attack from the direction of Bulgaria. The hinterland is narrow, communications are poor, and any attack down the Struma valley into Eastern Macedonia can easily cut off all the troops defending Thrace from any retreat by land. Realist strategy would dictate the abandonment of this whole area east of the Vardar, and, in fact, work on what was afterwards to be known as the Olympus Line was begun as early as November. But the Greek General Staff had shown a natural, if unstrategic, reluctance to leave these provinces unprotected against Bulgaria (as distinct from Germany) and had built a number of forts blocking the Struma entrance into Greece at Rupel and Nevrokop as well as the so-called Metaxas Line, really a very weak affair existing chiefly on paper, in defence of Kavalla and the coast.

But if Thrace was to be defended the danger of an attack cutting across the south-east corner of Yugoslavia and thence proceeding by the broad and easy Vardar valley to Salonika must be met, otherwise all the fortifications to the east would be turned. This gap is narrow at the Greek-Yugoslav frontier, extending from Ghevgeli, on the Salonika-Belgrade railway, to Lake Doiran. Adequate fortification here might be expected to hold up the Germans while British forces got into position on their advanced line on the Haliacmon.

In short, either the fortifications in Thrace and Eastern
Macedonia should have been abandoned or the Doiran gap
should have been fortified as well.  Metaxas did neither because
he believed or affected to believe that it would be a provocative
act towards Germany.  The result was that while divisions were
left in Thrace the Germans poured through the undefended gap
at Ghevgeli.  It took them just seventy-two hours from the
opening of the campaign to reach Salonika.

But far more serious was the political intransigence of the
Greek dictator.  Now, if ever, was the time for burying past
differences.  Metaxas could immeasurably have strengthened
his own position and immensely contributed to the Allied cause
had he made any attempt to widen the basis of his Cabinet by
taking in members of the Opposition.  The Venizelists had, in
the most patriotic spirit, declared themselves entirely behind
the policy of the Government.  Sophocles Venizelos, son of the
Liberal leader, had sent from America his adhesion to the foreign
policy of Metaxas.  But the opportunity was conspicuously
missed, and it was I think one of the gravest faults of the British
Minister that he failed to take advantage of the peculiarly
privileged position that Britain enjoyed in Athens, especially
during the first weeks of the ' honeymoon ' period, to insist—
as he had every right to insist—that in the interests of the more
effective prosecution of the war representatives of the Venizelist
party (always distinguished for its Anglophile sentiments)
should be included in a truly National Government.

But nothing of any significance was done.  A few exiled
leaders, such as Kafandaris, were allowed back to Athens on
condition they undertook to keep their mouths closed on all
political issues.  The more elderly of these exiles were allowed
the privilege of sitting dumbly in their homes in the capital ;
the younger were, in some cases, allowed to serve as privates
in the army.  This was the case with Canelopoulos, perhaps the
most distinguished mind among all the younger Greek politicians.  He offered his services to the Government in any
capacity.  The Government could find no better use for his
first-class brain than to send him to the front as a simple soldier.

Many were not so fortunate. About six hundred Venizelist officers, who had been under arrest or in exile for their part in the 1935 rising or for subsequent opposition to the régime, were refused re-admission to the army. They included at least three of the ablest Greek Generals—Protosyngelos and Theodore and Constantine Manettas. These three, and about a hundred others, being refused re-admission into their own army, applied to the British Military Attaché to serve in any capacity with the English forces. Whatever the views of the Military Attaché, and I believe he was favourably disposed, no action was taken to enable these men to serve with our troops.

These were no Fifth Columnists. Many of them had followed Venizelos when he established his Provisional Government at Salonika in 1916 on behalf of intervention in the last war. Their only crime had been their democratic sentiments which had led them to support the Revolution of 1935 or subsequently to fall under the disfavour of the dictatorship. To have received these back would not only have been a gesture of immense significance but would have reintroduced into the army a large proportion of its most technically experienced officers. Nothing was done, and here again the British Legation must take the blame for not having forced the Government to adopt a more conciliatory attitude. Pittsacus, the ablest of all the Greek Army Commanders, the victor of Koritza, had lodged a request that they should be recalled. He was refused. I understand that General Haywood was viewed with considerable disfavour in high quarters on the ground that he had received a deputation of these officers. Later, the Archbishop of Janina, a militant patriarch worthy to stand beside the heroes of the War of Independence, fell into disgrace for having urged the recall of these officers upon Korizis.

Not less harmful to the effectiveness of Greece's war effort was the suppression after the first week or two of the war of all inimical references to Fascism. At the beginning of the war, the relaxation of the Press censorship as regards hostile references to Italy naturally produced a spate of ' leaders ' in the Greek papers denouncing Mussolini, the Italian nation, etc., as well as frequent references to Adowa, Caporetto, Guadalajara and other

Italian feats of arms.  But it produced something else as well.
For the first time since 1936 the newspapers, under the guise
of attacking Italian Fascism, were able to indulge in attacks on
Fascism in general.  These only too closely interpreted the
feelings both of the bulk of the civil population and of the army
at the front.  I am convinced that the principal driving force
inspiring the Greek armies in the Italian war was the fact that
they felt themselves to be fighting against the type of régime
which had oppressed them during the last four years.  The
nearer one got to the front the less one heard about the glories
of the régime and the more about what the soldiers intended to
do with the leaders of the Fourth of August after they had
finished with the Italians.  " When we come back we are going
to fix those bastards."  " I'm keeping one shot in my revolver
for Manyadakis."  " Now they have given us arms they'll have
to take the consequences.  When the war is over we shall clean
out our own Fascists."

That was the spirit I found in my talks with soldiers at or
near the front.  One didn't find much enthusiasm for the glories
of the Fourth of August dictatorship ; while references to the
Neolaia and their heroic posturings, complete with band and
photographers, up and down the streets of Athens nearly made
them vomit.  I know of no better comment on the attitude of
the army to the régime than the story of the wounded soldier
and Metaxas.

The dictator, in the course of a visit to one of the hospitals
early in the war, stopped in his progress through one of the wards
to exchange a few words with one of the wounded soldiers.

" Where were you wounded, my man ? " he inquired.

" By the Italians, you mean ? " replied the soldier.

" Of course."

The soldier indicated his chest.

" That's where the Italian Fascists wounded me."  Then
rolling over suddenly in bed, he showed a back covered with
scars and weals.  " And that's where your bloody Secret Police
wounded me," he exclaimed.  " Get out, you old hypocrite ! "

The attitude of the great bulk of the Greek people and army

was of course symptomatic of the profound cleavage, which can be noted in every belligerent country, between those who see the war as yet another line-up between two groups of nation-states and those who see it as a struggle against the social and economic organization of society known as Fascism. The Greek soldiers in spirit were fighting the Fascist at home just as much as the Fascist abroad ; the Greek Government was fighting a fellow Fascist dictatorship because it had no alternative. That was the position.

Actually, the attitude of Metaxas over this issue became more rather than less intransigent. In mid-November in an address to the professors of Athens University he had spoken vaguely, but encouragingly, of cultural values and had even seemed to imply that he was not wholly unsympathetic to the idea of " cultural freedom ". But that was as far as he went. An inter-view given to the *Nike* (a ' yellow ' Greek weekly paper of the most vulgar and chauvinistic type), shortly before his death, gave great offence. In answer to the question, " To what do you attribute the remarkable victories of the Greek forces ? " Metaxas replied, " Entirely to the spirit of the Fourth of August ". It was not a reply calculated to endear the army or the nation to him. Except among the Neolaia and a small group around the dictator, the " spirit of the Fourth of August " was merely a joke, when it was not something much more painful.

The régime proved equally insensitive to public feeling in other respects. The réclame of the victories was entirely reserved for Metaxas himself and for the Commander-in-Chief, Papagos, a complete Metaxas ' Yes-man '. Papagos' military abilities were not of a high order ; he was, in fact, usually regarded in pre-war days as a mere carpet knight, a soldier who had risen by Court influence. It had been a standing joke in Athens before the war that the first step which was to be taken on the actual outbreak of hostilities was the transfer of Papagos, then Chief of the General Staff, to the post of aide-de-camp to the Crown Princess. This was, perhaps, scarcely fair. Judged by results, Papagos does not deserve to be put in the same cate-gory as Smigly-Rydz or Gamelin. But his merit lay chiefly in his ability to absorb and carry out the strategical concepts of the Premier, rather than in any evidence which he showed of original thinking. After the German occupation he remained behind in Athens and was among the first to be placed under arrest by the Germans. In this I thought he was unfortunate. I have no evidence of defeatism on his part, but I fancy he was overawed by the prospects of the German attack and not equal to the vigorous measures which might have kept the Greek army longer in the field.

No mention of other Generals was allowed in the Press. Pittsacus was the ablest of the lot. He was not a politician, either Royalist or Venizelist, and he was popular in the army. Neither of these qualifications did him any good, and at one time he was removed from his command ; but the feeling ran so strongly against this action that he was soon restored. The psychological ineptitude of Metaxas was further shown by his refusal to publish in the Press even the names of privates and junior officers decorated for conspicuous gallantry in the field— a serious failure to appreciate one of the elementary characteristics of the Greek nature. Even the King was kept studiously in the background. He was never a popular or spectacular figure in Greece, and it might have been assumed that Metaxas would make the most of the opportunity to build him up in the public eye as a Patriot-King. Nothing of the sort was done. Not once during the premiership of Metaxas did he visit the front. The first act of Metaxas' successor, Korizis, was to remedy this omission, and the King was despatched on a brief visit to the front. Actually, he never went further than Jannina, and this isolated attempt to make a popular figure of a hardworking but, as far as his own subjects were concerned, undoubtedly wooden monarch was not followed up.

Nor was adequate publicity given to the aid which Britain was bringing to Greece. Popular feeling, always Anglophile, was only too anxious to make the most of any evidence of British help. During the first weeks of the war the enthusiasm for Britain reached tremendous heights. The entry of a group of British airmen into a café or restaurant was again and again the signal for an outburst of spontaneous applause. Everywhere outside shops and restaurants one saw the legend " English Spoken " and a Union Jack displayed. Inside the restaurants the menus had frequently been translated into English, often of the quaintest and most pidgin variety. One proudly announced itself as " The Best Place for Good Eats ". Another confidently offered " Baconized Eggs " to its patrons. Most notable was the change on the kiosks. For months, owing to the lack of newspapers from England, they had of necessity displayed a large number of German and Italian papers. Now all these were swept away, not only the Italian, which was to be expected, but also the German. To cover their nakedness, copies of the English weeklies, months out of date, were displayed—*The Illustrated London News*, *The Sphere*, *Picture Post*. The German bi-weekly paper, *Athener Zeitung*, ceased publication after the outbreak of the Italian war. An English weekly had been started and was being eagerly bought by the large number of English-reading Athenian citizens. There had been some hitch in connection with the naming of the paper. The British Legation originally intended that it should be called *English News*. Nicoloudis, Minister of Press, though willing that the paper should be started, objected to this name. For some obscure reason, the word *English* in the title would be provocative to Germany. The Germans did not use the word *Deutsch* in their title, therefore the English must not be permitted to use the word ' English ' for their paper. The Legation acquiesced, and agreed upon the more innocuous title, *News of the Week*.

Nicoloudis was a queer fish. This fat, pompous, vain man was believed at one time to be among those members of the Cabinet who had anti-British leanings in spite of, or because of, the fact that his wife had been educated at Oxford. He was not taken very seriously in any quarter, so far as I know, being regarded as a mere windbag. On the first morning of the war, meeting *The Times* correspondent, Patrick Maitland, in the lobby of the Grande Bretagne Hotel (later the headquarters of the General Staff) while the welkin was being split outside

with the noise of practice alerts, he exclaimed with a snarl :
" So this is what your country has landed us in ! "  The remark
might have been dismissed as badinage, which in fact it was not
(Mavroudis, the Permanent Under-Secretary for Foreign Affairs,
was talking in much the same way), were it not for the fact that
it interpreted what some Greeks felt at the time, and many
more later on came to feel—that their country had somehow
become involved in " England's war " and would be left to her
fate by England.  That same morning Christopher Buckley of
the *Daily Telegraph*, a very typical-looking Englishman, tall and
fair, was surrounded outside the British Legation by a cheering
crowd, exclaiming,  " *Zito  Anglia !* "   " *Zito  Churchill !* "
(Long live England !  Long live Churchill !)  But through the
midst of this crowd one figure thrust his way to the English
journalist.  " Is your country going to help us ? " he exclaimed,
" or will she let us down as she has let down the others ? "

The doubts of the man in Loukianou Street were far more
justifiable than the accusation of the Minister in the Grande
Bretagne.  Poland, Norway, Holland, Belgium, France seemed
to tell only one tale, even if we omit Manchuria, Abyssinia,
Spain, Czechoslovakia—the invincibility of the Axis and the
absolutely reliable ineffectiveness of British aid whether diplomatic or military.  Why should Greece be any exception ?

Nicoloudis' complaint, on the other hand, represented what
I met so often—an apparent failure to grasp the very essence of
the war.  Even by people who were intelligent enough to have
known better, one found a strange resentment of the fact that
Britain, by being in a state of war with Germany, was producing
a disturbance on the Continent which threatened to involve the
small nations.  The same people who had blamed Britain,
correctly perhaps, for its refusal to risk war over Czechoslovakia
and other issues, were now equally critical because of the consequences when she *did* go to war with Germany.  Whether these
people really failed to realize that only British victory could save
them from becoming the vassals, economic as well as political,
of Germany, I doubt.  But they preferred to bury their ostrich-
like heads in the sands of wishful thinking.  Had they realized

that their best chance of security lay in coming in on the British side at the very beginning of the war there would not now be so many of them eating the bread of sorrow and drinking the water of affliction in London or Cairo.

Nicoloudis himself subsequently came down heavily on the British side, largely, I understand, because the extremely forceful lady who was his wife was anxious to be next Ambassadress in London. Like all the rest of the Cabinet, he was entirely dependent on the personality of the Prime Minister. When Metaxas died, the Ministers were like a ship's crew whose captain is drowned and who suddenly find themselves floundering about in the water, but, in the face of overwhelming catastrophe, continue to keep up their personal feuds and bickerings. On the morning of Metaxas' death, the British Press Attaché, David Wallace, called on Nicoloudis and was on the point of offering him formal condolences when the Minister burst into an uncontrollable fit of weeping. Rather impressed by this evidence of devotion to the dead leader Wallace waited patiently until the Ministerial blubbering began to subside. Nicoloudis then explained that his tears had been caused, at any rate in part, by the fear that his political career was at an end, as the new Premier, Korizis, whose appointment had just been announced, was a personal enemy. It was, in fact, rumoured for some days that Nicoloudis and two or three other Ministers were to be relieved of their posts, but neither the King nor the British Legation showed any desire for a change of personnel, and the opportunity of getting rid of a lot of dead wood, quite apart from potential defeatists, never recurred until the last days of the Greek campaign. It was unfortunate that the King saw fit at this time to publish a proclamation stating that the principles of the Fourth of August, which stank in the nostrils of the vast majority of his subjects, were to be continued under the new Premier.

When he learnt that he was not to be dismissed, Nicoloudis plucked up his spirits and sought to create the impression that he was the destined successor, the Elisha to Metaxas' Elijah. The method which he chose was astonishingly naïve. One

15

morning, about ten days after Metaxas' death, a singular article appeared in all the Athens newspapers, which of course were still under the control of Nicoloudis as Minister of Press. It stated that just a week before his death the late Prime Minister had called on Nicoloudis at the unusual hour of eight in the morning. Rushing into the Minister's bedroom he had (so it was stated) baldly announced that he was working upon the final stages of a new order of society for Greece and that Nicoloudis was to be his first confidant when the project was completed. The nature of this new order was discreetly left vague, as Nicoloudis obviously had not the remotest idea of what to say about it. This childish desire to assert himself as Greece's next Man of Destiny caused nothing but entertainment.

Nicoloudis in his handling of the Press never showed much desire to co-operate with the British, and no one at the British Legation saw fit to bully him as he should have been bullied. He rarely appeared before representatives of the foreign Press. One such occasion occurred in late November. All representatives of the Press were requested to attend the Minister at the highly inconvenient hour of noon, which was the time when the British correspondents normally filed their stories to their newspapers. Nicoloudis read a speech thanking the correspondents for their interest and sympathy which they had shown in the Greek struggle, but urging them to point out with all the evidence at their command that Greece needed great quantities of war material and that " she had practically no aircraft " and was therefore at a crippling disadvantage against the Italians. But this address most pointedly omitted any reference to the work which the heavily outnumbered squadrons of the R.A.F. were doing over the Albanian front, an omission which can hardly be regarded as other than a studied discourtesy.

This conference, though I took good care that my colleagues did not know it, was caused because I wrote a story begging that the British should send more aircraft to Greece. I mentioned the weakness of the small Greek air force. This was passed, not by the British censor (who, I regret to say, was not blessed with abundant grey matter) but by the senior British officer in

Greece, whose initialling the censor would have to accept against his own small-minded decision. But then the Greek political censor turned it down. I gathered that they did not want more British planes, in case it should prove provocative to Germany. It seemed to me that while the Greek nation was imploring that more help should be sent from England and America, the petty officials were too scared of their superiors to allow my story to leave the country. I made a fuss at the Ministry of Press, but they, like most organizations whose job it is to run anti-Axis propaganda, failed to see the value of the story. I took it to the British Legation and they acted immediately, making a great fuss, which resulted in Nicoloudis giving it to the whole Press.

Another example illustrating the uncooperative spirit of the Ministry of Press occurred in January when the British ran a large convoy containing great quantities of food, equipment and medical stores right through the Mediterranean to Athens. These goods were for the exclusive use of the Greeks, and great risks had been run by the convoy, which had been heavily attacked by Stukas from Sicily. A gesture of gratitude on the part of the Greek Government was, under the circumstances, reasonable and fitting. But the Government, either through the agency or with the acquiescence of the Minister of Press, banned all mention of this convoy in the daily papers long after its arrival and after repeated representations had been made by the British. Unfortunately small paragraphs were allowed to appear in obscure corners of the daily papers briefly referring to supplies which had been sent from England. It was explained to those who inquired the reason for this singular handling of the matter that to give greater prominence to the fact that Britain had sent supplies to Greece would be provocative to Germany. . . .

A great deal might have been done by the British Legation to compel the Greek Government to show a more co-operative spirit, but I could not feel that Sir Michael Palairet was the man to apply the necessary push. Sir Michael has many good qualities—a devout Catholic, like so many of our diplomats, an exemplary husband and father, he had all the domestic virtues. I personally always found him courteous and sympathetic. Sir Michael is every inch a gentleman : that is what is wrong with him. The situation demanded someone with more of a 'rough-neck' quality about him, someone who knew how to hector and bully. There were those who said, unkindly, that Sir Michael and Lady Palairet had wandered out of the pages of Evelyn Waugh's *Black Mischief* and were trying to find their way back. Anyhow, he failed dismally to cope with two of the major issues during these months—the task of keeping the Greeks free from Fifth Columnism and an anti-British trend and the task of compelling the Government to secure real national unity by broadening its own basis so as to make itself truly representative of the nation and by recalling to the services those elements whose patriotism was unquestioned and who would by their qualities have greatly strengthened the fighting forces of the country.

Sir Michael had the game in his hands, had he seen fit to adopt a more forceful line. Greece was like a girl who needed raping, but Sir Michael, alas ! was no raper. Though Greece was at war with Germany's partner, Italy, the German Legation remained in Athens, where it proved of immense value to its ally in transmitting information. Any intelligent observer foresaw that if the Italians could resist in Albania until the spring, the Germans would, in their own time, come down through Bulgaria to attack Greece. But nothing was done to forestall this, and Germany was allowed to choose her own time for an attack which was almost certainly inevitable from the moment the Italians began to retreat from the Pindus. The non-provocation fallacy was dished up for Sir Michael, and he swallowed it.

Again, one need not be a partisan in Greek politics to realize how much the inclusion of the Opposition in a National Government would have united the nation and strengthened its determination to fight to the end. Twice at least the opportunity occurred—on October 28, when Italy declared war, and at the end of January, on the occasion of the death of Metaxas—and twice it was let slip. A little judicious pressure, bullying if necessary, and Greece might have had a Government which would have enabled the people to feel that they were fighting in a truly democratic cause instead of for the maintenance of an internal tyranny which took its tone from Berchtesgaden rather than Westminster. It was impossible to feel that Sir Michael was very closely in touch with the Greek people, or at any rate with that not inconsiderable proportion of it which had not been educated at Eton and Oxford. The Legation did not cast the net of its invitations widely, and it was believed, perhaps unfairly, that the Minister spent an undue proportion of his time cultivating his garden and the domestic virtues in the rural retirement of Kephissia. Nor could his devout and regular practice of the Catholic religion be expected, as such, to make any particular appeal to a nation virtually one hundred per cent. Orthodox in faith.

I am very conscious that in these pages I may seem unduly critical of the various Ministers who represented my country in the Balkans. This is not due to any desire to be clever at their expense. But one can only write as one feels, and I am convinced that one of the causes, perhaps only a subsidiary cause, but certainly a cause of the loss of the Balkans, was the failure of British Legations in general to grasp the real essence of the struggle. In no country that I visited did I have any feeling that the British Legation possessed the initiative in relation to its German vis-à-vis. One saw extremely few evidences of any thinking ahead or far-sighted constructive diplomacy. There were several able First Secretaries, but ability seems seldom to survive appointment to the post of Minister. To discuss adequately the reasons for this would require another book. But I am convinced that there is no informed or unbiassed foreign correspondent who does not share my feelings.

But perhaps the worst fault which I found with British policy in Athens related to propaganda. The soil was so good, the population was so pathetically anxious to hear and accept the British point of view. To the vast majority of Greeks Britain was fighting for the overthrow of régimes such as that by which they were being ruled, and they may be forgiven if they showed themselves frankly puzzled and worried at the inconsistencies of the British attitude with regard to dictatorship.

There was a magnificent opportunity for constructive propaganda in Greece, but the hungry sheep looked up and most emphatically were not fed. There was a Director of Publicity in Athens. He had been for some years Director of the British School of Archæology. He had translated the epigrams of Callimachus. He was justly proud of his singing voice. He had an unrivalled knowledge of the works of Mr. P. C. Wodehouse. He was reputed to play a pretty game of patience. It is not easy to discover which of these qualifications caused him to be selected to direct British publicity, the more so as very early in the war he was heard to give expression to the sentiment that British propaganda was unnecessary in Greece as the Greeks were on our side anyway. An intense dislike of journalists and the journalistic profession and a retiring, almost monastic, nature hardly contributed to the effectiveness of his propaganda. The Press office suffered from a sort of publicational constipation. A great deal went in. Very little came out. A large amount of books and pamphlets of high propaganda value were either allowed to remain on the shelves of the Publicity Office, sent out for sale to the kiosks at their full English price, or sold for pulping. The daily news bulletin and commentary which constituted one of the very few forms of active propaganda was, by agreement with the Greek Government, available only for British subjects. Even so, the Director stated that it was his deliberate policy that the issue of this bulletin should be limited to 150 copies daily. This purely arbitrary figure was afterwards exceeded, and the number was gradually pushed up to nearly 500. But the Director of Publicity stated with conscious pride that he made a principle of opposing every request for copies of this bulletin. Such was the Mad Hatter's Tea Party atmosphere prevailing in the management of publicity that the receipt of this one poor shred of positive propaganda was treated as a privilege only to be granted after long argument, prayer and fasting. It was actually necessary for zealous subordinates who wished to increase its circulation to resort to the most lengthy process of cajolery or subterfuge.

Another British propaganda organ of which not the best use was made was the British Council. I have observed the work of this organization in every part of the Balkans, and I do not feel that the execution is worthy of the original conception. The idea is so sound—the spreading of the knowledge of the English language and culture and English standards and values ; but in practice it has not worked very well. In Athens there was a large and flourishing Institute, as also in some other parts of Greece. Some of the teachers were excellent—real live wires—but the chief qualification of many others to spread the "glories of our blood and state" appeared to lie in a high-pitched querulous voice, mincing manners and specialized tastes. Such young men, and there were too many of them throughout the Balkans, did more harm than good. The work they could have done would have been as useful as many jobs for which men are put into uniform, and it was, I think, a pity that it was not practicable to do this, as the spectacle of so many young men of military age in the cafés and restaurants of Athens was not helpful to the Greek appreciation of our war effort. Many of these youths were still in the undergraduate stage of development and their unformed minds were certainly not fit for the responsibilities which they were called on to assume. It would have been better to have sent out older men, but these would scarcely have come for the salaries which the British Council was in a position to pay. It is not easy to think of an ideal solution, but I am sure that the selection of young men for these posts has sometimes been anything but fortunate.

About a month after the outbreak of the war (throughout this chapter, "the outbreak of war" refers to the Greco-Italian War, unless specifically stated otherwise) the Greek Government decreed the closing of all foreign schools and institutes. This hit the British most hardly, as their Institutes were the largest and most flourishing. Three ostensible reasons were given for this odd and unfriendly step. It was said that the gathering of large bodies of persons in public buildings unprovided with adequate shelters was undesirable in view of the possibility of large scale air raids. These air raids on Athens never occurred, nor were they very likely to occur. Secondly, the closure was justified on the ground that as the elementary schools had all been closed since the outbreak of the war it was invidious that the Institutes, which were largely attended by the well-to-do, should be kept open. This rather artificial argument ignores the very special value of the English Institute as a vehicle stimulating Anglo-Greek friendship and understanding. Thirdly, the closure of the English Institute was held to be necessary in order to permit the Greeks to take a similar step with regard to the German. The English Institute in Athens had some four or five thousand students enrolled on its books; the German had barely as many hundred. Yet to close the latter without closing the former would have been considered provocative to Germany. So the principal channel of Anglo-Greek cultural contact was closed; and Sir Michael Palairet concurred.

Throughout the winter I followed day by day the slowing down of the momentum of the Greek offensive. At the beginning of December the Italians were really on the run, within a few days Koritza, Premeti, Argyrocastro, Santi Quaranta and Pogradetz had fallen, and the whole of the first defensive position of the Italians with its good lateral road had gone. This road was now available for the Greeks to transfer troops or supplies from one part of the front to another. The Italians fell back to the extremely formidable position formed by the gorge of the Aous between Tepelini and Klisoura and to Chimara on the coast.

Much was written in praise of Greek strategy during the early months of the war. The initial policy of keeping to the mountains, avoiding descent into the plains where the Italians with their greatly superior mechanization would be at a decided advantage, had served the Greeks particularly well in the early stages, particularly in the fighting leading up to the capture of Koritza. Equally effective on that occasion had been the method by which the Greeks avoided the actual entry into the town until it had been made completely untenable for the Italians.

But this cautious strategy, justifiable at the start, had less to recommend it when the Greeks were so definitely in the ascendant and should have been pushing their advantage home. Everyone knew that it was a race against time and that the weather, which would soon make the roads impassable, was the real enemy. Nothing else at that stage could have checked the Italian flight. Metaxas knew this, and knew that the only hope of decisive victory was to attain the Skumbi, the river which divides Southern from Northern Albania, by Christmas. At the northern end of the front the Greeks were working their way along the western shore of Lake Okhrida while their patrols on at least one occasion penetrated practically to the outskirts of Elbasan. In the centre their advance was directed towards Berat, while on the southern sector Valona, the second port of Albania, was the objective.

The original Greek strategy at this point aimed at an enveloping movement in the north. If the Greek forces could reach Elbasan over the mountains the road was open for an advance down the Skumbi to the sea, pinning the Italian forces in a Sedan between the mouth of the Skumbi, Berat and Chimara. I don't know when the hope of this really faded, but it was almost certainly before the end of December. Meanwhile the advance continued in the south. The cautious nature of Greek strategy at this time is exemplified by the criminal sluggishness of General Demestichas in failing to follow up the Italian retreat. An interval of four days was allowed to elapse between the evacuation of Argyrocastro and the entry of the Greek troops, during which period the Italians, after having abandoned the town in the utmost disorder, were able to return and fetch away all their stores and munitions. Demestichas was one of the many Generals who owed his position to Court and political services rather than to military merit. If not actually pro-German he was generally regarded as defeatist.

Even as early as December signs of defeatism, born of the disastrous fear of antagonizing Germany, which was certain to consider herself antagonized as soon as it suited her policy and as soon as her troop concentrations were ready, were apparent. There is an ugly story, on which I have no absolute check but

which I received from an excellent and patriotic source, which
I give for what it is worth.

About this time, when it seemed to many skilled observers
that nothing could stem the precipitate Italian retreat, the
German Minister in Athens handed a note to Metaxas. It
stated that Germany had no designs upon Greece, that she
regarded the Greek-Italian war as unconnected with the main
issue between Germany and Britain, and that she would not
intervene unless the Greeks took possession of Valona and
allowed the British to use it as a naval base. Metaxas gave
orders for the slowing-down of the advance.

Such is the story. The source from which I received it is
unusually reliable, and in military circles I have heard disappoint-
ment expressed that the Greeks did not pursue their advance
along the coast more speedily during the second half of December.
The weather by this time made serious operations in the northern
sector impossible. In the centre the Greek forces were held up
by the excessively strong Tepelini-Klisoura position, but in
the south the coastal road presented no such difficulties, either
natural or artificial, particularly as the Greeks had taken Porto
Palermo and Himara, where the main Italian stand had been
expected, before Christmas.

That was almost the end of the Greek advance. A final
and rather costly offensive in mid-January took Klissoura, but
after that the impetus of the Greek attack died down in sleet
and snow on the bleak heights of Albania. The troops had
suffered very severely indeed from frostbite, which was neither
early recognized nor adequately treated, and their losses during
the later months of the war were probably at a higher rate than
during the first few weeks when they chased the Italians back
from the Pindus deep into Albania. Tepelini became to the
Greeks what Krithia and Achi Baba were to our troops in the
Gallipoli campaign during the last war—always seeming on the
point of capture, never actually attained. Fires were observed
in the little town from time to time, Greek patrols were continually in and out of the place and Greek officers returning to
Athens assured their hearers that with the first three days of

fine spring weather Tepelini would fall and the victorious advance be continued. In fact, it was the Italians who took the offensive and, under a new Commander-in-Chief, Caballero, launched attack after attack upon the Greek positions. These assaults were on a considerable scale, and in the light of the collapse which followed later on the Greek front it is important to remember that at this time the Greek army was still fighting with extreme courage and tenacity and was showing itself as effective in defence as it had already done in attack. It was Italy's last attempt to pull her own chestnuts out of the fire before the senior partner in the Axis came in to take control of the situation. But the position was growing serious for Greece. She had neither the men nor the resources for a long war. After the first Italian defeats there had been high hopes of driving the enemy back behind the Skumbi before the winter set in, which would have given a strong defensive position against any subsequent offensive and would have given the British Fleet a base in the Adriatic.

Could it have been achieved? It will remain one of the great 'Ifs' of the war. If Mussolini had chosen to attack on September 28 rather than October 28, if the British had been in a position to throw into the air squadrons afterwards used in the African offensive, if Metaxas had been willing to place the Salonika base at their disposal, if the Greek Generals had shown more enterprise, if the armament of the Greek troops had been more adequate at the beginning of the campaign (as it should have been after four years of a dictatorship which claimed to have substituted Power for Liberty as the guiding principle of Government). . . . Metaxas must bear a heavy responsibility for the failure of Greece to push home her advantage during the fateful month of December.

The dictator died on January 29, after an illness of about a fortnight's duration, so well concealed that many pressmen did not know of it until two or three days before, and some members of the British Legation until the night before. If ever a man was *felix opportunitate mortis* it was he. This totalitarian General, who almost throughout his career had been regarded with mistrust by the vast majority of his fellow-countrymen and whose four years' premiership had probably brought him more unpopularity than any other Prime Minister in the history of modern Greece, died amidst an atmosphere of adulation, some of which was quite sincere. Many good, simple people were naïve enough to believe him a genuine supporter of democracy, an enemy of Fascism, which in fact he had been driven to fight by force of circumstances. Evidence that his views had in any way changed was singularly lacking, though many people who should have been less simple took faith from an address which he delivered to the University of Athens, about a fortnight after the outbreak of the war with Italy, in which he spoke in extremely vague terms of the importance of cultural values.

The British Legation would undoubtedly have liked the King to come forward at this moment and proclaim himself dictator, in spite of the constitutional difficulties involved by the combination of the two offices which would tie up the throne with the success or failure of the policy pursued by the Government. They were certain of his attitude with regard to the war and knew that he could be relied upon to stand to the end with the English. This was true enough. They believed also, however, that he represented the best hope of uniting the country, which was not so true. Those English who moved only in Legation circles never realized how bitter was the feeling against him. Broadly speaking one found that English democrats in Greece were more inclined to make allowances for the King, Greek democrats for Metaxas. The English could not forget his genuinely Anglophile sentiments and his apparent unobtrusiveness—always a quality that endears sovereigns to the English. Metaxas, on the other hand, appeared to the English of the Left the very incarnation of ruthless Totalitarian dictatorship ; that he was an able General and, according to his lights, a patriot interested them less. The very lack of an obviously adequate successor to Metaxas is a condemnation of his methods. The policy which banished or suppressed so many who should have been the natural leaders of the next political generation, and filled his Cabinet with an efficient chief of police and a number of ciphers and sycophants, hardly made for the training of statesmen.

Given the combination of the reluctance of the King to call in the Venizelists and the reluctance of the British to press him, Korizis was perhaps about the best choice that could have been made. He was an honest man, and probably loyaller and more sincere in his co-operation with the British than Metaxas had been, and some of the measures he adopted as soon as he became Premier were to his credit ; for instance, the attempt to build up the King with the army by sending him off to visit the front was a step which should have been taken much earlier. He cut down the budget of the Neolaia, removed their chief from office and instituted an examination of their accounts. But he was not dynamic, and the crisis ahead demanded someone with the gift of leadership on the grand scale.

The shadows were falling on Greece through March when the German troops were pouring down through the Bulgarian passes to the Greek and Turkish frontiers. Every week the centre of interest shifted further from the Albanian front to the political couloirs. About this time, *The Times* Balkan correspondent, afterwards captured by the Italians in Yugoslavia with the British Legation, submitted a memorandum dealing with the dangers of Fifth Columnism on the part of the régime. It was a moderate and well-reasoned document, and on the whole a very fair interpretation of the position. Everyone who had followed the developments of the past months knew perfectly well that Fifth Columnism, silent during the weeks of victory, was still latent in certain small but powerful sections of the nation. The British Minister, Sir Michael Palairet, however, chose to treat this memorandum, which Maitland had requested should be forwarded to his paper through the diplomatic bag, as a personal attack upon himself. He appears to have been convinced, as certain members of the Legation undoubtedly were, that " there was no Fifth Columnism in Greece ". He was with some difficulty restrained from recommending *The Times* to replace Maitland as their Balkan correspondent. In any case this honest and sincere statement of opinion, with which a number of representative English and Americans to whom it was shown were in substantial agreement, earned the unfortunate Patrick, to put it mildly, a black mark at the Legation.

It is no pleasure to me continually to criticize the handling of British policy by our Legations in the Balkans, as I do rather frequently in these pages. I regret it in the case of Athens because both the Minister and the First Secretary showed me great personal kindness. But if there be any lesson at all to be deduced from this book it is that the handling of the diplomatic issues which arose in the Balkans was far too often singularly unskilful, not to say amateurish, and that the old style of diplomat, who for the most part occupied the post of Minister in the various capitals, again and again proved quite inadequate. It is surely no accident that the two most successful Ambassadors we have had in recent years, Sir Stafford Cripps and Lord Lothian, were neither of them trained diplomats. One is placed in a peculiarly difficult position if one wishes to criticize the conduct of British diplomacy. If one is, as I have been, in the habit of being entertained at Legations, then one is accused of showing base ingratitude, biting the hand that fed one, etc. If, on the other hand, one is not as a rule received in this way, then it is simply a case of sour grapes. So either way one is wrong.

There are three main reasons for the growth of a defeatist spirit in Greece during the early months of 1941. The first was simply war - weariness. The country was approaching exhaustion as the result of a winter of war. There was less and less variety of food available. Retail prices had not as a rule risen so much as might have been expected owing to Government control, but the food simply could not be obtained, partly owing to lack of labour, partly owing to transport difficulties. In short, Greece had not been able to effect the change over from a peace to a wartime economy.

Secondly, there was the strange delusion found among so many Greeks (and among citizens of so many other neutral States which had been attacked by Germany or Italy) that their country had in some way been involved in " England's war ", that enough had now been done for honour, and that to continue would bring about the destruction of the country. This view was found among certain Ministers, and, more widely, in the highest ranks of the army. Defeatist Generals proved even more disastrous to Greece than defeatist Ministers.

But the chief reason was the very comprehensible awe of the military efficiency of the German war machine. France had packed up in a month, and what could Greece, which had been fighting for five months, do under the circumstances? She might make some sort of resistance with heavy loss and destruction of the property and resources of the nation, but surely it would be better to " call it a day " and throw one's hand in.

The sort of defeatism which set in was, as always, most marked at the top, and probably most of all on the general staff. But in the country as a whole the prevailing sentiment, when it was known that the Germans would be against Greece, was that Greece could no longer fight for victory but would retain her honour. Mr. Eden arrived, fresh from his much-advertised talks with the Turkish Government, and received a welcome no less warm than in Turkey. But there was little optimism in British circles at the beginning of his visit. There were some who felt that the venture of sending troops to Greece was in itself a mistake, and others who were conscious of the inadequacy of the force that was to be sent.

The question had risen acutely during Wavell's visit to Athens in January, when there had been a sharp difference of opinion with regard to the proposed expedition. Metaxas wanted an army of half a million men, a request which he afterwards modified to 300,000. Anything less, he held, would merely be a bait and an invitation to Germany to descend on Salonika. Wavell knew that under no circumstances would he have anything like that number of troops available for the expedition, but he had faith in the Olympus line, and he hoped that it would be possible to fight a delaying action which might yield strategical results justifying the tactical defeat which must almost certainly occur if Germany descended on Greece in force. I have far too much respect for Wavell's capacity as a General to suppose that he seriously thought the Olympus line to be impregnable, as was freely maintained in Athens at the time. Wavell, as Commander-in-Chief in the Middle East, had to see the campaign as a whole, and take decisions which appeared on the face either rash or half-measures with a view to obtaining long-term results. Metaxas, seeing the campaign solely from the point of view of Greece, was naturally bound to stress the danger of a small British force serving merely as a bait to the Germans. German Intelligence, incidentally, got quickly on to the story of the dissensions, and publicized a highly coloured account of the final meeting, ending with Metaxas (who died very shortly after) staggering out of the room with his hand to his heart, exclaiming, " This day Greece is lost ! "

There were those in Athens at the time, both Greek and British, who were inclined to feel that the whole venture of the expedition to Greece was one which should not have been undertaken in view of the very limited forces which General Wavell and Air-Marshal Longmore had at their disposal. Greeks argued that the effect would merely be more surely to attract the Germans—the non-provocation theory in modified form. British argued either that Turkey was in fact the real objective of Germany's *Drang nach Osten* and Greece a mere blind alley or, more frequently, that, taking the long view, the Greek expedition could not be justified strategically, that Wavell simply could not afford to dissipate his resources in gestures however chivalrous, however politically attractive. The theory held by this school was that, having the Italians so completely on the run in Libya, it was important at all costs to complete the conquest of that province, and that even if that proved impracticable for technical reasons, it was more important to keep the army of the Middle East in being than to endeavour to hold what palpably could not be held. Whatever force we put into Greece, Germany with her immensely greater *immediate* resources and with the advantage of interior lines could certainly throw in a decisively larger body.

The most consistent exponent of this view was Dennic, the

Yugoslav Press Attaché, certainly the most influential figure at the Yugoslav Legation in Athens. A good democrat and a convinced friend of England, he believed firmly in the certainty of British victory, but believed also that the only way in which we could overplay Germany was by ' feeding ' her army with victories. No army, he maintained, could stand against the Reichswehr. Therefore let them spread across the Continent until they reached the sea on every side. Let them conquer the Spanish Peninsula and the Balkans, let them spread over Asiatic Turkey. Their difficulties would increase the further they extended. They could not attack Turkey in safety with an unconquered and potentially hostile Russia lying on their flank. Therefore they would be driven to attack Russia. Many found this reasoning somewhat naïve at the time, and regarded the forecast of a Russo-German split as the wishful thinking characteristic of the Serbs in relation to Russia. Personally I do not think that this view makes enough allowance for the moral factor. How would Europe, and still more America, have reacted to these super-Fabian tactics which appeared to consist in the abandonment of positions, both moral and strategic, without raising a hand to defend them ? Nor, I think, does it take sufficient account of the effect of our probable loss of the whole Middle Eastern position subsequent to a German drive across Turkey and the swing-over of Syria, Irak and Iran to Germany. Nor can one view lightly the effect on the Battle of the Atlantic of the probable conversion of the Spanish and Portuguese western ports into bases for Germany.

However, these views were held only by a few, and those few diminished notably when Eden and Dill arrived at the beginning of March. In the critical talks the Greek General Staff were ' swung ' to a great extent by the influence of the King, also perhaps by the belief that having gone so far with Britain it was a moral and technical impossibility to withdraw. Yet throughout the period there seemed always something a little amateurish, not to say naïvely ostentatious, about the British moves. One felt that Eden's decorous journeying from Cairo to Ankara, and from Ankara to Athens, had somehow the

16

smack of the old diplomacy. It was picturesque, it impressed, and yet somehow it seemed remote from reality. It seemed to belong to the age of Castlereagh and Talleyrand rather than that of Ribbentrop and Molotov. Those communiqués stating that all was well, that complete unanimity of view existed between the two Governments, whether they referred to Britain and Turkey or to Britain and Greece, had we not heard something of the sort before ? One was reminded of the days when strong-man Daladier was Premier and honest Georges Bonnet at the Quai d'Orsay, and of a wet and gusty week-end between Bad Godesberg and Munich.

Anyhow Greece was committed after the Athens talks. The balloon went up in Athens about ten days later with the publication of "An Open Letter to Herr Hitler" by George Vlachos, editor of the *Kathimerini*, one of the three leading morning newspapers, Royalist by tradition but of late soundly pro-British. Vlachos had been tipped off by the Government and his letter therefore had a quasi-official significance. In tone it was still conciliatory, but its intent was clear. If Greece were attacked by Germany she would fight, there could be no question of sending away the British (a solution which had been whispered in Germanophile circles), and Greece, which had given an example to the world of how to live, would now give an example of how to die.

The release of this letter in a Press so rigidly muzzled and forbidden to publish anything directly or indirectly against Germany marked the fact that Greece had burned her bridges. Her position was now defined. It was no good sign that three army commanders had to be removed from their posts at this time for more or less unconcealed defeatism. But their action in asking for their retirement was at any rate more honest than that of some who stayed on to the detriment of their country. About the same time a group of Ministers were sent up to Thrace for a speech-making tour, presumably to stiffen civilian morale. The Ministers chosen included some of those least distinguished for Anglophile sentiments, and the purpose behind their selection remains obscure.

Meanwhile the bare three or four divisions which Wavell was able to spare were beginning to arrive. Their presence was, of course, perfectly well known to the Germans, for Greece was not at war with Germany and the German Legation still remained in Athens, but it could not be mentioned in the Greek or in the British Press. The whole world knew they were there and speculated on the number. It was perhaps fortunate for the peace of mind of the population of Athens, whether Greek or British, that such wildly inaccurate estimates of the actual strength of the Expeditionary Force prevailed. The estimates of serious observers who should have known better varied from 100,000 to over a quarter of a million. No one was more accurately informed than the German Legation.

With the coming of British and Dominion troops Athens became a decidedly gayer place at night though, in pursuance of the policy of the Greek Chief of Police, no Greek girl might associate with British soldiers or airmen, and any who did so were liable to arrest and cross-examination. Nevertheless, the arrival of the troops certainly acted like an injection upon the Greeks. At this time, too, we were sending a good deal of food into Greece, and the arrival of a large convoy of frozen meat for the use of the civilian population helped a good deal. It is astonishing how little one notices the decline in the quantity and quality of food if only it is progressive rather than sudden, and lets one down gradually. Even a year earlier there had been only two meat days a week. Now there was only one, and the meat obtainable was as a rule of the poorest quality. Greek cooks were quite skilful in producing various sorts of dish out of liver, brains and offal, which could be eaten with reasonable safety if not with positive pleasure. The supply of most vegetables was erratic. Coffee was at times unobtainable, and in the later months was ground almost exclusively from acorns. Rather surprisingly, fish was the most difficult food of all to obtain, this being due to the large number of fishermen called up. The sugar ration was small, and it was strange that the big cafés like Zonar and Floca were permitted to sell a profusion of cream cakes to the very last. This contrasted rather painfully with the long food queues which one could not fail to see in the poorer parts of Athens at any time during the winter. Those well enough off fared adequately, as eggs, which had been unobtainable just after Christmas, were available during the later months and one could always get most of the constituents which go to make up *hors d'œuvres*. Bread was of a very poor brownish-grey quality, and travellers from Athens subsequently arriving in Egypt fell with gusto on the beef-steaks and white bread of Alexandria and Cairo.

Greece knew her number was up. There was a welling up of enthusiasm at the time of the Yugoslav *coup d'état*. One could see again the same spontaneous enthusiasm which had been so marked during the early days of the war—complete strangers grasping one another's hands and telling one another that now all would be well. I don't quite know what everyone expected from it—a dozen divisions in southern Yugoslavia near the Strumnitza gap, perhaps. I think it was more generally believed than not that Hitler would pause to re-shape his plan and that there might be a further and more subtle attempt to lever Yugoslavia into the Axis. A British diplomat, arriving in Athens from Belgrade about 3 o'clock on the morning of April 6, expressed to a colleague of mine the view that no immediate attack seemed likely. The colleague agreed. An hour or two later the bombardment of Belgrade had begun.

That Sunday was rather tragically reminiscent of October 28, when the Italian attack was launched. In brilliant sunshine crowds surged round the British Legation carrying banners, just as they had done on the previous occasion. There were even larger crowds outside the American Legation, which is next door to the German, crying, " Zito Roosevelt ! " There was very little actually hostile demonstration against the Germans. One of the ironies of the war was the fact that the German Minister, disdaining the various means of transport that were put at his disposal, obstinately refused to depart from Athens. One route passed through a military area ; the ship that was to take him and his staff to Turkey failed to satisfy his requirements.

It was of course a gross breach of diplomatic privilege, and we should certainly have been justified in arresting him, as rumour had it that we had done. As it was, he stayed on in Athens, taking advantage of the private wireless transmitting set without which no German Legation is complete.

## CHAPTER XIII

## YUGOSLAVIA—THIRTEENTH-HOUR REPENTANCE

THE announcement that Yugoslavia, or rather its Prime Minister and Foreign Minister, had signed a treaty of adherence to the Axis came as no surprise to observers. It represented the culmination of a long period during which the Regent and his two successive Prime Ministers, Stoyadinovič and Cvetkovič, had moved closer and closer towards 'collaboration'. Partly this was the result of sheer timorousness; partly it represented a stealthy and quite conscious movement towards the Axis. The same combination of timorousness and treachery was apparent in the rulers of every European Power, great or small. What happened on March 25 was Yugoslavia's own particular Munich, and before we blame the nation for allowing its Government to drift under the bows of the Axis pirate ship, flying so ostentatiously its skull and crooked cross, we should pay a tribute to the spirit and political awareness of the people who so promptly and vigorously rejected it. It took England nearly two years after Munich to get rid of Chamberlain, and even then there was much talk—one has only to re-read his obituary notices to realize how much—of this narrow, selfish, cold-blooded, insular bureaucrat having acted for the public good " according to his lights ". " If the light of your body be darkness . . ." It took Yugoslavia just two days to reverse the verdict of her Municheers. And how much more violently and completely! One did not find Cincar-Markovič sitting in the new Cabinet!

In fact, the behaviour of Yugoslavia can stand comparison with that of any of the greater Powers threatened with the German menace. Of Italy and France it is unnecessary to speak. The one nation had long accepted, had been the pioneer of, the Fascist system; the other had acquiesced in a long series of surrenders in foreign policy and the rule of crypto-Fascists— Lavals and Bonnets—at home. And Russia never denounced her pact with Nazi Germany even when the armies of the Reich were massing on her frontier with no possible end but aggression in view.

The retreat from independence was slow, and in the case of many of the personnel involved, it was largely the result of force of circumstances rather than of any active desire to co-operate with the Axis. Like all other European neutrals Yugoslavia rejected the prophetic warning broadcast by Mr. Churchill in January 1940—the warning that unless the smaller nations of Europe were prepared to unite to act collectively against Hitler they would be destroyed individually.

The French collapse confirmed Yugoslavia in the attitude adopted by all other European neutrals, with the exception of Italy and Romania, who now openly threw in their lot with the aggressor—a determination to cling more tenaciously than ever to their neutrality. The real significance of the German victory over France was entirely lost. So was the Italian intervention. No one then or later appeared to realize that the fall of Paris spelt the doom of Belgrade. A colleague of mine arriving in the Yugoslav capital on the very morning after the Italian declaration of war and driving to the Srbski Krj Hotel asked the manager what he thought of the situation.

" England is in for a bad time," was the reply.

" But don't you see that your country, equally, is affected ? "

" But we shall remain neutral. We regret what is happening to France and England, but we cannot commit suicide on their behalf."

Just ten months later the hotel was completely destroyed by German bombers. An American journalist in Belgrade at the time told me that all that remained that was not a mere shambles of shattered masonry was a single gaunt and battered lift-shaft.

One of the aspects of these times which will interest post-war historians will be the extreme vitality and omnipresence of German propaganda in the years preceding the second World War. Where did this access of vitality come from ? How did it succeed in imposing so much Germanism, with all its unlovely characteristics, in so widespread a fashion throughout Europe, the Americas and the Middle East, not to mention other areas ?

The answer is, in part at any rate, economic. Trade did not follow but preceded the flag, and the German traders throughout the world formed a channel through which the Nazi ideas of political and social organization easily penetrated. One of the most natural channels for the outflow of German trade is the Danube valley via Yugoslavia.

Germany is the natural market for Yugoslav products, which are mostly of an agricultural character, although recently the minerals of the country—copper, lead and iron ore—have been developed, largely through foreign capital. As a mineral-producing country Yugoslavia is by far the most important in South-Eastern Europe, excluding the oil from Romania.

Germany had a clearing arrangement with Yugoslavia after the visit of Dr. Schacht to the Balkans. This greatly increased the percentage of trade between the two countries, and not only flooded the Yugoslav markets with unwanted cameras and aspirins but ruined a good deal of their trade. For example, from the time of the Austro-Hungarian Empire the main trade with Serbia had been in pigs. The Germans came along and insisted on buying fodder as part of their exchange agreement. This they used for developing their own pig industry in Austria, making the sale of Yugoslav pigs difficult if not impossible.

In the north of the country in recent years tremendous developments occurred in the textile industry. Small mills and weaving establishments were set up, worked by water-power, in the Sava valley. These small factories paid particularly low wages to the peasant and produced second-class goods which supplied almost all required for home consumption. The finer goods were still imported. Generally, a man would own a few of these small factories and be agent for one or two important firms from whom he imported goods. He was certain to be a Jew, and the entire administrative staff of his office in Zagreb and the overseers in his factories would be Jewish. The only Aryan was generally some poor weak mutt of good family, taken in as a partner, having his name on the notepaper, whose only job was to be a commercial traveller in Germany. I know such firms, not only in textiles, but in wood pulp and in leather.

As is the German custom, periods of economic penetration alternated with periods of diplomatic pressure. From the very beginning of the war she had made no secret of the fact that she regarded Yugoslavia as part of her economic reservoir. Early in September she had raised the vexed question of pigs, demanding the doubling of the number already exported to Germany. At the same time she was trying, as I have shown, to get the best of both worlds by buying up all available fodder and thereby threatening the whole of Yugoslavia's flourishing pig industry. She ran a pretty line in blackmail by detaining in German territory some seven thousand trucks and one hundred and seventy barges belonging to Yugoslavia. The Cvetkovič Government did its best to prevent the excessive stripping of the soil. The export of maize and of all vegetables was controlled, but similar methods adopted with regard to minerals were clearly biassed against the democracies, having special reference to the French-owned Bor copper mines in North-Eastern Serbia and the British-owned Trepka lead and zinc works near Mitrovitza.

The German propaganda was now turned on at full blast. There are only two papers of wide circulation in the country, *Politika* and *Vreme*, and the latter at about this time passed entirely under Government control. The staffs of the German Legation and Consulates were much increased after the beginning of the war, while the German Travel Agency was found to be employing over six hundred people. Leaflet campaigns accused Britain, among other things, of supplying poison gas to Poland. This was still almost the honeymoon period of the Nazi-Soviet Pact, and the Germans were in the peculiarly fortunate position of being able to play on agitators of both the extreme Right and the extreme Left as light skirmishers in the propaganda war. Communists were used to abuse the grasping western capitalists, Fascists distributed leaflets taunting the Communists for not having protested against German brutalities in Prague. To set against this there were student demonstrations in Belgrade and Zagreb against the spread of German influence in the country.

The conference of the Balkan Entente in February 1940 had provided a last opportunity for strengthening the waning prospects of peace in the Balkans by building the Entente into a real mutual assistance alliance. It would have been a task challenging the capacities of British diplomacy to the full. It was therefore left unattempted. It would also have been an admirable touchstone by which the sincerity of Turkish friendship could have been tested. Turkey, in alliance with Britain and a member of the Balkan Pact, was obviously well placed to exercise leverage if she chose, but British policy was still bound by the non-intervention tradition and, for all I know, by the principle that " Europe must not be divided into two ideological camps ".

The result was that the conference concluded with a series of platitudinous non-committal declarations which of course suited German policy admirably. Cincar-Markovič told the visiting Foreign Ministers at the close that they were justified in regarding the future with optimism. " The Balkans are not threatened from any side."

April 1940 was a month of invasion alerts both in Greece and in Yugoslavia. Large numbers of those remarkable ' tourists ' who continued to flood the Balkans throughout the summer arrived—young men of military age, furnished with diplomatic passports and bringing in large trunks not subject to search. After the tourist season ended these young men continued to come in, but they were now usually called technicians. There was some pleasing light comedy stuff with faked banknotes which were widely circulated. Leaflets offering Yugoslavia " one last chance " of avoiding the fate of Czechoslovakia and Poland were being distributed. The German Consul-General at Belgrade told a conference of the Yugoslav Press that the Reich Government disapproved of the amount of space given to the news of the Norwegian campaign from Franco-British and German sources respectively. He threatened to cut down the supply of newsprint available and made it clear that Germany was prepared to work up a violent Press campaign against Yugoslavia.

This was the mailed fist with a vengeance, and the combination of suggestive troop concentrations beyond the north-western frontier with the threatening expansion of husky Teutonic tourists, estimated in some quarters at about 30,000, looked ugly. The Cvetković Government showed some spunk, arrested some of the foreigners and expelled others. At the same time there was a drawing together of the Danubian States, Hungary, Yugoslavia, Romania and Bulgaria, to co-operate in the policing of the river. This was one of the few moves in the Balkans in which German intentions were clearly forestalled by intelligent combination, but that combination was destined to be still-born and the action of the riparian States was subsequently over-ridden by Germany.

But the sensation of the month was the arrest of the former Germanophile Premier, Stoyadinović. This action was however completely misinterpreted by wishful thinkers in the democratic countries. It did not represent any sort of defiance of Germany ; there was no political principle underlying it. In Britain such an action would indicate a major change in policy. In accordance with the simpler principles prevailing in South-Eastern Europe, Stoyadinović was arrested because it was considered a " good thing " to have him out of the way—one less complication in the task of governing the country and dividing the spoils. That was all.

Stoyadinović, a big husky Serb, tall and broad-shouldered but running to fat, was a typical product of the small group of rich post-war bourgeoisie. Of peasant origin, he had made his pile very rapidly by some skilful jugglery with war bonds in the nineteen-thirties. Unfortunately he had lost the virtues of the peasant without acquiring those of the bourgeois. It was said of him that within six months of becoming Finance Minister he was quite unable to look his closest friends in the face.

His foreign policy has frequently been misunderstood. In the opinion of English observers well qualified to judge, and uncontaminated by the complacency so characteristic of the period, he was not Germanophile, politically speaking, but hoped by improving relations with Italy to form a bloc against the penetration of Germany towards the Mediterranean : at the same time, while opposing Germany politically, to benefit economically by fostering Yugoslavia's export trade with the Reich. It was a tricky policy. Stoyadinovič, in supping with the Devil, omitted to take a long enough spoon, and was soon drawn into the Axis economic, and therefore political, orbit. I don't think he deserves much pity. He certainly succeeded in queering his pitch pretty successfully all round.

The Regent, always nervously, though unnecessarily, apprehensive that Stoyadinovič (who had in fact learnt his parlour tricks) would use the wrong forks at lunch or dinner, even if he did refrain from drinking out of his finger-bowl, never liked him, and was not concerned to defend him. The English could not be expected to bestir themselves on behalf of a Premier who had played such an equivocal part in foreign policy. His intransigent policy during his premiership (1935-39) alienated the Croats, with whom he made no serious attempts to establish a *modus vivendi*, and he had caused a positive furore by his ill-advised Concordat with the Catholic Church. This was surprising, as religion does not play a deep part in the life of the Serbs, who are essentially Erastian ; but they were quite ready to kick up a shindy at the idea of privileges being extended to the Catholics of Croatia. So no one was much interested in championing Stoyadinovič. But his arrest signified just about nothing as far as any real change of policy was concerned.

Personally, I doubt whether there was ever quite so much of a crisis as was made out by the Press, and I suspect some of my more imaginative colleagues of earning their pay during a prolonged dull season. There were, however, authentic stories going about during those days of German aircraft violating the frontier and large stores of German arms being discovered in police raids. Yugoslav authorities were clearly worried, and the trade pact with Russia was an indication of the desire to seek an alternative commercial link with the possibilities of political alliance with a great Power with whom her Government had steadfastly hitherto refused to have diplomatic relations. The Yugoslav people did not share the reluctance of their Government or the Regent to establish good relations with Russia. There has always been a strong sentimental feeling for Russia as the great Slav brother. This facile metaphor, which seems to smack of *Little Arthur's History of England*, really does mean something in Serbia. "Uncle Ivan has dyed his beard red, but he is Uncle Ivan still" summed up the attitude of all but the extreme Right in Yugoslavia. And there is, after all, no extreme Right in the sense of a big landowning class, and very little in the sense of a large body of *native* capitalists.

I was interested to know whether German pressure in Yugoslavia was as active as it was in Romania, and so in July, not long after the cession of Bessarabia to Russia, although Romania was still very much in the news, I took a plane to Zagreb and immediately sought out my friend Bicanič. When I asked him what the aim of the Yugoslav Minister of Commerce was at that time, he said, "To break the British blockade". Shocked and horrified I said, "But you are pro-British"! He told me that the British blockade had prevented rubber, cotton, wool, yarn, jute and manila from reaching his country, which was ruining the new industries of Yugoslavia and causing much discontent, unemployment and pro-German feeling. I was delighted to hear that the British blockade was so efficient, especially as I would not have put it past the Yugoslav merchants when they had got the stuff through to sell it to Germany. Apparently the Italians were more forthcoming in what they allowed to pass into the Adriatic. He complained that they were in serious trouble with the Germans for having sent 120 waggon-loads of lard to Palestine, obviously for the use of the British Army. The German Minister had been to see him to protest and had even said it would be considered as an act of hostility. Not only were the Germans playing up the unemployment in Yugoslavia caused by the British blockade, but they were ruining Yugoslavia's trade by forcing prices down, and, for example, insisting on Yugoslavia's exporting fodder to Germany, thereby ruining her oldest trade of exporting pigs.

At this time the Yugoslavs did not know where they stood or what to think. They quietly asked various English journalists to leave, as their despatches from Belgrade were upsetting the Germans. An ex-journalist who had worked for the *New York Times* in Belgrade, and had married a Czech refugee wife, was sent as British Consul to Skoplje. His journalistic feelings twitched when he came across a very good story which gave the Italian plans for invading Greece and increasing the size of Albania at the expense of Southern Yugoslavia. There is, it must be clearly stated, a large Albanian minority in the south of Yugoslavia. This map he felt too good a thing to miss, and he gave it to the representative of the *New York Times*. The Yugoslavs asked that he should be quickly removed.

The Legation in Belgrade remained on extremely friendly terms with Prince Paul and the Court set. The Minister was a bachelor, and his entertaining, by reason of the genuine friendliness which inspired it, was famous in the country. But even in the British colony in Yugoslavia there was dissension between those who supported the Serbs and those who supported the Croats. I am confident that to the Consul-General in Zagreb, Mr. Rapp, great credit is due for having Yugoslavia fighting with us in the war. Had his influence with the Croats not been so strong, Maček would never have joined the Government which finally entered the war. But at this time the Legation in Belgrade looked upon Zagreb as an unwanted provincial town, and Zagreb looked upon the Legation as being in the wrong place.

The history of the autumn and winter in Yugoslavia is really, in all essentials, a repetition of what had happened in the spring and summer, at any rate as regards her relationship with Germany. When Yugoslavia agreed to the formation of a camp near Belgrade to accommodate the 120,000 Germans who were being moved from Bessarabia after the Russian occupation, still more when it became known that she had allowed German troops moving in to occupy Romania to pass down her territorial waters of the Danube to Turnu Severin, there was much dis-appointment in Britain and among her allies.   There was still a sentimental feeling that Serbia, our ally of the last war, should have been found in our camp.   There was certainly not enough recognition of the degree to which Germany had drawn Yugo-slavia into her commercial net, and that, short of actually sur-rendering the independence of the country, Yugoslav policy would be determined by her ability to sell her produce abroad. Nor was there enough realization of the extent to which the " internal discipline " of Yugoslavia differed from that of pre-war England.   It is only when one has lived in a Balkan country for at least some months that one begins to realize how, behind the respectable façade of political or scientific progress, violent and sadistic oppression by the police is still the rule, not the exception.   This does not imply that the State in question is Fascist, but merely that it has adopted Fascist methods to maintain the internal authority of the Executive.   If in the following passages Yugoslavia is quoted as an example, it is not because I consider Yugoslavia more oppressive in this respect than the other Balkan countries.   Whether one considers the Romania of King Carol, the Greece of Metaxas, or any of the others, it is the same story.

In Yugoslavia, as elsewhere, there were movements that were avowedly Fascist or Nazi.   One Lijotič led a strongly pro-Nazi and anti-Croat organization known as the " Yugoslav National Front ", whose meetings were usually attended with disturbance. Maček and his friends gave constant warnings to the peasants and to the students of Zagreb not to be led away by foreign ideologies, since the needs of the peasants and the Croat national cause were considered sufficient to occupy their energies, and neither Fascism nor Communism would improve their lot.

Yugoslavia, however, whether under King Alexander or later under the Regent, was not a Fascist State, but rather a " Police State ", as this term was understood in the nineteenth century, particularly under Metternich, the Russian Tsars, and the Kings of Naples and of Spain.   A Police State is charac-terized by spies, by *agents provocateurs* and by arrests and questionings of suspected persons. In a Police State the one great danger that is run by ordinary citizens is that they will become suspect, be dragged away to prison, and possibly kept shut up for months or years without a trial.

The prisons of Yugoslavia, like those of other Balkan countries, are not relatively well-run institutions such as those in our own country. Political prisoners in the Balkans have generally to put up with severe hardships. An influential person, such as Korošeč or Radič, is interned in a pleasant Adriatic island, or guarded in a private house; but, apart from torture or suffering deliberately inflicted, prison buildings are often old and insanitary, rat-ridden and damp, and would long ago have been scrapped but for the desire of the Government to inspire in the peasants and students a wholesome dread of arrest. Only the strong can survive imprisonment, and only the rich can bribe themselves out.

Part of the system is to arrest people and keep them in prison for some months together before trial, while the police 'investigate' their cases. During this time they are often treated with special brutality, in order that they may be induced to confess. The men are ferociously beaten; the women beaten with rubber batons between hips and knees. Such is the thoroughness of this agonizing method that many of the younger women are disabled for life. Particularly severe treatment is meted out to persons suspected of Communism, especially University students, who generally hold extreme views. After arbitrary arrest and months of horror while awaiting trial, they are frequently given long sentences and emerge as bitterly Communistic, revolutionary enemies of the State. The cells are often tiny, two or three paces each way, and for months together the prisoner stays in this confined space, without even the relief of exercise in the prison yard. It is admitted by the authorities that there is a large number of suicides in prison, and middle-aged persons come out as nervous wrecks and soon die.

A woman friend of mine was accused of being a Communist and arrested. Her views were in fact similar to those of English

Left-Wing Conservative members, such as Vivian Adams or Victor Cazalet. I saw her body after her release was secured by means of pressure brought to bear by important foreigners visiting the country. On her thighs were still deep sores. Owing to her enormous strength and vitality doctors had been able to get rid of the festering. She told me that during her period of menstruation she asked for cotton-wool. The guards laughed and said they would see she didn't need these luxuries again. Soon afterwards they tied her hands behind her and raped her night after night, even after they were aware she was pregnant. Mercifully, through fear, lack of food and greatly reduced vitality, she had a miscarriage when beaten once more with rubber truncheons.

I quote this case in some detail at the risk of upsetting my more squeamish readers, but I know the girl and I know her story is true. This might have been equally true of a young woman in Hungary, Romania, Greece or Bulgaria. There is nothing much to choose between Balkan prisons. They are all places which no tourist is ever shown.

I managed by accident to penetrate one prison near Belgrade. It was damp, unheated in winter. No English horse would have been allowed to use it as a stable. The place stank; none of the water-closets functioned—though this shortcoming is scarcely limited to prisons in Yugoslavia. No prisoner had a bed or a chair unless he was rich enough to have relations who brought them to him and bribed the warder. Otherwise he slept and spent his time sitting on a bundle of straw and eating the filthy food provided by the prison. An English friend of mine was arrested in Zagreb (her papers were not in order) and spent one night in tremendous discomfort with prostitutes, verminous refugees, ancient gipsies and drunken women from the streets and brothels. As neither water nor any sanitary arrangements were provided, the atmosphere can be imagined.

English readers aware of the standards prevailing in their country, and of the protests of humanitarian bodies such as the Howard League against British prison conditions, can hardly be aware of the appalling conditions obtaining in the correspond-

17

ing institutions throughout the Balkans, especially in Yugoslavia, Romania and in Greece under Metaxas. No public-spirited person dare make a fuss or try to bring about reforms, lest he experience the inside of a cell for himself.

Apart from the small Fascist movements, and the unpleasant methods of the Serbian police, there was another non-democratic feature of Yugoslav politics unfamiliar in the West. That is the existence of secret societies, particularly among the officers, where the well-known rival cliques are the Black Hand (which organized the assassination of Alexander of Serbia in 1903) and the White Hand. There are also the terrorist societies such as the Croat *Ustashi*, operating mainly from abroad. That the terrorists are really dangerous is proved by the frequent occurrence of outrages, the greatest of them the assassination of Alexander the Unifier in 1934. They have also been largely responsible for maintaining the quisling Pavelič in power. A somewhat caustic foreigner, exasperated for some reason with the Serbs, once said that they think themselves civilized because one of their kings has died in his bed. The remark has a foundation of truth. In 1868, in 1903, and in 1934, Serbian sovereigns perished at the hands of assassins. King Peter the First was fortunate to live out his days and die a natural death.

The British were fighting what inevitably appeared a losing battle. It is unfortunate that in nearly every Balkan country they have backed the kings, and the kings have with one exception let them down. Only King George of Greece has stood by the British, and unfortunately he has never been popular in his country, where he is regarded as a foreigner with neither understanding of nor interest in Greece, and is now probably unacceptable to fully eighty per cent. of the people.

For the other sovereigns there is much less to be said.

> King Zog
> Was always considered a bit of a Wog,
> Until Mussolini quite recently
> Behaved so indecently,

runs a well-known clerihew. Before the war began Zog had ingloriously lost his throne. He had tried to play with the

Italians in the hope of retaining it. He had failed. Yet he has been heavily played up by British propaganda rather recently. Carol was another whom we backed until the rude shock of his repudiation of our guarantee to Romania in June 1940. He trusted to German support, forgetting how much they hated him for his suppression of the Iron Guard. He, too, had to go. Boris of Bulgaria appealed to those circles in Britain which could never quite stomach Carol. They saw in this king another bourgeois monarch, a second Louis Philippe. His reputed devotion to wife and family brought faint nostalgic memories of the Prince Consort, while his somewhat adolescent taste for driving railway engines was regarded with the indulgence due to the eccentricities of an English milord. And so we did our best to play him up. We didn't succeed because Boris never blotted his copy-book with the Axis, and so he keeps his throne, which is nice for him. He did, however, when the British Legation left the country, place a special train at the disposal of the British Minister, Mr. George Rendel, which was nice for the British Minister.

But the most interesting case is Prince Paul of Yugoslavia. Perhaps no one will ever know to what extent he was playing a double game. Although educated at Oxford and married to a sister of the Duchess of Kent, he was very much under the influence of the White Russians, who at that time were decidedly pro-German. He was heavily committed to the Germans, at any rate after September 1940, shortly before the Germans violated the neutrality of his country. He and Princess Olga paid many visits to Germany, and he had certainly enjoyed one State visit. I was informed by friends of his at the time that until about February 1941 he was in very close touch with the Wilhelmstrasse, and constant secret envoys came to Belgrade from Berlin who always stayed in the palace. Whether Germany wouldn't pay the price Paul wanted, or whether it was the other way round, I don't profess to know. I do know that Prince Paul went often to his villa at Bled, which is within a few kilometres of the German frontier.

Yugoslavia's part during the Greek war, right up to the time of the March *coup d'état*, was not a particularly glorious one. Like Greece she was subject to intermittent Press attacks from Italy during the weeks which preceded October 28, and she found it prudent to ignore them. There were menacing hints about Albanian rights in Serbian Macedonia and suggestions that other nations had better claims to Skoplje than Yugoslavia. Notwithstanding all this the Prime Minister could remark, with fatuous complacence, in a public speech at Nish just one week before Italy attacked Greece, " Thank God, events are now fairly crystallized. We have to-day a clear international situation, and our foreign policy must avoid any adventure which might lead us from the peace we now enjoy."

The Government wasted no time in declaring its neutrality when the Italian attack developed against Greece at the beginning of the following week. It was contrary to any really far-sighted policy of " enlightened self-interest ", but by this time one had ceased to expect anything in the way of far-sighted policy from the rulers of any European State. " We are all pacifists now " might have been inscribed over the doors of any European Chancellery except Berlin or Rome. Unfortunately the wrong people were pacifists, and at the wrong times.

On November 5, Italy " tried it out " on Yugoslavia. Three planes " of unknown nationality ", identified by observers as Fiats, dropped about a hundred bombs on the important town of Monastir, in the extreme south-west of the country, killing or wounding forty people.

It is possible, of course, that this incident was due to a loss of direction by the Italian pilots who may have thought they were bombing Florina. But it is much more likely that Italy wanted to test Yugoslav reactions to this sort of attack. The technique has a certain familiarity. One recalls the German planes which flew far over the Pyrenees to bomb the Dordogne valley in Southern France in the spring of 1938, at a time when there appeared to be some slight (very slight) hope that the French Government of the day (strong-man Daladier) might relax its policy of refusing to supply arms to the Spanish Government. Needless to say, the threat which had worked in the case of strong-man Daladier was equally effective in paralysing strong-man Cvetković.

Cvetković found whatever sand there was and buried his head in it. But the Serb people and much of the army was seriously provoked. Two days later General Nedić, the Minister of War, resigned his office. He is believed to have favoured a direct breach with Italy on this issue and to have resigned because he could get no support from the rest of the Cabinet. It is strange that months later this same General should be at the head of the quisling Government in Belgrade. Yet it seems certain that he really did feel at the time of the Monastir bombing that his country should and could have intervened with effect. There is no need to underline the importance which a flank attack from Yugoslavia in mid-November would have had upon the retreating and discomfited Italians. Probably it would have finished off the Albanian campaign before the end of the year. It is very doubtful whether Germany had enough troops concentrated to strike speedily at Yugoslavia, but in any case the position of the latter country could not have been worse than it was in the following April and her armies would at least have had a line of retreat open.

For Yugoslavia it was a wasted winter. No assistance was given to Greece, at a time when military assistance would still have been of great and probably decisive value; no adequate progress was made with the still embryonic rapprochement with Russia. Meanwhile she watched the Albanian campaign slow down to a virtual standstill and the German armies cross the Danube and sweep down through Bulgaria. Her one positive achievement in the diplomatic field, the Pact of Eternal Friendship and Permanent Peace with Hungary in December, proved just as ephemeral and valueless as all similar treaties in recent years which have conflicted with the aggressive designs of the Totalitarian Powers. I doubt if anyone in Yugoslavia or elsewhere really had much faith in the efficacy of the Pact. It is significant that three days after its signature a crowd of fifty thousand people demonstrated before the palace of the Regent of Hungary and demanded the return of the pre-Trianon frontiers. It is difficult to see how this could be interpreted as a gesture of peace and eternal friendship towards Yugoslavia, one of the beneficiaries by that treaty at the expense of Hungary. When Hungary concurred in the attack on Yugoslavia in April, she justified her action on the ground that the *coup d'état* of March 27 had created an entirely new situation which made the treaty no longer binding on Hungary, that Yugoslavia had attacked her first, that by the creation of an independent Croatia Yugoslavia had ceased to exist, that the Hungarian troops were marching in purely as a defensive measure to protect their own people. All, all were there, the old familiar phrases.

From the German occupation of Bulgaria, Yugoslavia became more than ever the Sweden of the Balkans, sitting paralysed while her neighbours one by one were raped all around her. Except for the short Greek frontier she was now completely surrounded by Axis-occupied territory, and accordingly Axis demands for ' collaboration ' began to stiffen. In theory, Germany was demanding no more than adhesion to the Tripartite Pact without military clauses, though German trains, war material and wounded were to be allowed to pass through the country and the national economy of Yugoslavia was to be brought into ' harmony ' with the Reich. In practice, of course, these were simply Trojan Horse demands of the familiar type with which we have all become so wearisomely accustomed, even those who have not read *Mein Kampf* or followed the campaign for the dismemberment of Czechoslovakia. Even if Germany had kept strictly to the terms, an eventuality so improbable as scarcely to be worth considering, acts of sabotage by Yugoslav patriots would certainly have brought down reprisals in the form of a German occupation. As for economic collaboration, the ' harmony ' indicated by Germany would commit Yugoslavia to the precise and unenviable position of the Young Lady of Riga.

The dramatic story of the *coup d'état* which overthrew the Regent and the Germanophile régime is too well known to require to be told here. There are, however, certain aspects of it which have not always been sufficiently stressed, and the motives behind it have been misunderstood. Though it was in fact engineered by the Air Force chiefs it was really a spontaneous national uprising. Several aircraft had already been flown across the frontier to Salonika where their pilots had put themselves and their machines at the disposal of the Greeks. Large portions of the army were practically in a state of mutiny; there were riots in every part of the country. The leaders who got in on the ground floor of the *coup d'état* were not necessarily the most representative of the nation.

For the moment the nation indulged in an orgy of defiance. The tramwaymen at Belgrade burned Hitler in effigy in front of the German Travel Bureau, which week after week had been displaying sometimes flamboyant but always extremely skilful propaganda photographs; a distinguished Serbian General marched about the streets with a Union Jack pinned to the front and back of his uniform; the car belonging to the German Press Attaché was destroyed and he himself publicly ' de-bagged ' in the streets of Belgrade.

But this ebullience of anti-German sentiment was very far from being welcome to the new Government of General Simovič. Even now he was working for a pact with Germany; an innocuous pact it is true, but still a pact. What he wanted was something to hold off the Reich while he negotiated with Ankara and, above all, with Moscow. The Press was instructed to soft-pedal the ' incidents ' which had occurred on March 27 in so far as Germany was concerned, and a ' stop ' was put on the story of the de-bagging of the Press Attaché.

It is not my purpose to describe in detail the military campaigns of Yugoslavia and Greece in April 1941. It is too late for reportage and too early to know the full facts which account for the unpreparedness in one country and the Fifth Columnism in both.

The two broad and obvious failures which must occur to everyone who glances at a map were (1) Why was the Yugoslav army not concentrated in the south of the country, in view of the fact that an attack from the side of Bulgaria would cut off the one line of retreat—down the Vardar or by Florina into Greece ?

(2) Why did the Yugoslav army not take advantage of the one opportunity that presented itself for effective action by advancing into Albania directly upon the rear of the Italian forces ?

The official explanation given for the former omission is that the Cvetković Government had avoided the one form of military concentration which could have saved the army as an effective fighting force on the grounds that this concentration would be ' provocative ' to Germany. There was the additional problem of the Croats. As I have shown earlier, the Croats, who were always a doubtful quantity from the military point of view, had made it quite clear that unless Croatia was defended they had no intention of fighting. I doubt whether they fought very vigorously at any time during the brief campaign. Nevertheless, the Cvetković Government had not been so remiss with regard to mobilization as its successors chose to assume. From July 1940, when the intervention of Italy brought the war to the Mediterranean, there were never less than 500,000 men under arms. From the time of the Italian attack on Greece there were never less than 700,000 and the number had been raised to about a million by the time Simović took over. These figures have been checked by reference to the sums expended by the Ministry of Finance for rations and pay. Yet General Simović has declared in a broadcast that of the twenty-eight Infantry Divisions and three Cavalry Divisions which composed the Yugoslav army only five Divisions of Infantry and one and a half of Cavalry were able to play an effective part in the decisive battles.

It was not, therefore, the failure to mobilize but the failure to reconcentrate speedily or adequately that was the cause of the rapid break-through in Southern Serbia. Under the Regency the concentrations had certainly not taken sufficiently into account the danger of an attack from the side of Bulgaria. After the Germans went into Romania in the autumn of 1940 some hurried fortification was attempted on the open north-eastern frontier where the great Hungarian plain gives every advantage to an invader. But the grouping of the divisions had remained very faulty. There do not seem to have been more than five or six to defend old Serbia, and only two on the Romanian and Hungarian frontiers ; but there were apparently as many as eight grouped along the Dalmatian coast and about four more in Slovenia and Croatia.

Expert opinion which I have consulted on this point has assured me that in the ten days which elapsed between the *coup d'état* and the German attack much re-concentration could have been carried out had the General Staff really settled down to tackle the task with the energy which the urgency of the situation demanded. But they proved anything but co-operative. General Sir John Dill had hurried to Belgrade in the hope of initiating military conversations. But his proposals for a close military alliance and the co-ordination of the efforts of the two armies were turned down by the Yugoslav General Staff, still anxious to avoid ' unduly provocative ' action, and convinced that Germany, for technical reasons, could not attack before April 20 at the earliest. The nation knew that the decision of March 27 meant war, and they were facing up to the consequences bravely, but the Higher Command does not appear to have acted with sufficient vigour or alacrity. It has been unkindly stated that General Simovič seemed more preoccupied with his daughter's forthcoming wedding than with the impending catastrophe which was threatening his country.

Again, Allied opinion confidently and reasonably expected a vigorous drive into Albania on the rear of the Italian armies. This task had been allotted to the Third Army, which failed dismally to execute the plan. The army when fully concentrated should have been composed of more than four divisions. Two of these, operating from Podgoritza, were to enter Albania from the extreme north and take Scutari ; another, advancing from Prizrend, was to advance through the Kukus Pass in a south-westerly direction upon Tirana, while a fourth was to cross the frontier by way of Dibra to Tirana and by way of Struga to Elbasan.

The plan, which involved a sweep through Northern Albania towards the rear of the Italian army rather than a direct attack upon its left flank, was sound enough, but it never got going at all.    Troop concentrations were behindhand, the attack was terribly slow in getting under way.  When the Blitzkrieg methods employed with such success by Germany should have been a stimulus to the Yugoslav army to move rapidly upon their objectives they appear to have spent the first two days engaged in a decorous artillery bombardment across the Drin in the most approved 1917 manner.  Meanwhile the rapid advance of the German forces from Bulgaria upon their rear appears to have exercised a paralysing influence upon the divisions in the Struga, Dibra and Prizrend areas.  Only the advance from the north appears to have made any progress whatever, but there is extremely little evidence to support the Yugoslav claims to the capture of Scutari, much less Durazzo.

Viewed generally, it was simply the Polish War over again. Overwhelming German mechanized strength, a plan of campaign well thought out and executed with the utmost speed and skill ; against this the Yugoslavs could only set the unquestioned courage of their troops.  The High Command never had the situation in hand.  Like the Poles, they endeavoured to defend too many frontiers at the same time ; like the Poles contact was almost immediately lost between the Government and General Staff on the one hand (Simovič combined the post of Prime Minister with that of Commander-in-Chief) and the various army commanders on the other.  As the result of the air bombardment on the opening day of the war, Belgrade radio closed down for forty-eight hours.  The first official war bulletin, broadcast by wireless on Tuesday morning, opened with the remarkable statement, " On all fronts the situation is in our favour ".    In fact, the Government, shifting constantly across North-Western Serbia and Bosnia, from Belgrade to Ushitze, from Ushitze to Sarajevo, from Sarajevo to the coast, and constantly bombed from the air, can never have had very much idea of what was going on in other parts of the country.

The main German drive came in the south of Serbia, and it met with instantaneous and spectacular success.  It was an attack in force at the very place where a child could have foreseen that it must have occurred—the ' hinge ' of the whole Yugoslav-

Greek front. It took the form of a two-pronged drive in great strength upon Skoplje and Monastir by way of Kriva Palanka and Strumnitza. The attack began early on the morning of Sunday, April 6. By the evening of Monday the heavy out-mechanized Yugoslav forces in the neighbourhood of Strumnitza had collapsed (there was apparently tougher resistance in the Kriva Palanka sector) and the German mechanized forces were pouring through, across the Vardar, where bridges were left unbroken (the Meuse over again !). Both Skoplje and Monastir were in German hands by the end of Tuesday. Skoplje, after being bombed all day long until a thick pall of smoke hung over the dazed and shattered town, was taken by five hundred para-chutists. This effectively cut the Yugoslav forces off from retreat into Greece either by way of the Vardar or of Monastir. The hardest fighting, and that in which the Serbs showed to best advantage, occurred during the following days when the Germans, thrusting up north-west from Skoplje in a huge enveloping movement, were held for some days in the Katchanik Pass, losing heavily in tanks, a stand which perhaps enabled a considerable proportion of the Yugoslav army to make a get-away into the mountains of Bosnia and Montenegro.

But apart from the Katchanik battle the Germans were at no point seriously held up for long. Nish, where the Belgrade line forks to Istanbul and Salonika, was captured on Wednesday, April 9, the day that Salonika fell. Zagreb, capital of Croatia, fell on the Thursday without putting up any defence, and Kragujevac, the principal manufacturing town of Central Serbia. On Friday German and Italian troops established contact with one another north of Lake Okhrida. On Saturday Belgrade was entered by German troops coming in from the north. After a week's fighting organized resistance was practically at an end. Sarajevo, one of the last centres of inland resistance, fell to the Germans on Tuesday, and Split on the Adriatic coast to the Italians. All regular fighting came to an end with the formal capitulation of the Yugoslav armies on Thursday, April 17.

## CHAPTER XIV

# GREECE—THE END OF AN EPIC

GREECE'S war against Germany opened in the most ominous manner. At 3 a.m. on the very first night an immense explosion, followed at intervals of about half an hour by two others, shook every house in the Peiraeus. Even miles away in Athens doors were blown in and windows broken. A twelve-thousand-ton ship, heavily laden with TNT, had been blown up by a delayed-action bomb. Seventeen or eighteen ships in the neighbourhood were destroyed. The work of unloading the ship had apparently been suspended for the whole of Sunday, which in itself appears inexcusable in view of the fact that it was long odds on a heavy raid that night. Under these circumstances, it was an act of criminal negligence to have left the ship in port still largely unloaded. It is an elementary rule of modern warfare that ships carrying cargoes of this nature put out to sea at the approach of night. The chief error appears to have lain in faulty liaison work, for which both the British and the Greek harbour authorities must be held responsible. Again, though we could ill afford to lose the cargoes, the moral effect of the explosion was perhaps even greater than the material loss. It suggested that fatal amateurishness which was coming to be associated with the management of the British war effort in the Balkans.

The great explosion shook the nerve of the population of Athens and the Peiraeus rather badly. Having heard and seen its effects, they were in no way deceived by the official communiqué of the Ministry of the Interior which announced that " a steamer and some buildings had been damaged ", an example of litotes which must surely stand high among official announcements. The incident was nicely calculated to give a foretaste of the thunderbolt quality of the German offensive which had just been launched in Thrace and Macedonia. Coupled with the news of the destruction by air bombardment of Belgrade, news which, though fragmentary and incomplete, does not appear to have gone beyond the facts, it convinced many of the inhabitants of the Greek capital and its port that the hour of the destruction of their own towns was at hand. As a matter of fact, apart from a little machine-gunning of roads in the out-skirts of Athens during the last days of the campaign, the German raiders confined themselves strictly to military targets, at any rate in Attica. Athens remained unbombed, but the port was raided with considerable thoroughness and efficiency night after night, though there was nothing more so spectacularly disastrous as the explosion of the munition ship on that Sunday night.

The whole course of the Greek campaign was conditioned by the events in Yugoslavia, both political and military, between March 27 and April 7. The original British plan contemplated a stand on the Olympus line, the front line of which ran along the Vistritza River, a little south of Salonika, across to Kozani and Grevena in the Pindus. The right flank of the Greek army in Albania was to have been drawn back some way behind Koritza to bring it into line with the new position. Nothing more than a covering action in Eastern Macedonia or Thrace or north of Salonika was ever intended, and the Greek forces there were small, certainly not more than three divisions; more probably about one and a half. The Simovič *coup d'état* in Belgrade, and the certainty that Yugoslavia would resist a military attack, led to a hasty last-minute alteration of plan, based on the assumption that the Yugoslavs could hold the invader from Bulgaria for some days, at any rate in the neigh-bourhood of their frontier. The right wing of the Greek army was not drawn back from Albania, and the left wing of the British forces, including an armoured brigade, was swung for-ward to Florina to cover the Monastir gap in the hope of linking up with the Yugoslav forces.

As we know, Yugoslav resistance in the extreme south of their country was broken down within some thirty-six hours. The small armoured force pushed up towards Monastir, and the Greeks on their left among the mountains had to effect an improvised withdrawal. Fighting holding battles at Ptolemais and Edessa, they drew back once more to the original position.

Unfortunately while the mechanized British forces in the plain were able to make the withdrawal in good order on account of their mobility, the Greek infantry on their left flank in the mountains could not keep pace and, battered both in front and rear by artillery and dive-bombers, its transport and supply completely broke down, with the result that by Friday, April 11, when we were back on the original line, it was clear that the Greek corps in the mountains, which was serving the double purpose of acting both as our flank guard and as our link with the army of Albania, had practically to be counted out as a fighting force.

In the holding action in Macedonia during the early days of this week the Greek forces had fought with extreme gallantry at the forts in the Struma gap and on the Nevrokop plateau to the east. German attacks with dive bombers, parachutists, heavy artillery and tanks were repulsed. The Greek troops here do not seem to have been in the least contaminated with defeatism, though it was otherwise with their High Command. A Greek junior officer, wounded in the fighting at Fort Rupel, gave currency to a phrase which achieved considerable publicity in Athens during these days.

" These Germans," he said, " are all right as fighters in their tanks, but once you get them out of their machines they are nothing but chauffeurs."

Nothing but chauffeurs ! The phrase caught on in Athens, and people cheered themselves up by repeating it to one another.

This relative optimism was not shared by the Greek Cabinet, still less by the General Staff or the army commanders. The top of the political and military hierarchy was as rotten as the base was fundamentally sound and courageous. Defeatism in high quarters had been growing for months. The collapse of the Yugoslav resistance in the Vardar valley, which was known on Monday evening, caused something of a panic. The news was published in a special midday communiqué on Tuesday, which referred baldly to the uncovering of the left flank of the Greek forces in Macedonia by the Yugoslav withdrawal from the Strumnitza region. The announcement gave an uncomfortable jolt to the man in the street. Special communiqués had been extremely rare in the course of this war, and the publication of this one at noon in addition to the customary midnight communiqué drew all the more attention to the disaster.

The Fifth Column, believed in certain official British circles to be non-existent because it did not pursue the precise methods employed in Norway or in Holland, was excessively active during these days. That same Tuesday morning a rumour circulated with the utmost speed throughout Athens that Turkey had entered the war on the Allied side. In some quarters of Athens the whole population was in the streets saluting the advent of the new Ally. Turkish flags were carried alongside the British and the Greek, and there was a procession to the Turkish Legation, where the Minister very prudently refused to show himself. Within an hour or two, of course, the cold truth had broken, but the people who had been demonstrating were at first reluctant to believe it. The morale of Athens, always so sensitive to news currents, was gravely lowered by this incident, which caused a sharp disillusion throughout the civil population. The sense of uncertainty and general bewilderment was greatly increased. But because the Fifth Column chose this different method of going to work, certain British circles chose to believe that " there was no such thing as a Fifth Column in Greece ". One important Legation official petulantly refused to see patriotic Greeks who called with information concerning the activities of these elements. Less than a week later he was tumbling over himself with anxiety to pass on to the overworked First Secretary the most inadequately authenticated rumours concerning the impending formation of a Germanophile Cabinet.

The Press Ministry had little information to give, and the censorship in its usual unhelpful way tried to restrict the telegrams of foreign correspondents to a mere parrot-like repetition of the day's communiqué. Such an attitude could only strengthen the conviction that a badly rattled Government was distrustful of all military comment, just as it had long been distrustful of all political comment. At the same time it signally failed to discourage the rumours that were being disseminated from day to day to the effect that the German forces had shattered the British defensive position at Olympus and that the British were already making all plans for a speedy withdrawal of their forces, and had asked the Greeks to cover their retreat with their fleet.

Wednesday, April 16, and Thursday, April 17, were among the worst days in respect of defeatist rumours. It was said that the British line had been broken on the Olympus front, that the Australian Division had been cut to pieces and that the Germans were swarming over the Larissa Plain. As a matter of fact, though the retreat from the Olympus position to Thermopylae all the way across the plain of Thessaly had been decided on as early as the previous Saturday, the line of the Peneios immediately south of the mountain block was still being held by a New Zealand brigade and two Australian battalions.

Athens was badly rattled during these days. One symptom of the spirit now abroad was the tearing down of anti-German posters. On the first day of the German attack a number of these had appeared, the most effective being one which depicted Hitler as a butcher leading to slaughter a number of fat pigs— Poland, Denmark, Norway, Holland, Belgium, France, Romania and Bulgaria, and calling out for more blood. Between nightfall on April 17 and dawn on April 18 these all disappeared from the hoardings.

The tension in the capital was much heightened during these last days by the sinister pickets of slow-marching armed police which patrolled, in groups of half a dozen as a rule, up and down the Athens streets. This certainly did nothing to calm the general nervousness. It was difficult to feel sure whether these patrols were to be used for or against the British. On the Thursday there were rumours of an impending Germanophile *coup d'état*, and the names of the members of the new Government which was to seize power that evening were being bandied about. There was a sudden and mysterious disappearance of every single taxi from the streets of Athens.

The rot was setting in both among the High Command and

the Government. Bacopoulos, the Greek commander in Thrace and Eastern Macedonia, had thrown in his hand and capitulated on behalf of his army which, though isolated by the fall of Salonika, was still fighting bravely and in good order and which might, in part at any rate, have been withdrawn by sea. Already the defeatist Ministers in the Government were acting without taking the trouble to consult the Prime Minister who, sick and disheartened, was clearly feeling overwhelmed by the situation. Papademas, Minister of War, was responsible on April 17 for the order declaring further resistance impossible and giving a free hand to the Generals to behave as they saw fit. The same day an Army Order was issued, releasing for a period of two months' leave all those classes which were just about to be called up for military service. Nothing did more to convince the nation than this latter order, which was the first to become known, that the Government considered that the game was up. Still more reprehensible was the conduct of Oeconomou, Minister of Communications, who took it upon himself to give an order that, to prevent unnecessary loss of life, the remaining Greek aircraft should be grounded and the petrol dumps at Tatoi and Eleusis destroyed. British influence with the King was successful in obtaining the revocation of this order, and British ground staffs at the aerodromes prevented the intended sabotage, but Oeconomou's proposal is an indication of the lengths to which the defeatists were prepared to go to bring the struggle to an abrupt end.

On the next day, Friday, April 18, Good Friday in the Orthodox Calendar, General Papagos delivered an exceedingly depressing report to the Cabinet on the military situation. This probably came as no particular surprise to anyone, in view of the fact that the Greek force on the British left had ceased to exist as an effective fighting unit for the past week, while the Albanian army, which had delayed its retreat too long, was now falling back in some disorder. The British forces who were carrying out a retirement across the Larissa Plain were now suffering just as the Greeks had suffered a few days earlier from incessant dive-bombing attacks on their lines of communication.

18

One cannot help wondering whether when the Olympus position was planned the problem of supply was sufficiently considered. Transport had to come up the long road from Athens with its numerous bottle-necks in the mountain passes, and break-downs and blockages were constant. The port of Volo, much nearer to our front line than the Peiraeus, was absolutely battered to pieces by the German bombers. The conclusion is unavoidable—the Olympus line could have been held only if the British had something approaching equality in air strength, and this, of course, we never had. There were, I suppose, at the time when the attack on the Olympus position was launched, about a hundred British fighters available to cope with upwards of twelve hundred German planes, and this disparity increased with every day that passed. The Germans had got our bases absolutely taped—a squadron and a half was destroyed on the ground near Larissa in the early stages of the battle—while after the withdrawal from Olympus to the Thermopylae position, waves of enemy bombers followed one another practically without intermission in attacking, from a low altitude, the bases at Tatoi and Hassani.

German air superiority must therefore in any case have determined the result of the campaign. As the American Military Attaché remarked : " The British have sent a boy to fight a man." It was also exceedingly doubtful whether the Greek army of Albania could make its way back by the difficult mountain roads of Epirus to Attica or the Peloponnese. Papagos clearly thought not. It was now a question of when, not of whether, the King and Government should retire to Crete. The Cabinet was on the verge of breaking up. The King and Korizis were known to be for continuing to the last, but the latter was at this time a very sick man. Torn between a desire not to betray his ally and the realization of the scale of the misfortune that was now befalling his country, he wavered backwards and forwards over the question of the removal to Crete. It seemed an inevitable step now, but apart from the fact that it would certainly confirm the impression that all was lost on the mainland, it would give a signal to the Germanophiles to rise and take control, thereby acutely embarrassing the withdrawal of the British forces.

Ziphos, the young Minister of Shipping, was at this time acting as link between the British Legation and the Greek Prime Minister. He was charged with finding out the intentions of the latter with regard to the proposed change of the seat of Government. Korizis, in an agony of indecision, torn between evenly balanced alternatives, again and again refrained from a positive answer. Ziphos became more and more insistent. " I *must* have your reply, Mr. President. It is essential that there should be no further uncertainty or delay in this matter." Korizis at last roused himself. He rose and walked slowly towards an inner room. At the door he paused and turned. " In one minute, Mr. Ziphos," he said, " you shall have your reply." The door closed behind him. A moment or two later Ziphos heard the sound of a revolver-shot. Korizis was the second Prime Minister (Count Teleki of Hungary had been the first) to commit suicide as the result of the German drive through the Balkans in April.

The news rapidly spread with additions and amplifications. The next appointment came as a surprise. It was announced that the King had taken over the Premiership himself, a step which British official circles had desired in January after the death of Metaxas. Remarkably, the Vice-Premier was Kodzias, Minister-Governor of Athens, who had achieved such notoriety in the previous summer as a Germanophile.

It was a strange appointment, but it lasted only for one day. This large, vain, talkative man was nobody's choice except the King's, and it appears that through the advice of Thomas Bowman, the British Vice-Consul in Athens, who at this time was practically running the country, the King was informed that Kodzias was not an acceptable choice. It was obvious that the King must resort to the Venizelists. He first tried non-Party Premiers—General Mazarakis and Admiral Sakhellariou in turn. He approached Sophoulis and several of the elder Liberal statesmen. None of them were willing to take up such a sticky heritage after having been excluded for so long. In any case, few of them had approved of the restoration of the Monarchy. " Have you, too, turned against me ? " the King inquired of Pericles Argyropoulos, a former Foreign Secretary of Venizelos. " Your Majesty," replied Argyropoulos, " those who have never been for you cannot turn against you."

In the end, Tsouderos, a very moderate Venizelist and former Governor of the Bank of Athens, accepted the post. His appointment was regarded as likely to conciliate the Liberal and Democratic majority in the country, while his character and temperament were not of the sort which makes revolutions. He was indeed an admirable ' compromise ' Prime Minister—he was in addition, a Cretan. In the opinion of many Greeks, however, he signally failed to take advantage of the opportunity which his position gave him to make a clean sweep of the discredited relics of the August Fourth régime. It is widely felt that though new wine is available the Premier insists on retaining the old bottles.

Kodzias, during his day of Premiership, did something to pull things together and to counteract the ugly atmosphere which had prevailed on the Wednesday, Thursday and Friday of that week. Such news as came through from the front was at this point rather better. The immediate danger of a break-through to the very suburbs of Athens was seen to be a product of the whispering campaign of these days. British forces were retiring across the Plain of Thessaly to the Thermopylae position, and the Germans, badly mauled in the Olympus battle—the Le Cateau of this campaign—did not follow up the retreat at all closely. But no one really believed that this position could be held when the carefully prepared Olympus line had fallen.

However, spirits in Athens rose, in the mercurial Greek fashion, on the Saturday. Kodzias managed to stage a pro-British demonstration in front of the Legation ; there were cries of " Zito Polemos ! " " Zito Anglia ! " and young men who had been given their discharge from the army a day or two before were crying " Give us arms ! " About a hundred and fifty German prisoners who had been taken at Rupel during the fighting on the first day of the attack and had been brought to Athens were marched through the streets. This proved a spectacular and effective gesture, and it was a pity that no one thought of it earlier. The credit for the idea should, I believe, go to a British Staff officer.

Things were in a bad way, nevertheless, at the Legation. The Minister had been slow to recognize the existence of highly-placed Fifth Columnists on the Greek General Staff, though this was not for lack of information. He had also taken the view that the evacuation of any of the women and children of the British colony at an earlier stage would be detrimental to the morale of the Greeks. Consequently, the ships bringing British troops from Egypt were allowed to return empty, though for the life of me I cannot feel that the evacuation of British civilians carried out *pari passu* with the arrival of British troops would have been as damaging to the morale of our ally as the spectacle on Thursday, April 17, of swarms of British subjects besieging the forecourt of the Legation. The British Legation, formerly the private house of Venizelos, was one of the most conspicuous buildings in Athens (it had recently been painted a pale, sickly pink), and it was so much a barometer of the situation, in peace as well as in war-time, and so closely watched by enemy spies and agents, that I cannot think of anything more disastrous than what actually occurred. Careful arrangements had been made in the previous autumn to evacuate the entire British colony had the Italian aggression proved successful, but the ship which had been chartered for the purpose had been turned over to the Greek Government for use as a hospital ship, and now these unfortunate people had absolutely no idea whether they would be evacuated at all, and if so by what means. The British subjects swarming round the Legation that day do not form a mental picture on which one wishes to dwell. If only the wives and children and governesses and British Council teachers had been shifted earlier, or had been informed what measures, if any, were being taken for their evacuation, they would, in fact, have proved patient and co-operative, as British people, whatever their other faults, normally are in a crisis. It is greatly to the credit of the Director of Publicity, of whom

I have spoken rather hardly elsewhere in this book, that almost alone among members of the Legation, he was at pains to enforce this view upon the Minister. As he pointed out with justice and force, it was not a case of these people " demanding a couple of battleships escorted by half the Mediterranean fleet ". They merely wanted to know what was going to be done. The danger, too, that at the last soldiers' lives might have to be sacrificed to getting civilians away ought to have been apparent.

In the end the English-born part of the British colony was, in fact, successfully evacuated, a large part on Friday, April 18, the day of Korizis' suicide, the remainder four days later, when the Thermopylae line was in the process of being abandoned and evacuation of the army had already been decided on. It was a great pity that there had to be so much unnecessary publicity in connection with the evacuation of the civilians, and it certainly played right into the hands of those who were working anti-British propaganda.

The Cypriots and Maltese, of whom there were some thousands in Greece, were less fortunate. They nearly all belonged to the poorer classes, and were naturally among the most ignorant of the plans of the Legation on their behalf. American subjects who subsequently arrived in Cairo from Athens have described to me the pathetic spectacle, on the morning when the German troops arrived, of hundreds of these people, who had collected outside the British Consulate (from which all the officials had of course departed days earlier) in the vain hope of some miraculous intervention on their behalf.

" Every schoolboy " has heard of Thermopylae, and connects it with the dramatic resistance of Leonidas and his three hundred Spartans in the pass to the Persian hordes. But however alluring the prospect of history repeating itself may have been to the observer and commentator sitting at the safe distance of some hundreds of miles, its value as a defensive position at the present day is considerably decreased by the fact that the sea has receded in the course of the centuries, leaving a distance of some three miles between mountain face and water. Anyhow, in these days of three-dimensional warfare, mountain passes, so beloved by pin-and-paper strategists, are not what they were as defensive positions, as they are liable to cause a bottle-necking of supply. At the best, Thermopylae could only be held by a covering force long enough to allow the embarkation of a fair proportion of the force. The remarkable thing was that our troops were able to retire to it unmolested save from the air. The Germans had, in fact, been severely handled on the Olympus line and were at this point beginning to outrun their transport. For some unaccountable reason, having forced the gap between the Greek and British troops to which I have referred, they never successfully exploited it by coming straight into the Larissa Plain by Kalabaka and Trikkala. There was an Australian brigade defending our flank at Kalabaka, but there was at least one German division, and possibly two, in the immediate neighbourhood. Instead of turning directly in upon the re-treating British, they appear to have executed a lengthy sweep right round to the west through Janina and Arta, which eventu-ally brought them to Delphi and the Gulf of Corinth, but too late to play an effective part.

The last of the British troops had withdrawn to the Therm-opylae line on Monday, April 21. On that day, General Tsolakoglou, on behalf of the Greek army in Epirus, acting on the defeatist broadcast of the Minister of War three days earlier, after hasty overtures to the Germans, capitulated on behalf of all the Greek armies on the Albanian front. The original terms were suspiciously generous. The Greek victory in Albania was recognized; their armies were required only to withdraw to the Greek frontier, which the Germans undertook to prevent any attempt by the Italians to cross; the officers were to be allowed to retain their equipment, while the soldiers, after surrendering their arms, were to be free to return home.

No doubt the Germans could have extracted much harsher terms from the hapless Tsolakoglou, but presumably from sheer force of habit they preferred to adopt the *Mein Kampf* technique of the 'advance by stages' even when there was no need for it. The next day, the capitulation having once taken place, the Germans promptly revoked the conditions on the ground that the King's " Fight to the end " broadcast nullified the terms on which the armistice had been arranged. As a matter of fact, the Generals, by taking the decision into their own hands, had tacitly repudiated the royal authority. However, the excuse was good enough (any excuse would have done), and the German Command, withdrawing the previous armistice, issued fresh terms by which all Greek equipment was to be handed over and all Greek soldiers became prisoners of war, though this latter condition was not, in fact, acted on.

The rest of the fighting, so far as the British were concerned, was simply an affair of holding actions while the troops were evacuated. German landings on the island of Euboea, which lies close to the mainland, gave them the opportunity of crossing back at Chalcis, where the strait is less than a quarter of a mile wide, and cutting across the line of retreat from Thermopylae. A similar enveloping movement from the south was held up for some valuable hours by effective road demolition in the neighbourhood of Delphi and Arachova. It was among these very crags and boulders that, according to legend, at the time of the Persian invasion of Greece, the god Apollo had turned back a group of the invaders by rolling down rocks upon them in protection of his sanctuary at Delphi.

The British were faced with an evacuation which, except that there were fewer troops to be withdrawn, was in almost every respect more formidable than that from Dunkirk. The distance to be traversed to Crete was much greater than the width of the Channel. The Saronic Gulf, which is the natural route of evacuation from Athens, had been heavily mined. The heavily-bombed port of Peiraeus was therefore virtually useless, and it seemed impossible that any considerable body of troops would be able to get through the isthmus of Corinth to the ports of the Peloponnese. Moreover, R.A.F. fighter defence was by this time non-existent, largely as the result of the almost incessant low-altitude bombing of our airfields. I hesitate to interfere, as a layman, with the technicalities of air warfare, but it does appear that our aircraft were too concentrated on the landing-grounds rather than being more widely scattered in separate pens, as had long been the custom adopted at home. Nor, even allowing for the difficulties involved by the fact that we had only the months of winter to prepare fresh aerodromes, do I feel that this problem was tackled with sufficient vigour. Some excellent aerodromes were under construction in the Peloponnese, notably one at Cape Araxos near Patras, which might have been, but in fact I believe were not, used as bomber or fighter bases during the later stages of the retreat. But they mostly appear not to have been used, probably because in the last part of the campaign there were no more fighters available. In short, our air support was simply not able to cope quantitively with the job. We had too few airfields and too few planes to operate from them, and, of those few, too many were lost by carelessness or misfortune in the early stages of the battle.

Our Command was faced with the unenviable alternatives of evacuating by night, which, though relatively safe from the point of view of air attack, meant that the bulk of the crossing to Crete had to be done by daylight with enemy bombers swooping down on our convoys from above ; or by day, with all the attendant disadvantages which an embarkation under observation of the enemy implied. The latter was considered, on the balance, to represent the lesser evil. Moreover, the destruction wrought on the ports of Attica meant that a large proportion of our force had to be evacuated by the ports of the Peloponnese, which had never been contemplated in the original plan.

The Germans made a second extraordinary blunder in failing to seize the isthmus of Corinth by parachute troops (of which they must have had large numbers available, as we learnt next month in Crete) until Saturday, April 26, when the advance guard of their mechanized troops was already approaching Athens, which they entered early next morning. A large proportion of our force got away from Nauplia and Kalamata. The remainder fought their way back to the beaches at Rafina and Porto Rafti on the east coast of Attica while the Germans were coming down upon Athens from the west.

Months later, in Cairo, I met the last British officer to leave Attica—he had been in the capital the evening before the German armoured column entered.  He told me of the friendliness of the people to the very last and their warm appreciation of the British effort.  This attitude of the ordinary Greek contrasted now as always throughout the war with the reluctant and grudging co-operation accorded by so much of official Greece.  It was rather mournful to reflect that the most eminent of the true Fifth Columnists, at any rate among the civilians, the men who had been responsible for maintaining and supporting five years of Fascist dictatorship, were now comfortably outside the country, and from Crete or Cairo were professing the most whole-hearted pro-British sentiments.

## CHAPTER XV

## RETREAT TO AFRICA

•

*May* 29, 1941.

GERMAN planes were daily reported to be flying over small parts of Turkish territory. These were without doubt making reconnaissance flights over Syria. I was staying with the Consul and Mrs. Brenan in Mersin. They had previously been posted at the Consulate in Sofia, and are amongst the most charming and efficient British officials that I have ever been privileged to meet. Their object is to help British subjects and to overcome difficulties, not to make them greater. Naturally they are universally respected, and I imagine, now that the consular and diplomatic services have been amalgamated, he will be promoted rapidly to the senior service. But at this time Mersin was very important. Large numbers of British subjects had been evacuated there from the rest of Turkey; added to these were Poles, Belgians and other Allies who did not wish to take the risk of going through Syria, and many Allied nationals who could not get a Syrian visa.

When I arrived the only subject of conversation was the possible evacuation of Crete. The whole staff of the Consulate came upstairs to the drawing-room every morning to hear the news.

I was anxious to get to Egypt as quickly as possible. The Syrian frontier was closed and trains had ceased to run. There was virtually no shipping at all from Mersin. Turkish ships were not allowed to leave Turkish territorial waters. No Romanian or Bulgarian ship dare leave the safe waters of the Straits. I was lucky, for a small sailing-boat, known in that part of the world as a caique, flying the Palestinian flag, was taking the risk of sailing to Alexandria. The owner of this boat had had some "arrangements to make" in Turkey, which I think must have been most profitable to himself, or he would never have taken the risk of going there. He agreed that I might travel on the boat. There was, of course, no sort of accommodation for passengers, no food, no water. Mrs. Brenan supplied me with cooked chickens, bread, water, wine and fruit.

The boat which was made of wood had a total tonnage of one hundred and fifty. There was a small engine as well as the six large sails. The lifeboat as well as the entire deck space was full of cargo. Unhappily the cargo consisted of bags of nuts well covered with fleas and bugs (how did I ever believe the story that one never had the two together?); these were lumpy and uncomfortable to sit on or for sleeping purposes. The Consul arranged all the formalities for me, and so great was his influence that I had no difficulties in leaving.

We all rowed out to the caique which was lying in the harbour. I was sad to leave Turkey at that moment. I knew the Brenans would have liked me to stay with them longer, and no guest ever has a pleasanter feeling than that. I spend so much time with people that I have to mix with because I am a journalist that I felt it hard as I climbed up a rope ladder from the rowing-boat to the caique. I watched them row back to shore and saw the lights of Mersin appear as the mountains behind grew fainter.

We were waiting for the one other passenger, an officer who had been advising the Turkish army and was rushing back to Egypt. I hoped he might be interesting, as the other people on the boat—a German woman married to an Indian, and two hearty Belgians out to join the British Army—were rather disappointing. At least I felt I should have a chance of learning some German and brushing up my French. But the people were dull. The officer, too, when he arrived was dull. So dull, that in desperation I asked what was to him the most enjoyable event in his life. He replied, " The pub crawl I go on every Saturday evening when I am in England ".

During the last century few people have been foolish enough to cross the Mediterranean Sea in a small open boat. I thought it was going to be something of an adventure, as I expected that the German planes which were bombing the ships evacuating soldiers from Crete would come down to machine-gun us, though I knew they would not think the ship worth a bomb. The captain of the caique carried no radio of any kind, in order that the crew should not get nervous. This was rather bad for one who is used to hearing the news two or three times a day. It was especially bad for me, who depended on news for my bread and butter.

As we drew anchor the Palestinian flag was pulled down. The captain enforced a strict blackout. This was difficult, because three of the passengers were ill almost at once. The sea was quite calm. My ideas of learning German and brushing up my French were to receive a rude shock, as both the Belgians and the German were ill throughout the voyage. It was hard to find anywhere to sleep. The nights were very cold, and the sea washed over the side of the boat, soaking all my clothes and luggage, ruining my only expensive garment, a Persian lamb coat. It was obviously impossible to change or get warm. So I just slept and let the fleas and bugs do their worst.

At dawn on the first day we could see the coasts of Turkey and of Cyprus. When we were within sight of the lighthouse on Cape St. André the flag was hoisted. There was no wind, and although the crew hauled the sails up and down a good deal, our speed never exceeded five knots on the whole trip. During the first day at sea and part of the second, spent sailing round Cyprus, we were protected from the breeze by the hills of the island. The sun beat down on the boat. There was no shelter from it. Luckily I am dark and did not suffer, but the other passengers were ill for a fortnight afterwards with the effects of sea-sickness, cold and sunburn.

We were all glad to see the last of Cyprus. I was most disappointed, as I imagined that the coastline would be beautiful. It is bare, just like the south coast of Asia Minor. Behind the white sand which almost shone by the light of the moon there are low hills covered with scrub. Apart from one harbour, which we could not see owing to a heat haze, the island was deserted. We were often only a hundred yards from the coast, and I had powerful field-glasses (these were greatly in demand, as the Arab crew had never used any so powerful and enjoyed playing with them). I saw about three houses and one monastery. Now as I write in September 1941 I hear of continuous streams of military transports passing along the roads as the final preparations are made in case Germany should attack.

After the coast of Cyprus had disappeared I sat in misery on the boat, in the misery of boredom. The sea was blue and beautiful, but there was nothing to do by night or by day but sleep. Maybe I was crazy, but I often looked out hoping to see a German plane. Here in the most exciting and dangerous part of the world there was nothing but boredom. I drank all my wine and ate all my fresh food before it turned with the heat. Afterwards I lived on tinned Turkish sardines, which are not so good. I don't in the least mind not washing for a week, but I do hate getting fleas into my hair. As there was nothing to be done, I read every printed word on the ship, and between sleeping watched the sailors. At that time I was unused to living in a Moslem country that took its religion seriously, and it surprised me to see the sailors say their prayers five times a day without any self-consciousness at all.

The engine went wrong. The man who looked after it was quite amusing. He hated engines and all modern gadgets. The owner had recently insisted that a ship's log be kept, and it fell to the poor engineer (as he called himself) to do it. I helped him. During the time we were doing the job together he told me that the owner had insisted, too, on compasses being used, but he struck at this, as he had sailed about the sea for forty years without a compass. As we thought we were nearing Alexandria the crew climbed up the mast every few minutes with my field-glasses to look for land. I wondered whether we might find ourselves miles out, as no compass was used. But no ; we struck land exactly at Alexandria.

It was fun sailing into Alexandria harbour amongst all the warships. Many of these had only recently returned from Crete, and bore obvious signs of battle. Sailors looked at us and not unnaturally laughed. There were Greek ships, French ships being maintained by skeleton crews, and a Polish ship. I was really more impressed and excited than a schoolboy.

The ships signalled to one another as we spent the whole morning and a large part of the afternoon waiting for the Egyptian authorities to allow us to land. (The British gave their permission after examining the ship's papers in about five minutes.) I was concerned only for the sick people on board.

Dirty but cheerful, I left the caique with all my luggage and took a taxi to the best hotel. Rather to my surprise they allowed me to enter. The British Consul-General in Alexandria is an excellent man. He ought to run a Foreign Office school before he retires in order to teach young Vice-Consuls their job. He telephoned and asked me for an account of the journey, lent me twenty pounds, and invited me to lunch with some most interesting people who had that morning arrived from Crete. I met many familiar faces from the Balkans in Alexandria, among them Christopher Buckley, just returned with one of the cruisers which had taken part in the evacuation.

The story of the Battle of Crete was a grim epilogue to the disastrous history of the twelve months during which Germany had eaten up the Balkans. Perhaps this moment after the evacuation of Crete was the blackest since the fall of France almost exactly a year previously. Victory looked further away than ever. It was beginning to seem as if we could never hold any position in the face of a German attack, much less carry out an offensive of our own. We had been in Crete more than six months; plenty of time, one would have thought, to put the island into a thorough state of defence. I wonder whether any of the successive British commanders in the island ever really got down to the job. They were changed far too frequently. Perhaps they did not have time; perhaps it was regarded as not sufficiently urgent.

Anyhow, we had been in Crete for more than six months and were not ready. Mr. Churchill had stated in the House of Commons only a week or two earlier that we had every intention of holding Crete and Tobruk, and we were not ready. Our command knew that the attack was imminent, and we were not ready.

At least no one tried to sell the Press or the Public the story of yet another brilliant retreat and successful evacuation. Neither Press nor Public would have bought it. There was a general feeling of exasperation abroad, and a very strong disinclination to be put off with any further sedatives. No one wanted any more of the "Between the bombs our boys played football" nonsense.

Why was it necessary to evacuate Crete?

The answer can be found in two words—Air Power.

Crete obviously presented, in little, some though by no means all the problems that an invader of Britain, possessed of air superiority though not of sea power, would have to face. But there was absolutely no comparison between the strength of the defence in the two cases. Our air forces in the Middle East were still terribly inadequate numerically. In his masterly exposition some days later in the House of Commons, Mr. Churchill compared the ease with which the Germans could switch units of the Luftwaffe rapidly across Europe with the time taken to send our material by the Cape route, with all the loading, unloading and reloading involved. Even if we had had total air superiority *vis-à-vis* Germany, which of course we had not, the enemy would still have been able to display a considerable local superiority, owing to the advantage he possessed in holding interior lines. The chief benefit which the intervention of Italy brought to Germany was that it opened up a second front which was as advantageous to Germany as her Russian front is liable, on a long view, to be disadvantageous. And Axis communications with this front are reckoned in terms of hundreds of miles; ours in terms of thousands.

In other words, owing to the loss of the bastions of Central Europe, thanks to "the peace in our time" mentality of a Prime Minister and his advisers who appear to have known as little of the elements of strategy as they did of firmness, consistency or honesty of purpose, we have been placed in a position in which what we really needed was an air force not equal to, but double the combined Axis forces. Fundamentally, the men really responsible for the loss of Crete were those statesmen—most of them still unfortunately alive—who failed to inform themselves of the elementary needs of Imperial strategy. Repeated recrimination on this point is the only way of avoiding another generation being slaughtered somewhere in the nineteensixties. Every one of the dangers of the German drive to the south-east was, in essentials, pointed out by Mr. Churchill in a brilliant speech in the House of Commons just after the occupation of Austria.

The whole lesson of the Greek campaign was underlined by the events in Crete. There were additional carelessnesses. We had only the three air bases Heraclion, Maleme, Rethymno, because, as the Prime Minister showed, it was useless to have more bases than we could effectively operate. But, that being so, there should have been no time lost in providing the strongest possible defence for those three. Again, the Prime Minister pointed out that there simply were not more anti-aircraft guns available, bearing in mind our wide commitments in the Middle East. In that case one feels that far more should have been done to render the airfields impracticable landing-places for enemy planes. The probable capture of the airfields by the enemy ought to have been more effectively guarded against.

The Germans got their footing at Maleme, and then proceeded to pour in reinforcements by troop-carrying planes, which in the last stages of the battle were arriving at three-minute intervals. They had set to work from the moment of their occupation of Greece on preparing for the attack on Crete. With a rapidity which contrasted rather painfully with British methods they set about the construction of fresh bases in the Peloponnese as well as on the island of Cythera. Their air superiority was such, particularly after the compelled withdrawal of our fighter support half-way through the battle, that from dawn to dusk through the long summer days they were able to pound our troops with 1000-kilogram bombs without interruption or interference. The miracle is that our men held their positions for as long as they did, and secondly that any of them remained alive.

It is difficult to realize, until one has actually experienced it,

19

how much an air attack against which there is no fighter defence immobilizes the whole functioning of an army from Divisional Headquarters downwards. Under such circumstances direction and execution are completely paralysed, and the initiative is entirely surrendered to the enemy. The only hope of avoiding extinction from dive-bombing or low machine-gunning was to lie huddled in prepared positions practically motionless. Here there was a tolerable degree of safety, though enemy prisoners frankly stated that they found the tin hat of the British soldier makes a conspicuous mark from the air, in spite of attempts to decorate it with foliage in the manner of the soldiers in Macbeth.

After being bombed all day in this summer it takes a deal of heroism to have to face a determined infantry attack. The miracle is that this heroism was in fact shown again and again, though at a cost which made the continued retention of Crete impracticable. Both by land and sea, but especially by sea, we were suffering losses which did not justify a continued endeavour to retain the island. The Navy was set the task of preventing a sea-borne invasion by patrolling the waters between Crete and the mainland and between Crete and the Dodecanese without any, or with wholly inadequate, air support. The loss of four cruisers and six destroyers was far too heavy a price to pay for what proved to be the retention of Crete for only a few days longer.

And yet I am convinced that the original decision to hold Crete was justified, that we came near to success, and that the battle will go down in history among actions in which decisive success only just eluded us. A few more guns of heavy calibre in the neighbourhood of Maleme aerodrome should have been sufficient to wreck the landing-ground and would have made further landings impossible. Our lack of air power was nearly as disastrous when it was a case of dealing with isolated bodies of troops already landed. Again and again, some small knot of enemy troops who could easily have been dispersed from the air contrived to seize and hold on to some point of strategic importance, thereby immensely hampering our operations. At

Rethymno, for example, a body of 150 German parachutists obtained possession of a monastery in a strong position controlling the road between the town and the airfield. They cut off all communications passing between them and hamstrung the movements of our troops in the whole sector. It proved impossible to retake the monastery by infantry attack, whereas a single bomber would have made quick work of it.

This is only one of many occasions in which our lack of air support enabled small bodies of the enemy to carry out operations whose importance was out of all proportion to the numbers of men engaged. To say this is not to belittle the achievement of those airmen who were present in the earlier part of the battle. They did all that could be done, but once our air bases could no longer be used the position rapidly became hopeless.

The one encouraging feature in this depressing episode appeared to be that the parachute bogey had been largely exploded. There seemed complete unanimity of opinion among all who had taken part in the battle, and all felt that parachutists, while potentially formidable in a sparsely inhabited country or against an unarmed population, would have little opportunity in a country such as England. They went further. Parachute troops, it seemed agreed, were jam to the armed infantry man. Even though in Crete they were dropped from a much lower altitude than in Poland or Flanders, they were still as a rule about twenty seconds in descent, during which time they form an excellent mark. " We fire at their feet and we can be almost certain of getting them," was one of the comments made by a little New Zealander. Moreover, during the period of a minute or two after landing the parachutist is still an extremely vulnerable target.

The attack had, of course, been beautifully conceived, as is the German method in warfare. Phase One had consisted of the methodical bombing and machine-gunning of the areas selected for attack ; phase Two the dropping of parachutists who themselves established defensive positions and prepared bases for the arrival of air-borne troops by plane and glider, which formed the Third phase.

The parachutists were marvellously equipped. Their maps were miracles of detail and accuracy. They indicated the points where British artillery posts and British ammunition dumps were to be found and sites for their own. They contained the most detailed markings of the positions of British units. But it is known now, of course, that the Germans very seriously underestimated the amount of troops we had actually landed in Crete, though they were accurately enough informed about their dispositions. This misjudgment contributed materially to prolong the struggle and prevented the hoped-for runaway conquest. The result was that in ten days of hard fighting the Germans seemed to have used up practically all the parachutists available, but, alas, they had already fulfilled their task.

It is impossible otherwise to account for the failure of the Germans to drop parachutists at Sphakia on the south coast, from which many of our troops were evacuated. A comparatively small number of parachutists could have held the little port and destroyed our troops piecemeal as they came wearily straggling across the Cretan mountains—no longer a force in being, merely some thousands of exhausted individuals, some with rifles and a few rounds of ammunition, some without. Yet this was not done, though the Germans knew that we were using Sphakia for evacuation. The only solution is that they had no more parachutists to drop.

I felt very depressed when I heard of the perfect quality of all the equipment which the parachutists carried, particularly their first-aid outfits. It really knocked on the head the idea that there was any shortage of war material or supplies in Germany.

The Crete campaign might be regarded as symptomatic of our failure in the whole conduct of military operations and of the international developments which preceded them. It was important to hold Crete. We had publicly committed ourselves to holding Crete. It was lost because at a vital stage of the battle we had no air support. There was no air support because we had lost one aerodrome and could not effectively operate the other two which we possessed. We had no more aerodromes because we had not the anti-aircraft equipment, or for that matter the planes at our disposal to make use of them. We had not got planes and A.A. guns in sufficient quantity because the enormous length of our line of communications to the Middle East imposed a terrible time-lag on the delivery of war material. We had this long line of communications because our rulers, knowing less about the political and strategic problems of Central Europe than they knew about the municipal drainpipes of Birmingham, allowed the bastions of Central Europe to fall, just as, cherishing an admiration in their hearts for the Fascist order of government which they condemned with their lips, they made smooth the way of the aggressor while feeding their own people with lies and evasions.

I was in a very despondent mood as I travelled up to Cairo past the mud villages of the Nile delta, not reading but letting my gaze dwell on the enormous number of flame trees, mostly in avenues by the side of the railway line. There was no green on the trees to moderate the effect. We passed many soldiers on the way and a trainload of wounded.

I was sunk in reverie. "*Partir, c'est toujours mourir un peu,*" and I looked back on a year of varied experiences which had taken me from one end to another of South-Eastern Europe. I had many happy and many poignant memories. But above all I reflected on the melancholy spectacle of one country after another succumbing to the aggressor.

I looked back on the years I had spent working for the League of Nations Union, lecturing in town and village on behalf of collective security. How right we had been! Men who should have been better informed, but who were not, told us that we were wrong, or they told us that the League was a "beautiful ideal" when actually it was a rather prosaic but eminently practical way of achieving some degree of international order. They told us that it was impractical. I hope that those who told us so regard the ruined cities of Warsaw, Rotterdam and Belgrade as a monument to the practical results of *their* policy. I hope that the vested interests, of whose baleful influence it is impossible to write, because the truth must not be told, may come to regret the way in which they worked to make smooth the path of the Nazi aggressor.

Looking back on nearly ten years of struggle one has to fight against the danger of relapsing into a sense of despairing defeatism in oneself. It is wearisome being a Cassandra, destined always to prophesy truly and always to be disbelieved.

They told us that the re-arming of Nazi Germany would be in the interests of European peace, and they were wrong. They told us that we must not impose sanctions upon Italy because that would drive Mussolini into the arms of Hitler; that we must not oppose the re-occupation of the Rhineland because that was German territory; that we must avoid the danger of dividing Europe into two ideological blocs, to which Mr. Churchill pungently retorted that there was already an aggressor bloc, in any case, on one side but a mere rabble on the other. They told us that the sacrifice of Spain and Austria and Czechoslovakia would bring us peace; and they were still wrong.

Everyone who has followed international developments during the last ten years knows the reason for these things, though they are too seldom said in print. Everyone knows that the power of international finance capital has inflamed and aggravated the diseases of a world already sufficiently tormented by political, racial and religious divisions, the power without responsibility or control is as noxious in the economic sphere as it is in the political.

The irresponsible power of the nation-state and the irresponsible power of finance-capital have, in combination been the cause of our " present discontents ". Between them they have frustrated the greatest constructive idea that arose out of the last war. Unless the lesson of the events of the last twenty years, underlined by the events of the last two years, is studied and taken to heart at the close of this war, we shall have nothing better to provide for our children than a holocaust on an even more titanic scale in 1960 or 1970.

The white train drew in to Cairo station. The crowd was enormous. I drove through the town for the first time in what seemed an old and broken-down taxi, but I afterwards found that it was merely a normal taxi for Cairo. It looked as though there had been an air raid. This, however, on the Fifth of June was not the case, but all the Egyptian houses are unfinished— often only half-built. If they are finished the owner has to pay the full house tax.

It requires little ingenuity to avoid this taxation law.

BUCHAREST—ISTANBUL—CAIRO,
      *September* 1941.

# INDEX

*Aeroput* Air Line, 31
Albania, 28, 122–3, 138 ff., 232 ff.,
    254, 265, 269, 279
Alexander, King of Yugoslavia, 18,
    20–3, 255
Alexandria, 286–7
Alexandroupolis, 147, 175
Alexandrov, Feodor, 22
Anglo-Turkish Treaty (1939), 11
Antonescu, Gen., 68–9, 72 ff.,
    95 ff., 105, 178 ff.
    Mme., 68
Aous Gorge, 232
Arachova, 280
Arad, 61
Araxos, Cape, 281
Argyrocastro, 232–3
Argyropoulos, P., 276
Arta, 279
*Astra Romana*, 109–10
Athens, 151–4, 171–2, 243–5,
    268 ff.

Backa, 15
Bacopoulos, Gen., 273
Balcic, 209–10
Baldwin, Earl, 63, 203
Balkan Entente (1934), 11, 17, 63,
    250
    League (1912), 16
    War, Second, 16
Banffy, Count, 39, 57
Baranyay, Z., 54
Barnes, Ralph, 151
Beck, Col., 87–8
Bela Kun, 56
Belgrade, 30–1, 244, 247, 254 ff.,
    268
Berat, 233
Bessarabia, 28, 45 ff., 62, 79, 86
Bethlen, Count, 38–9, 57
Bibesco, Prince Antoine, 44, 80
    Princess Elizabeth, 82, 197
    Princess Marthe, 44
Bicanič, 25, 28, 253
Biklichta, 146, 156–7
Bismarck, Prince von, 16
Bled, 259
Boris, King of Bulgaria, 12, 200–1,
    204, 206–7, 259

Botosakis, 139
Bowman, Thos., 131, 275
Boyle, Sir Edward, 204
Braila, 208
Brasov, 37, 61, 78, 87–8, 182
Bratianu, C., 80
    G., 73, 75, 81
Brenan, Mr. and Mrs., 204, 283–4
Brewer, Sam, 147–8
Bridge, Ann, 53
British Council, 54, 124, 231
    Expeditionary Force, in Greece,
    243 ff.
    Guarantee of, 1939, 51
    Intelligence Service, 178, 184
Brown, Mr., 87
*Bucegi*, 110
Bucharest, 32 ff., 68 ff., 178 ff.
Buckley, Christopher, 129, 152–3,
    166, 244, 287
Budapest, 65
Bukovina, 49–50, 79
Bulgaria, 50–1, 63, 141, 179, 191–3,
    199 ff., 217
    claims on Yugoslavia, 15–17
Bunjevacs, 15
Burgas, 193
Butculescu, Mme., 85

Caballero, Gen., 235
Calinescu, A., 32–3
Campbell, Ronald, 29
Canelopoulos, 218
Carol, King of Romania, 12, 43,
    45, 48 ff., 58, 68 ff., 81 ff., 90,
    120, 259
Cernauti, 12, 50
Cernozemsky, 22
Cetatea Alba, 67
Chalcis, 280
Chamberlain, N., 246
Chimara, 232–4
Chisinau, 46–7
Churchill, W. S., 224, 247, 288–9,
    294
Cincar-Markovič, A., 246, 250
Clark, Percy, 113–14, 117
Cluj (Klausenberg), 38–9, 56, 61,
    81

Codreanu, C., 43, 69, 73, 76, 90 ff.
  *père*, 93-4, 97
Constanza, 107, 111, 119, 186,
  192-3, 197, 212
Corinth, Isthmus of, 281
Cosmavici, 93
Cosutič, 25
Craiova agreement, 209
Crete, 274, 287 ff.
Cripps, Sir Stafford, 41-2, 238
Croats, 14-15, 18 ff., 30, 64, 252,
  264
Cvetkovič, D., 144, 246, 251, 261,
  264
Cyprus, 285-6

Dalmatia, 17, 31
Danube, 35, 51, 118, 208, 212 ff.,
  251
  Commission, 208
Davidescu, 48
Delane, 129
Delphi, 280
Demerdjis, 125
Demestichas, Gen., 233
Dennic, 240-1
Dietrich, Major, 179, 184
Dill, Gen. Sir John, 241, 265
Dimbleby, R., 160
Disraeli, B., 16
Djumaya, 22
Dobrudja, 58, 62, 70, 209-10
Doiran-Ghevgeli gap, 217-18
Dragalini, Gen., 182
Drossos, 170
Duranty, Walter, 32, 43, 45-6, 71
Durazzo, 16, 266
Dushan, Stephen, 16

Earle, George, 205-6
Earthquake, Romanian (1940),
  102-4
Eden, Anthony, 239, 241
Edessa, 269
Elbasan, 233, 265
Erseka, 146
Euboea, 280
*Evening Standard, The*, 157

Fabricius, Dr., 72, 78-9, 85, 115
Federal Union, 18
Filoff, 179
Florina, 144, 269
Focsani, 213
Fossy, Treaty of, 60
France, sale of loot from, 193-4

Franz Ferdinand, Archduke, 21
Free Thought, Party of, 125-6

Gabrovo, 199
Gafencu, G., 33-4, 36-7, 42-4,
  87-8
Gafencu, Mme., 43
Galatz, 79, 210-11, 213
Gambier-Parry, Gen., 154, 170
Gennock, Ted, 160
George, King of Greece, 132, 222,
  225, 236-7, 258, 274 ff.
  Crown Prince of Yugoslavia, 20
German Foreign Policy, 64
  Gestapo and Secret Service, 35,
    61, 85, 131
  Propaganda and Trade, 27, 40,
    87, 107, 177, 190, 201-4,
    223, 243, 248-9, 252, 263
  Tourists and Fifth Columnists,
    23, 43-4, 49, 58, 70, 73, 83-5,
    92, 191-3, 208, 250, 271, 282
Gheorgiev, 22
Gibson, Archie, 99
Gigurtu, I., 37, 73, 79
Giurgiu, 35, 99, 105, 107, 118,
  120, 181, 185, 212-3
Glenconner, Lord, 172-5
Goga, O., 99
Goumenitza, 146
Grazzi, 140-1
Greece, 28, 64, 89, 122 ff., 215 ff.,
  268 ff.
Gunther, Mr., 68

Hankey, R. M. A., 35, 109, 193
Hansen, Gen., 86, 182, 186-7
Hapsburgs, 65
Harrison, of Reuters, 53
Hassani, 274
Haywood, Gen., 171, 219
Helen, Queen of Romania, 76-7
*Helle*, 122, 135-7
Henderson, Sir Nevile, 53
Herriot, E., 62
Hitler, A., 37, 48, 73, 126, 242
Hoare, Sir R., 23-3, 103, 117
Hofmann, 119
Hoggia, Daout, 138
Hohenzollerns, 65
Holler, 53
Horthy, Admiral, 65
Hungarian-Yugoslav Pact, 261-2
Hungary, 17, 50-1, 53 ff., 202,
  261-2
Hvar, 23

Iorga, Prof., 105
Iron Gates, 31, 34–5
    Guard, 33, 43, 51–2, 69, 71–2,
        76 ff., 90 ff., 111 ff., 178 ff.
Italo-Greek War, 142 ff., 232 ff.
Italy, 13, 17, 23, 28, 64, 111, 135 ff.,
    219 ff., 259–51

Jacobici, Gen., 186–7
Janina, 144–5, 219, 279
Jevtič, 24
Jews, 26, 47, 65, 91, 99–102, 104,
    177–8, 185, 248
Jilava, prison of, 104

Kafandaris, 218
Kalabaka, 279
Kalamas River, 146
Kalamata, 281
Kastoria, 155
Katchanik Pass, 267
Kavalla, 174
Kendall, Mr., 186, 193
Kephissia, 229
Klisoura, 232–4
Kodzias, K., 135, 138–9, 275–6
Kondylis, 125
Konitsa, 145
Koritza, 126, 144, 146, 154–60,
    167–70, 232
Korizis, A., 129, 222, 225, 237,
    274–5
Korošeč, 23
Kozani, 155
Kragujevac, 267
Kriva Palanka, 267
Kyriakos, G., 137

Lamia, 154
Lares Air Line, 47
Larissa, 154–5, 170
Lausanne, 13
Laval, Pierre, 63
Lavrentiev, 42
Le Rougetel, J. H., 116, 90
Libya, 240
Lijotič, 255
Little Entente, 17
Logothetopoulos, 135
London, Treaty of (1915), 17
Longmore, Air-Marshal, 240
Lothian, Lord, 238
Louvaris, 135
Lupescu, Mme. M., 44–5, 74–5,
    82, 99, 120

Macartney, C. A., 54
Macedonians, 15–16, 22
Maček, A., 19, 23–5, 80, 254–5
Macnab, Col. Geoffrey, 115
Madgrearu, M., 105
Maitland, Patrick, 153, 223, 237–8
Maleme, 289
Manettas, C., 219
    T., 219
Maniu, J., 42, 62, 69, 80–1, 188
Manyadakis, I., 131–3
Marghiloman, 60
Maria Theresa, 15, 38
Marie, Queen of Romania, 209–10
Masterson, Ted, 109
Mavroudis, 137, 224
Mayers, Norman, 113
Mazarakis, Gen., 275
Mediterranean, 284 ff.
Melas, Col., 153
Melaxa, 78, 81–2
Mersin, 283
Merton, Arthur, 160, 166, 172
Mestrovič, I., 26, 29
Metaxas, Gen., 12, 124 ff., 216 ff.
    Line, 174, 217
Metsovo, 144–5
Michael, King of Romania, 75–8
Mihailov, I., 22–3
Milan, 13
Miller, A., 114–7
Mitrovitza, 249
Molotov, V., 28, 48
Monastir, 144, 260, 267, 269
Mussolini, 20, 126, 140, 142–4,
    163, 235

Napoleon Bonaparte, 146
Nauplia, 281
Nedič, Gen., 261
Negru Voda, 212
Neolaia (Youth Movement), 130–
    131, 220, 237
Neubacher, 85–7
Nevrokop, 217, 270
Nicoloudis, 223–7
Nish, 267
Non-provocation, 216

Obrenovič, Alexander, 21
Odessa, 50
Oeconomon, A., 273
Oil engineers, arrest of, 111 ff.
Oilfields, Romanian, 34–5, 40, 49,
    106 ff., 190
Okhrida, 30, 169, 233, 267

Olympus Line, 217, 239–40, 269 ff., 276
O'Malley, 53
Oradea Mare, 61

Palairet, Sir Michael, 227–9, 237–8
Pan-Slavonic Federation, 17–19
Papademas, 273
Papagos, Gen., 221, 273
Parachutists, 291–2
Pares, Peter, 58
Paris, 9
Pašič, N., 18
Patmore, Derek, 198
Paul, Prince, of Greece, 138
    Prince, of Yugoslavia, 12, 24, 29, 252, 259 ff.
Pavelič, A., 26, 258
Peiraeus, 268, 280
Peneios, 272
Peter I. of Serbia, 258
Peter, King of Yugoslavia, 29
Peter, Prince, of Greece, 154
Pindus, Battle of, 143, 145
Pinsk, 46
Pirot, 17
Pittsacus, Gen., 219, 222
Platys, 135
Ploesti, 106, 111–12, 181, 190
Podgoritza, 265
Pogradetz, 232
Poland, 10, 55
Poles, in Romania, 87–9, 194
Police State, 255–6
Porto Palermo, 234
    Rafti, 281
Pow, Mr., 44–5
Predeal, 68
Premeti, 232
Preveza, 144
Prisons, Balkan, 256–8
Prizrend, 265–6
Protogerov, 22
Protosyngelos, Gen., 219
Ptolemais, 269
Pythion, 147

Radič, S., 19–20
R.A.F., 216, 226–7, 243, 274, 280–1, 289, 290–3
Rafina, 281
Rapp, Mr., 254
Rasputin, 91
Ratay, Major, 36, 205
Regensburg, 110–11, 118
Rendel, G. W., 201, 259

Rethymno, 291
Romania, 12, 32 ff., 56 ff., 68 ff., 177 ff.
Romano-Russian Commission, 50
Rothermere, Lord, 66
Rupel, 217
Russia, 28–9, 40, 48 ff., 70, 179, 193, 207 ff., 241, 252–3
Russo-German Agreement, 12, 40, 55, 249
Rustchuk, 121, 212–13
Ruthenia, 55

Sakhellariou, A., 275
Salonika, 144, 149–51, 173, 216–8, 263, 273
Salter, Cedric, 83
San Stefano, Treaty of, 16
Santi Quaranta, 232
Sarajevo, 266–7
Saronic Gulf, 280
Sava River, 30
Saxons, in Transylvania, 56
Schacht, Dr. H., 203, 248
Scutari, 265–6
Secret Societies, Yugoslav, 258
Seferiades, G., 152
Seres, 174–5
Servia, 155
Shipka Pass, 199–200
Sighisoara, 61
Silesia, 38–9
Silistria, 209
Sima, Horia, 51, 76, 91–5, 97, 101, 104–5, 178 ff.
Simeon, Tsar of Bulgaria, 16
Simovič, D. T., 263–6
Sinaia, 85, 191–2
Skoplje, 23, 26, 30, 260, 267
Skumbi River, 233
Skylakakis, 135
Slem, 27
Slovenes, 23
Smigly-Rydz, 88, 221
Snagove, 43, 88, 114
Sofia, 200 ff.
Sophoulis, 125, 275
Spain, 85, 146
Sphakia, 292
Split, 267
Srb, 24
Stambulisky, 22, 207
Stampar, Dr., 26
Stavroso, 174
Stokes, Henry, 154–5, 160
Stoyadinovič, M., 246, 251–2

*Straja Tarii* (Youth Movement), 39, 130
Struga, 144
Struma Valley, 217, 270
Strumnitza, 17, 267, 270
Subotica, 15
Suez, 122–3
Sulina, 209, 211
Šušak, 13
Sulzberger, C., 83
Swabians, in Transylvania, 56
Switzerland, 13
Syria, 283
Széklers, 61

Targoviste, 106–7
Tatarescu, 78
Tatoi, 274
Tchamouria, 141
Teleki, Count, 275
Temesvar, 15
Tepelini, 234–5
Theiss, river, 61
Theotokis, 125
Thermopylae, 272, 274, 276, 278 ff.
Timisoara, 66
Tirana, 265
Tirnovo, 199
Titulescu, N., 11, 63
Tracy, Mr. and Mrs., 112, 116–7
Transylvania, 16, 38 ff., 55 ff., 69–71, 86, 118
Trianon, Treaty of, 55
Troyan, 200
Tsaldaris, P., 125
Tsolakoglou, Gen., 279
Tsouderos, E. L., 276
Turkey, 63, 111, 119, 179, 193, 195, 210, 214, 240–1, 250, 271, 283–4
Turnu Severin, 58–60

U.K. Commercial Corpn., 172
Ukraine, 28, 37
Urdarianu, 51, 73, 82
Ushitze, 266
U.S.S.R., 36, 42, 46, 51, 179, 188, 207, 210–11

Valona, 233–4
Vardar River, 217, 267, 270
Varna, 202, 211
Venizelists, 124, 218–9, 275, 277
Venizelos, G., 11, 125–6, 219
S., 218
Vidovdan Constitution, 18, 21
Vienna Diktat, 60–1, 73, 80
Vistritza River, 269
Vlachos, G., 242
Volo, 274
von Felsen, Baron, 43
von Killinger, 85, 186
von Kohler, Edigh, 41, 85
von Ribbentrop, J., 61

Wallace, David, 225
Waterlow, Sir Sydney, 135
Wavell, Gen., 239–40, 243
Wilhelm, Prince, of Wied, 169

Yugoslavia, 14 ff., 63, 211, 244, 246 ff., 269
Yugoslav National Front, 255

Zagoroff, Dr., 203–4
Zagreb, 14, 18, 19, 26, 28, 254, 255, 267
Zemun, 79
Ziphos, A., 133, 137, 274
Zivkovič, 21
Zog, King of Albania, 169, 258–9